MW00637240

DIVINE
PATTERNS

DIVINE
PATTERNS

Seeking the Blessings of Heaven

New York Times Best-Selling Author

ROGER CONNORS

DESERET BOOK

SALT LAKE CITY, UTAH

To my grandchildren, Chase, Everett, Carter, Allie, Connor,
Caleb, Anna, David, John, Kade, and those yet to come.

May this witness fortify your faith in times of need.

© 2022 Roger Connors

All rights reserved. No part of this book may be reproduced in any form or by any means without permission in writing from the publisher, Deseret Book Company, at permissions@deseretbook.com. This work is not an official publication of The Church of Jesus Christ of Latter-day Saints. The views expressed herein are the responsibility of the author and do not necessarily represent the position of the Church or of Deseret Book Company.

DESERET BOOK is a registered trademark of Deseret Book Company.

Visit us at deseretbook.com

Library of Congress Cataloging-in-Publication Data

CIP on file
ISBN: 978-1-63993-042-5

Printed in the United States of America
Jostens, Clarksville, TN

10 9 8 7 6 5 4 3 2 1

CONTENTS

Introduction 1

Foundational Principles

1. How Do Blessings Come from God? 11

2. How Does God Decide Which Blessings
   to Grant and Which to Withhold? 19

3. Does God Have a Specific Plan for Me? 28

4. Why Do Some Blessings Seem Delayed or Never Come? 38

5. Will God Keep His Promises? 47

Divine Patterns

Part 1 – Experiencing God's Power

6. Motivated by Love: Loving God and
   Keeping His Commandments 59

7. Deliverance from Trials: Trials and Witnesses 69

8. Overcoming Doubt: Doubting Not and Seeing God Act 79

9. Seeking Miracles: Faith and Miracles 88

Part 2 – Adopting a Fresh Perspective about God and Yourself

10. Approaching God: Broken Hearts,
    Contrite Spirits, and Forgiveness 99

11. Obtaining Forgiveness: Confessing and Forsaking
    and Remembered No More 107

12. Renewing Covenants: Worthily Partaking
    of the Sacrament and Becoming Unspotted from the World 115

13. Staying Forgiven: Forgiveness and Being Forgiven 125

CONTENTS

Part 3 – Walking the Covenant Path

14. Becoming a Disciple: Thy Will, My Will,
    and God Performing His Perfect Work 137

15. Relying on God: Keeping the Commandments
    and Prospering in the Land 146

16. Practicing Holiness: Virtuous Thoughts
    and Confidence in the Presence of God. 155

17. Taking Accountability: Cheerfully Doing
    All Things and His Arm Is Revealed 164

Part 4 – Enjoying the Divine Privilege to Hear Him

18. Constant Companion: Entering in by
    the Way and Showing You All Things 177

19. Being Guided: Asking and Seeking and Receiving and Finding 187

20. Getting Answers: Trusting in the Lord
    and God Directing Thy Paths 196

21. Overcoming Adversity: Receiving the
    Comforter and Being Filled with Hope. 208

Part 5 – Striving to Stand Firm, Faithful, and True

22. Accessing the Power of the Atonement of Jesus Christ: Always
    Remembering Him and Having His Spirit to Be with You 219

23. Search, Ponder, and Pray: Hungering and
    Thirsting after Righteousness and Being Filled 228

24. Overcoming Weakness: Becoming Humble
    and Weakness Being Made Strong. 238

25. Staying on the Path: Continually Holding
    Fast to the Rod of Iron and Partaking of the Fruit. 250

    Conclusion 261

    Acknowledgments 265

INTRODUCTION

This is a book about seeking and obtaining God's promised blessings in our lives.

The scriptures are filled with tremendous promises made by God, all of which are taught extensively in the talks and writings of Church leaders. These promises are about the spiritual and temporal blessings He wants us to have—blessings that are available to each of us and that can bring greater joy and happiness into our lives in profound ways. Knowing how to obtain these blessings is important. Understanding how God grants blessings, when and where, is vital.

You may be one who has frequently experienced a divine hand lifting and blessing you in promised ways. If so, you will find this book reassuring and confirming. Or you may be someone who feels that God has not kept up His end of the bargain—that blessings have not come as expected, hoped for, or promised. If that is the case, I hope you will keep reading. There is a lot to share about why that may be so, and about the hope that you can have moving forward.

One of the keys to gaining God's blessings is understanding that He often uses repeating patterns to maintain order in His creations. These patterns are found in all areas of naturally occurring things, including the spiritual. Understanding this great truth helps us better appreciate not only how the Father and Son govern Their creations but also how They work with each one of us in our individual lives to help and bless us. One of the great realizations we can gain about what God wants from us is that spiritual blessings are most often granted by Him as we apply the particular patterns He has revealed that are associated with those blessings. A key takeaway: *patterns* are important.

A pattern is "an arrangement or sequence regularly found in comparable objects."[1] Patterns serve as a model or guide to help us repetitively accomplish something. We find patterns everywhere we look. In nature, there are at least five repeating patterns: spiral, meander, explosion, packing, and branching. These patterns are found all throughout the natural world—from spiral bacteria to spiral galaxies, the contours of sand dunes, the branching of lightning and the formation of tree limbs. In other words, patterns are naturally occurring; that's the order of things.

Elder David A. Bednar taught that "the scriptures are full of spiritual patterns."[2] These scriptural patterns repeat themselves, showing they can be relied upon as truth and act as a guide for approaching and connecting to heaven. Elder Bednar illustrated this concept with the instruction given to missionaries early in the Restoration found in Doctrine and Covenants 62:7–9. After reviewing this scriptural example, he pointed out, "Please note the basic elements in this pattern: (1) a thankful heart in all things; (2) act according to judgment and the directions of the Spirit; and (3) the Savior is with the faithful always. Can we begin to sense the direction and assurance, the renewal and strength that can come from following this simple pattern for inspired and righteous judgment? Truly, scriptural patterns are a precious source of living water."[3]

Patterns help us better understand what to do.

My little three-year-old grandson illustrated this truth one day when he wanted to get dressed to go outside and play in the snow. He was in such a hurry that he put on his shoes before his pants. After quite a bit of effort and no success, he cried in frustration, asking for help. *Pants before shoes*—that's an important pattern! There are many others: *look before you leap, think before you speak,* or *save before you spend.*

Often, with patterns, something comes before something else in order to get where you want to go. Go out of order and you may not get the result you're looking for. Instead, you will likely experience frustration and failed progress—like my grandson putting on his shoes before his pants.

In this book, the term "divine patterns" is used, differentiating it from all other patterns one may find in any discipline of science or life. These divine patterns are found in the scriptures and the words of living prophets. They pertain to our spiritual and eternal lives and govern our ability to receive blessings from God—blessings that will ultimately come if we seek to apply the divine pattern provided. God's prophets continually teach us of these divine patterns, such as *inspired questions lead to inspired answers, true doctrine changes behavior, faith precedes miracles,* or *seek before you find.* These patterns can be key to our happiness and to the happiness of those we love.

The Lord refers to patterns in the scriptures many times: David, the prophet, provided Solomon directions on building the temple: "And the pattern of all that he had by the spirit." Regarding the Tabernacle, Moses was told by God to "make all things according to the pattern shewed to thee in the mount." The Lord directed Church leaders in how the work was to be carried out in Ohio: "And let this be a pattern unto the elders until further knowledge." Finally, the Lord taught Joseph and the Church to discern the spirits: "I will give unto you a pattern in all things, that ye may not be deceived."[4]

Understanding divine patterns helps us know what we can do to enjoy each and every blessing God has waiting for us. Scriptural patterns point out how what we do and think is connected to heavenly blessings the Lord has promised—important pairings of interconnected ideas God wants us to know and understand. This isn't meant to imply that the gospel is formulaic: following steps on a checklist rarely yields the desired result with God. The principles of the gospel are interconnected and always require sincerity, true intent, and deep humility. There are, however, patterns in gospel principles that help us understand how to come unto Him with full purpose of heart and to ultimately obtain the blessings we seek—divine patterns that always lead to our good and ultimate happiness. This is heaven's promise.

I had this lesson reinforced to me early in my married life while serving as a new stake president. My wife, Gwen, and I had five young children. I had not been serving very long but felt the weight of a busy Church assignment while traveling the world to build an international consulting and training company—all while trying to stay connected at home.

At the time, one of our sons, Seth, was having some challenges in elementary school. He would often come home in tears and share that he was being bullied—something on a parent's list of things they never want to hear. Partly because of the effect you know it's having on your nine-year-old, and partly because you know how near impossible it is for parents to solve these problems.

Gwen and I labored over what to do—looking for the blessings of heaven for our son. Our prayers were constant. Still, every day after school we would hear the teary-eyed reports. Discussions with teachers were helpful, but this was not an easy thing for teachers to solve either.

Then one day, Gwen said to me, "Why don't you go to school and sit with him at lunch and see what's going on?"

"Can I do that?" I responded, a little shocked.

It sounded like a great idea, so I cleared my calendar and offered a heartfelt prayer for guidance.

When I arrived, Seth was wide-eyed and excited. A surprise visit from dad! (In elementary school that's still cool.) I joined him in the lunch line and got my tray, with what had to be the smallest carrots and hot dog I had ever seen. As we sat and began eating, I noticed my son tense up as the biggest boy in school sat next to us. I knew this must be the school bully, coming to check on what was going on with one of his regular victims.

As we ate, the bully asked me, "What're you doing here?" That question led to a surprising conversation. As we talked, I noticed he didn't have a lunch, so I offered to share mine, which he readily accepted. After visiting for a while, I thought that maybe my purpose had been fulfilled and it was time to head back to work.

"No Dad, you can't go now! We always play soccer after lunch. You need to come play."

Soccer?

When I grew up, the game was baseball. The last thing I wanted was to embarrass my son and undo any good we might have just done at lunch with the bully.

A moment later, as I squeezed into my tiny jersey, one of the class-mates, and apparently the smartest kid in class, instructed me to "just stand in front of the net with your arms out!"

Big dad. Little net. It made sense to me.

As the game moved along, the bully eventually came up to me to continue our lunch conversation. I thought, "Well this is good, we're con-necting." Then I heard shouts from the field. "Kick the ball!" "Just kick it!" Everyone on Seth's team was yelling at me! I suddenly realized that the ball was rolling down the field directly at me.

After a quick and desperate prayer for some degree of athleticism—more for Seth than me—my foot connected. It was somehow perfect. The ball screamed through the air, over the enemy goalie, and landed in the net on the other side of the field.

For a moment, there was just silence. I couldn't believe it. The bully couldn't believe it. Seth couldn't believe it. And then it happened; half the field erupted into a cheer. Victory! The time elapsed and the fourth-graders won (for the first time, by the way). Someone shouted, "Whose dad is that?"

The bully quickly responded, "That's Seth's dad!" The bully was some-how proud, and Seth was beaming.

After passing through a line of fourth-grader high fives I could see that for Seth, this was an important moment.

"Dad, thanks for coming. This was so great!"

Another high five, a big hug, and I was gone.

On the drive back to my office I felt satisfied that lunch had been a perfect idea, and that Gwen and I had done something important that day. As I took a quiet moment to offer thanks and reflect, the Lord spoke to me. It wasn't an audible voice but might as well have been. It was that direct. The instruction was clear: *If you take care of mine, I will take care of yours.* I knew He was teaching me a truth. I was learning a pattern. A divine pattern. He was saying, "You're sacrificing time now to serve in a busy Church assignment to help *mine*, and I will not forget that. I give you the promise that I will also be there helping *yours*, as you do."

Now this didn't mean we could be neglectful as parents and let God do everything. Not hardly. When we do our part, *then* God takes over, filling in the gaps for us. But we don't believe in a God of *just* our gaps. Of course, He often steps in when we can do no more, but His help doesn't begin there—it comes far earlier. We have the joyous reassurance that as we strive to do our part, through the Atonement of Jesus Christ, He is there to strengthen us *every step* along the way, not just at the end when our efforts appear to fall short.[5]

Back to my soccer career takeaway. In this moment of inspiration, Heavenly Father gave me the reassurance that He would not be neglectful of our family and our needs as we serve Him—I could be assured that He was serving, blessing, and helping us along the way.

I have never forgotten that lesson.

It is important to note that there is no way to shortcut or "hack" your way to the finish line when it comes to living the gospel. For spiritual success, we must follow the covenant path and the many patterns that God has revealed.

While there are hundreds of patterns in the scriptures, I have chosen twenty-five that are foundational to our faith and relationship with God, like "Faith and Miracles," "Forgiveness and Being Forgiven," and "Trials and Witnesses." They are based on the scriptures and teachings of living prophets, and they show us how to seek after the important blessings we want in our lives.

These scriptural patterns won't feel new to you, as they are based on scriptural teachings you have undoubtedly heard many times. However, looking at these divine truths from the perspective of a "pattern" may help you understand even more about what the Lord would have you do to receive the blessings He already has in store. That, in the end, is the objective of anything God has revealed—our joy and happiness.

It's also important to recognize that these patterns aren't the only way that God works with us but are good places to start when we want to better understand what *we* can do to seek the Lord's help and blessings. You will find many other ways He works with us to help us and bless us. In the end, all gospel principles are interconnected with each other, ultimately tying back to one great overarching truth: our reliance on Jesus Christ, His Atonement, and His grace.

In the first section of this book, the Foundational Principles, I begin by introducing the most commonly asked questions about when and how God chooses to intervene in our lives. Why He grants some blessings and seems to withhold others. I have heard these five questions asked repeatedly throughout my Church experience and know that the answers provide an important anchor in the foundation of our relationship with God. You may already be very familiar with these answers. However, reviewing this doctrine prior to our journey through the twenty-five divine patterns in the second section will prove useful and important.

It is impossible to have a real discussion about seeking the blessings of heaven without reviewing the Lord's own qualifiers to the blessings He has promised—the purpose of the Foundational Principles discussion in the first section of this book. These qualifiers are not heavenly *excuses* about "why God can't deliver"; they are God's *explanations* about how He works to bless our lives as fully as possible, with His eternal perspective in mind.

As you will see in these first five chapters and your own life's experience, it's not just black and white that you're either blessed or not. This topic is much more nuanced, particularly when we take a closer look at how and when these blessings show up. Laying this essential foundation early in the book will help clarify the obvious questions that arise as we review the promised blessings associated with the divine patterns identified.

Once you've read the Foundational Principles section, you can continue reading each of the chapters in the Divine Patterns section of the book in order, or you can jump to whatever pattern is most applicable and interesting to you. The objective is to help you better understand what the Lord would have you do to receive the blessings you seek—blessings that He already has planned for you.[6]

By the way, you will notice that most scriptures and quotations throughout this book have some portion of the text italicized. Unless otherwise noted, I have added these italics to emphasize a particular part of the scripture or statement.

As an author, my objective is to help direct your attention to what has been revealed by the Lord through Church leaders and the scriptures—revealed truth that will provide clarity and maybe even some answers you have been looking for. Understanding the divine patterns associated with obtaining God's promised blessings will empower you with even greater faith, knowledge, courage, and desire. My hope is that this book will help you draw even closer to God and provide you with greater clarity about how you can seek the blessings of heaven in your life and the lives of others.[7]

Notes

1. "Pattern," lexico.com.
2. David A. Bednar, "A Reservoir of Living Water," BYU devotional, February 4, 2007, https://speeches.byu.edu/talks/david-a-bednar/reservoir-living-water/.
3. David A. Bednar, "A Reservoir of Living Water," BYU devotional, February 4, 2007, https://speeches.byu.edu/talks/david-a-bednar/reservoir-living-water/.
4. 1 Chronicles 28:12; Hebrews 8:5; Doctrine and Covenants 73:5; 52:14.
5. "The Lord sees you. . . . If you trust your life to Him, His hand will guide you every step of the way until you are happy and at peace with all the desires of your heart" (Sharon Eubank, "A Letter to a Single Sister," *Ensign*, Oct. 2019).

   "One young man wrote me the following e-mail: 'I know God has all power, and I know He will help me if I'm worthy, but I'm just never worthy enough to ask for His help. I want Christ's grace, but I always find myself stuck in the same self-defeating and impossible position: no work, no grace.' I wrote him back and testified with all my heart that Christ is not waiting at the finish line once we have done 'all we can do' (2 Nephi 25:23). He is with us every step of the way.

   "Elder Bruce C. Hafen has written, 'The Savior's gift of grace to us is not necessarily limited in time to 'after' all we can do. We may receive his grace before, during and after the time when we expend our own efforts' (*The Broken Heart* [Salt Lake City: Deseret Book, 1989], 155)." (Bradley R. Wilcox, "His Grace Is Sufficient," BYU devotional, July 12, 2011, https://speeches.byu.edu/talks/brad-wilcox/his-grace-is-sufficient/.)
6. See Bible Dictionary, "Prayer."
7. See Dale G. Renlund, "Abound with Blessings," *Ensign*, May 2019.

FOUNDATIONAL
PRINCIPLES

CHAPTER 1

How Do Blessings Come from God?

It should come as no surprise that even God follows rules, including when it comes to how He blesses His children. We might wonder, why would He need to follow any rules when He can do anything He wants? The answer is found in the very nature of who God is: a being who obeys eternal law.[1]

We all understood this truth in the pre-earth life because we knew the Father well there. Church leaders have taught that "there is not a soul of you but what has lived in his house and dwelt with him year after year (in the premortal existence)."[2] In fact, He not only knew Joseph Smith by name; "He also knows each of us by name."[3] Finally, Elder Bruce R. McConkie said, "We are talking about someone who is a literal parent, who is the Father of the spirits of all men. You and I were born as members of his family. We have seen his face; we have heard his voice; we have received his counsel, personally as well as through representatives and agents; we knew him in the preexistence."[4]

"You and I were born as members of [God's] family. We have seen his face; we have heard his voice; we have received his counsel."

—Bruce R. McConkie

Here are some of the principles and rules that guide God's intervention with us, His earthly children—all are principles we knew well before we came to this earth:

- He is a God of order.[5]
- He is bound to keep His promises.[6] He keeps His word, no matter what.[7]
- He requires the expression of our agency before He can intervene in our lives.[8]
- He will not compel anyone to act.[9]
- He does not vary from what He has said.[10]
- He is the same God, yesterday, today, and forever.[11]
- He does only that which will result in our eternal happiness.[12]
- He knows all things, past, present, and future—from the beginning.[13]
- He is more intelligent than us all.[14]
- He has ordained that blessings come only in obedience to divine law.[15]
- He has all power and does all that He takes into His heart to do.[16]
- He will continue His work of salvation and exaltation "so long as . . . there shall be *one man* upon the face thereof [earth] to be saved."[17] He is motivated by love. In fact, God is love.[18]

It is comforting to know that the God we worship is not only in authority but is in possession of all those qualities that make us glad He *is* in charge. Consider the extent that He loves each one of us with these words from President Dieter F. Uchtdorf: "Think of the purest, most all-consuming love you can imagine. Now multiply that love by an infinite amount—that is the measure of God's love for you. . . . Though we are incomplete, God loves us completely. Though we are imperfect, He loves us perfectly. Though we may feel lost and without compass, God's love encompasses us completely. He loves us because He is filled with an infinite measure of holy, pure, and indescribable love. . . . He loves every one of us, even those who are flawed, rejected, awkward, sorrowful, or broken. God's love is so great that He loves even the proud, the selfish, the arrogant, and the wicked."[19]

With all that said, here are three experiences from my own life that illustrate common ways blessings from a loving God are granted—or withheld—all of which are consistent with the principles of divine intervention we cover here in the Foundational Principles section of this book.

Miraculously

When blessings come instantaneously, they are often clearly an act of God. For this case, I turn to my time as a young missionary in the Georgia Atlanta Mission. I was a new convert to the Church, having been a member for only about a year and a half. As the only member of the Church in my family, I was learning every day about how the Lord works with His children.

My companion and I were just leaving an uplifting zone conference where our mission president, Russell C. Taylor, had mentioned that we, as missionaries, should be paying our fast offerings. Typically, missionaries do not pay tithing on funds they receive for their mission, but we had apparently made a mistake in thinking that we did not pay any other contributions during our mission either.

My companion and I were both anxious to please the Lord and be obedient to our mission president, so decided we would fix this error and immediately pay our fast offerings when we got back to our apartment. I can still see the two of us sitting at the "not-so-gently used" kitchen table, staring at each other, when we realized that we each had only five dollars left in cash to last us the last five days of the month.

We discussed how we would eat going forward, as the cupboards were near bare. Should we pay the fast offering? Would the Lord really expect us to give up our last five dollars? I was being supported financially by contributions from members of my home ward, so I was on a very tight budget.

Still, there we were, wanting to be obedient and desiring the blessings we believed would come from paying our fast offerings. So, we each took our last five-dollar bill and inserted it into the contribution envelope and put it in the middle of the table. We looked back up at each other and smiled and said, "Okay, we've paid our fast offering!"

As we sat at the table thinking about how we would make this work, the phone rang. It was our ward mission leader, a very quiet and unassuming man. He was calling to invite us out for dinner. He said, "I will take you wherever you want." Immediately, we knew where we wanted to go . . . "Sizzler for the all-you-can-eat shrimp dinner!" Our strategy was simple: eat all the shrimp we could and see if that would last us the rest of the week!

On the ride home from dinner, our ward mission leader asked if we would mind stopping at the store while he went in to get a few things he needed. We offered to come in with him, but he declined, so we waited in the car. While waiting, we marveled how the blessing of food had come so instantaneously after making our offering. The fact that this ward mission leader had been prompted to reach out so immediately in our time of need and feed us dinner was equally impressive.

After what seemed like a long time, we saw him walking to the car with a store clerk, who was pushing a cart stacked with several cases of canned food. As they loaded the car, we laughed, asking him if he was stocking up on his food storage. He responded that the food was for us!

Astonished, we told him our fast-offering story—having just given our last five dollars when the phone rang. He obviously had no idea of our circumstances, but the Lord did, and He impressed this good man to help us. Miraculously, within a short couple of hours, we had an all-you-can-eat shrimp dinner from Sizzler and seven cases of canned food from the local grocery store! Quite amazing and very instant. A miracle.

Receiving blessings in an immediate and miraculous way is admittedly more unusual. It happens, but it's not common. More typically, the blessings come "by and by" (meaning eventually or after a while),[20] which is how the next experience came.

By and By

For many years as a growing teenager, I dealt with a complexion problem. It bothered me greatly. I was not a member of the Church and did not have the sensibility to wait to have a girlfriend. I wanted one. Of course, a complexion problem presented a challenge to getting this done.

While I was not schooled in religious things, I did know that I could pray. I recall lying in bed night after night asking God to take this problem away. I did my part and tried everything for many, many years. Went to doctors, tried creams, got shots, watched what I ate. I even gave up sugar for two years straight. (Anyone who knows me can tell you that sacrifice meant I was desperate.) Still, nothing seemed to work. It didn't get better. In fact, my complexion got worse.

It wasn't until about halfway through my mission that I was healed of this problem. I recall my mission president's wife being so impressed with how completely the problem was resolved that she asked me to coach other missionaries struggling with the same thing. But I really had no idea why I was now healed. I had done nothing special and guessed that it was just time for my prayers to be answered—so many years later.

Looking back, I think I can see why those prayers were not answered when I wanted them to be, and today, I am very grateful they were not. You see, the "problem" saved me from having a girlfriend too early in life. I did not have the religious training, understanding, or testimony that I would need to stay morally clean. One might say this was just a naturally occurring skin condition for someone my age—and maybe it was. Yet, it is easy for me to think that the delay in granting the blessing I was seeking was one way God was helping *me* stay safe during a very vulnerable time in my life—safe until I would become deeply rooted in the gospel and the Lord's law of chastity.

A loving and caring God uses discretion in answering our prayers. Elder Jeffrey R. Holland taught, "There will be times in our lives when even our best spiritual effort and earnest, pleading prayers do not yield the victories for which we have yearned. . . . So, while we work and wait together for the answers to some of our prayers, I offer you my apostolic promise that they are heard and they are answered, though perhaps not at the time or in the way we wanted. But they are *always* answered at the time and in the way an omniscient and eternally compassionate parent should answer them. My beloved brothers and sisters, please understand that He who never sleeps nor slumbers cares for the happiness and ultimate exaltation of His children above all else that a divine being has to do. He is pure love, gloriously personified, and Merciful Father is His name."[21]

Not Now/Never

My last example of how blessings come from God happened when I was in a university MBA program. I wanted to land a high-paying job at a specific, well-known strategic consulting firm. I knew I wanted to be a consultant, and this company had the diversity of clients I was after. This company rarely came to recruit at my business school, typically recruiting only from Ivy League schools. However, I knew they were coming to my school that year, and my sights were set solely on them.

I worked hard through the year, taking every assignment seriously and making sure my grades would be in line with the company's expectations. Everyone in the program knew that very few of us would get a first-look interview, yet everyone wanted to work for them.

I often prayed about this, hoping to have heavenly help to be prepared to land the job. Finally, the time came, and they visited campus looking at candidates. As it turned out, they interviewed only two people out of our entire program of over one hundred. You can probably guess that I wouldn't be telling you the story if I had been one of the ninety-eight. I made it in!

They flew me to their San Francisco office, where I interviewed with seven different people. It seemed to go well. I felt good. They then flew me to their Boston office, where I interviewed with seven more. Again, it seemed to go well. I felt even better. When the highly anticipated call finally came a week later, I was told that I had not gotten the job. They had taken my buddy but passed on me. What? Excuse me? Disappointment was an understatement. It was devastating. I had no backup plan. That job was plan A, B, and Z. I had prayed hard, worked hard, tried hard, yearned, sweat, asked, knocked, and pleaded. Yet nothing. All to no avail.

Yet, the answer "no" ultimately became an incredible blessing in my life. Yes, I was disappointed, but the closed door with this opportunity led to an open door with another even better suited to me. That door opened to an exciting and rewarding career, tailor-made for me. When God's answer is "no" or "not now," I have learned to trust that He has something better planned.

When God's answer is "no" or "not now," I have learned
to trust that He has something better planned.

In this chapter, I've given three examples of how the blessings we seek are typically granted—immediately, over time, or not now/never. If the average person could chart how the Lord answers the request for blessings in his or her life, it may look a bit like the typical bell curve below: a few come immediately, most come by and by, and a few seem to never come.

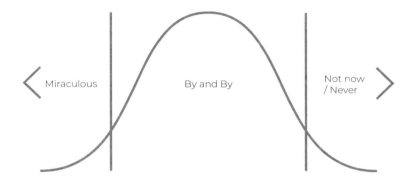

Why does it happen this way? Why are there those rare times that God grants the request almost miraculously, while more often they seem to come over the course of time? Then, why are there times that the request is never granted at all—when heaven is seemingly silent?

Underpinning all these questions is an important assumption: God's motive for intervening in your life is driven by His unending love for you. Sister Sharon Eubank, First Counselor in the Relief Society General Presidency, taught, "I appeal to each of you to put yourself in a place where you can feel the generous love God has for you. You cannot put yourself beyond the reach of that love."[22] How reassuring to know that, however hard we may try, we cannot alienate a loving God who will never give up on us and who will always be working to bless us, no matter what we do, because of the "matchless bounty of his love."[23]

The answers to many of these questions about why and when God allows blessings to come into our life lie in understanding how He works with His children, the subject of our next chapter.

Notes

1. See Doctrine and Covenants 88:13.
2. L. Tom Perry, "Be the Best of Whatever You Are," BYU devotional, March 12, 1974, https://speeches.byu.edu/talks/l-tom-perry/best-whatever/.
3. "I testify to you that God has known you individually . . . for a long, long time (see D&C 93:23). He has loved you for a long, long time. He not only knows the names of all the stars (see Ps. 147:4; Isa. 40:26); He knows your names and all your heartaches and your joys!" (Neal A. Maxwell, "Remember How Merciful the Lord Hath Been," Ensign, May 2004).
4. Bruce R. McConkie, "Celestial Marriage," BYU devotional, November 6, 1977, https://speeches.byu.edu/talks/bruce-r-mcconkie/celestial-marriage/.
   Also, "In the premortal realm, spirit sons and daughters knew and worshiped God as their Eternal Father and accepted His plan by which His children could obtain a physical body and gain earthly experience to progress toward perfection and ultimately realize his or her divine destiny as an heir of eternal life" ("The Family: A Proclamation to the World," ChurchofJesusChrist.org).
5. See Doctrine and Covenants 132:8.
6. See Doctrine and Covenants 82:10.
7. See 2 Nephi 10:17.
8. See Doctrine and Covenants 130:20–21.
9. See Alma 42:27.
10. See Mosiah 2:22; Alma 7:20.
11. See Doctrine and Covenants 20:12, 17.
12. See 2 Nephi 2:25.
13. See 1 Nephi 9:6; Doctrine and Covenants 130:7.
14. See Abraham 3:19. Neal A. Maxwell taught, "In intelligence and performance, He [the Savior] far surpasses the individual and the composite capacities and achievements of all who have lived, live now, and will yet live! (See Abr. 3:19)" (Neal A. Maxwell, "O, Divine Redeemer," Ensign, Nov. 1981).
   Also, "Moreover, what the Lord knows is, fortunately, vastly more—not just barely more—than the combination of what all mortals know" (Neal A. Maxwell, All These Things Shall Give Thee Experience [Salt Lake City: Deseret Book, 1979], 22).
15. See Doctrine and Covenants 130:20–21.
16. See Abraham 3:17.
17. Moroni 7:35–37.
18. See 1 John 4:7–8, 16.
19. Dieter F. Uchtdorf, "The Love of God," Ensign, Nov. 2009.
20. "By and by," dictionary.com. See also Alma 32:41–42.
21. Jeffrey R. Holland, "Waiting on the Lord," Ensign, Nov. 2020.
22. Sharon Eubank, "Turn On Your Light," Ensign, Nov. 2017.
23. Alma 26:15.

CHAPTER 2

How Does God Decide Which Blessings to Grant and Which to Withhold?

As a priesthood leader, I have conducted over ten thousand missionary interviews and been involved with hundreds of people as they have repented and improved while working out their salvation. Throughout these experiences, I have been careful not to talk about the people or their circumstances. Having served as a common judge in Israel, keeping confidences has always been essential. When I do draw upon some of these experiences so that all may benefit, I will change the name and context to keep the situation anonymous.

One such situation involves a young man I will call Tony. Tony was frustrated and felt that his prayers were not being answered. He desperately pled for blessings that he wanted but that were not coming. He was largely on his own; his parents and family were not engaged much with the Church. He worked a job while friends around him were going to college. His great love was snow skiing. He enjoyed the sport and did it as often as time and finances would allow.

Tony had served a mission and was "active" in the Church, but at the time that meant just showing up to Sunday meetings most of the time. In reality, his personal worship was suffering, as he had largely stopped praying and reading his scriptures. I could also tell that he was not hanging with the right friends in his spare time. Essentially, Tony was drifting from the fold and just barely hanging on to his faith.

When we met the first time, I asked Tony why he wasn't praying. His response was that God had stopped listening—Tony felt he had made too many mistakes, like being a disobedient missionary and persistent struggles with pornography. In addition, nothing seemed to be going Tony's way. Life was getting tougher, not easier. Tony essentially stopped trying. Yet there was still a strong part of him that wanted God to prove He still loved him—despite his lack of effort.

Do Blessings Require Work?

As you read about Tony you may be thinking, *well this is an easy one* . . . He wants blessings but isn't willing to work for them. The scriptures are clear on this point: "For all who will have a blessing at my hands shall abide the law which was appointed for that blessing, and the conditions thereof, as were instituted from before the foundation of the world."[1] Meaning, if you want the blessing, you must work for it. Obey the law, get the blessing.

Simple. Case closed.

But is it really that simple?

How do you know you've done your part—all that God would expect? And why are there people who work really hard to obtain certain blessings that still don't come? What about Tony? He had made the effort at one time and acknowledged that he felt blessed for it. But then, for whatever reason, he ran out of steam, while still hoping blessings would be given.

Answers to these questions are easier to come by when we understand the principles the Lord uses to determine how He intervenes in our lives— the principles of divine intervention.

Here are a few to consider:

First, the Lord will not do for us that which we can do for ourselves. He wants us to be self-reliant.[2] His purpose is to help us learn and to prepare to live the life that He lives. In this regard, the scriptures teach the law of the harvest: we reap what we sow.[3] Meaning, we get out of life what we put into it. However, there are inequities—times when we put in a lot and get back only a little. There are also times when we get more than we deserve. In fact, the truth probably is that we *always* get more than we deserve.

It's important to see that gospel principles are interdependent; they rarely stand on their own. In fact, all gospel truths relate to one another and interconnect in some way: justice and mercy, repentance and forgiveness, faith and works, and so on. You can generally never fully understand one gospel principle without understanding how it fits neatly into the whole. Ultimately, every gospel principle belongs to a divine pattern of truths that all lead back to the Savior and His Atonement.[4]

In this vein, the law of the harvest is interconnected with and tempered by grace. In the Guide to the Scriptures, we read this definition: "Grace is *the enabling power from God that allows us to obtain blessings in this life* and gain eternal life and exaltation in the life to come. It is this power that can change our sinful nature and turn our weakness into strength. This divine help is given through the mercy and love of God to those who exercise faith, repent, and earnestly strive to keep the commandments."

"Grace is the enabling power from God that
allows us to obtain blessings in this life."

—Guide to the Scriptures

As we strive to do all we can, we access God's grace—divine help that is given *when God feels we need it*, in His all-seeing and all-knowing perspective. But there is another application of the principle of grace: it is by the grace of God that all blessings come, regardless of how hard we have worked—it's always a gift, regardless of our effort.[5]

Fortunately, when the gift of grace is operating in your life, it means that you don't have to be perfect (in fact, perfection, as most of us understand it, is not even possible in this life[6]), but you do need to be trying to keep the commandments "as best you can."[7] Because our efforts often fall short, the Father's plan called for an Atonement—doing for us that which we *cannot* do for ourselves.

This principle of the law of the harvest is particularly applicable in our spiritual lives. As Second Counselor in the Sunday School General

Presidency, Matthew Richardson taught, "The Spirit leads, guides, and shows us what to do. *He will not, however, do for us what only we can do for ourselves.* You see, the Holy Ghost cannot learn *for* us, feel *for* us, or act *for* us because this would be contrary to the doctrine of agency. He can facilitate opportunities and invite us to learn, feel, and act."[8]

Second, God honors the agency He has given us.[9] One example of this can be found in how God answers prayer. In the Bible Dictionary, we learn that "the object of prayer is not to change the will of God but to secure for ourselves and for others blessings that God is already willing to grant but *that are made conditional on our asking for them.* Blessings require some work or effort on our part before we can obtain them. Prayer is a form of work and is an appointed means for obtaining the highest of all blessings."[10]

God wants us to authorize His involvement in our lives by asking for help and blessings through prayer—He will not force His way into our lives.[11] Then a counselor in the First Presidency, President Dieter F. Uchtdorf taught: "[God] will not force anyone to choose the path of righteousness. . . . [He] will invite, persuade. God will reach out tirelessly with love and inspiration and encouragement. But God will never compel— that would undermine His great plan for our eternal growth."[12] Prayer is an important way that we exercise our agency, and it qualifies as real work when it comes to seeking the blessings of heaven, either for ourselves or for others.[13]

President Uchtdorf provides an important clarification: "We cannot force God to comply with our desires—no matter how right we think we are or how sincerely we pray. . . . No, the purpose of faith is not to *change* God's will but to empower us to *act on* God's will."[14]

Third, God takes into consideration our personal worthiness when granting the blessings we seek. The scriptures teach that you must "deny yourselves of all ungodliness."[15] Whatever blessing you seek as you walk the covenant path, no matter how temporal the desired blessing may be, God also requires you to be clean.[16] Striving to have a clean mind and a pure heart is not optional with God and can supersede almost any other requirement for obtaining desired blessings.[17]

A good way to gauge your own personal worthiness is in how you answer the questions in the temple recommend interview—questions made public by Church leaders and that can be found on the Internet.[18] Your answers to these questions are a good indicator as to where you are on the covenant path—measuring how you are striving to keep the covenants you made with the Lord when you were baptized and received the priesthood (for males), and how you are honoring your temple covenants.[19] If we are unable to answer these questions in the way the Lord would hope, He may not be able to grant us the blessings we seek, even if He, as a loving parent, yearns to.[20]

Before a temple recommend is valid, we, as applicant, must sign it. It is not the priesthood leaders' job to determine the truthfulness of each of our responses (although the spirit of discernment may guide and direct them). It is their role to represent the Lord and ask the questions, *receive our answers* and, ultimately, determine our worthiness to hold a recommend. In the interview, it is our accountability as the applicant to truthfully respond to each question, as though we were declaring directly to the Lord, who knows all things.[21] We then sign the recommend, certifying that our answers are true, correct, and complete. In fact, every time we present the recommend to enter the temple, we are certifying to our continued worthiness.[22]

Important note: there are many reasons blessings do not come in the time or way we would hope—personal worthiness *may not* be one of them. As I said earlier, God does not require perfection if you are walking the covenant path—we can be worthy of certain blessings without being perfect. The speed in which we are moving along the path is not as important as the direction.[23] If blessings are not forthcoming, and you are *striving* (i.e., "making great efforts to achieve or obtain something"[24]) to keep your covenants, then it is quite likely worthiness is *not* the explanation. If you struggle with perfectionism, take heart: remember, we will be judged not just by our actions, but also by our intentions.[25]

The speed in which we are moving along the
path is not as important as the direction.

One good friend who is a faithful and strong priesthood leader, very successful father, and talented man shared these heartfelt concerns with me. I share them here (with permission) because I think there are many who either feel this way or know someone who does:

> One of the problems with not feeling God's involvement, answers, or love is that when blessings don't come, the blame seems to always come back on the person—they aren't worthy enough, working hard enough, trying hard enough. But what if one thinks they really are being good enough, they are reading and praying and fasting and serving and churching, but still feel God is ignoring them? They are empty inside and yearning for a light that never comes. These people are then inevitably told it's because, somehow, they still aren't worthy or good enough. People in this state then tend to beat themselves up and spiral into depression and self-harm (physically or emotionally), then lash out at God for being too darn persnickety. It can quickly become a never-ending dysfunctional, decaying relationship with deity. I'm not sure what the answer is, but I have lost many close family members from the gospel for this very thing, even struggling with it myself at times: "Why doesn't God just answer me in a way I can understand?" "Why has God abandoned me?" "Why doesn't God care?" "Why are others so blessed when I know they are doing less spiritually?"

Poignant feelings. Sincere questions. I'm sure we can all relate in one way or another.

Hopefully, this discussion of the principles of divine intervention can help any who experience these spiritual frustrations. Understanding the big picture for how God determines to bless us reveals that there are *many* variables involved in His intervention.

Fourth, faith is required for the Lord to do His work for us. When Jesus went to minister in His hometown of Nazareth, the scriptures recount: "*And he could there do no mighty work*, save that he laid his hands upon a few sick folk, and healed them. And he marveled because of their unbelief."[26] The people of Nazareth saw him as a local carpenter; they did not have faith in Him as the Son of God, so Jesus could do no mighty works among them.

He may not be able to do any mighty work in your life, either, without your faith.

The best manifestation of our faith in Jesus Christ is to be obedient, and our obedience yields even greater faith.[27] Our Heavenly Father prizes obedience, even above sacrifice.[28] President Russell M. Nelson, while a member of the Quorum of the Twelve Apostles, taught: "We cannot *wish* our way into the presence of God. We are to obey the laws upon which those blessings are predicated."[29]

A favorite statement that I heard as a young missionary goes something like this: Faith is belief, plus determination on the part of the individual to respond to the requirements of God, plus an added strength and power and force for righteousness from God Himself. Exercising our faith by showing our obedience is an essential requirement from God.[30]

Remember Tony, my friend I told you about at the beginning of this chapter? Despite feeling that God was not coming through for him, Tony exercised great faith and started to pray again. That eventually helped him make great efforts: attending addiction recovery meetings for pornography, choosing better friends, meeting with his bishop, and so on. He made the effort to come unto Christ and experience the Lord's promise: "Draw near unto me and I will draw near unto you."[31]

Note that in this scriptural pattern, we must take the first steps to draw near unto Him. Those steps, however small, show our desire and faith, which allows God to act. He might not be looking for some great thing from you; all He may need is an indication that you are willing to take that first step. The Lord's promise to Tony and to anyone making the effort: "Seek me diligently and ye shall find me."[32] That is the prize—finding Him—becoming a true follower of Jesus Christ. We may not get exactly what we want, but we will get exactly what we need to ultimately obtain the most glorious of all gifts, even eternal life.[33]

Notes

1. Doctrine and Covenants 132:5.
2. See *General Handbook: Serving in The Church of Jesus Christ of Latter-day Saints*, 22.1. "Church members are responsible for their own spiritual and temporal well-being. Blessed with the gift of agency, they have the privilege of setting their own course, solving their own problems, and striving to become self-reliant. Members do this under the inspiration of the Lord and with the labor of their own hands" (ChurchofJesusChrist.org).
3. See Galatians 6:7; Mark 4:3–9.
4. See *Teachings of Presidents of the Church: Joseph Smith* (2007), 54.
5. See Moroni 7:16
6. President Russell M. Nelson said, "Be patient with yourself. Perfection comes not in this life but in the next life. Don't demand things that are unreasonable. But demand of yourself improvement. As you let the Lord help you through that, He will make the difference." ("Men's Hearts Shall Fail Them" [video], ChurchofJesusChrist .org.)
7. President Gordon B. Hinckley taught, "Just do the best you can, but be sure it is your very best" ("A Challenging Time—a Wonderful Time," *Teaching Seminary: Preservice Readings* [Church Educational System manual, 2004], 18). He also said: "Please don't nag yourself with thoughts of failure. Do not set goals far beyond your capacity to achieve. Simply do what you can do, in the best way you know, and the

Lord will accept of your effort." ("Rise to the Stature of the Divine within You," *Ensign*, Nov. 1989.)
8. Matthew O. Richardson, "Teaching after the Manner of the Spirit," *Ensign*, Nov. 2011.
9. See Jeremiah 17:10; Doctrine and Covenants 101:78.
10. Bible Dictionary, "Prayer."
11. Joseph Smith taught that "God would not exert any compulsory means, and the devil could not," meaning God will not force us to do good, and Satan cannot force us to do evil. (*Teachings of the Presidents of the Church: Joseph Smith* [2007], 214).
12. Dieter F. Uchtdorf, "Fourth Floor, Last Door," *Ensign*, Nov. 2016.
13. See Bible Dictionary, "Prayer."
14. Dieter F. Uchtdorf, "Fourth Floor, Last Door," *Ensign*, Nov. 2016.
15. Moroni 10:32.
16. See 3 Nephi 20:41; Mormon 9:6.
17. See Marvin J. Ashton, "On Being Worthy," *Ensign*, May 1989.
18. See "Church Updates Temple Recommend Interview Questions," *Ensign*, Jan. 2020.
19. See Russell M. Nelson, "Closing Remarks," *Ensign*, Nov. 2019.
20. See Doctrine and Covenants 82:10.
21. "Temple recommend interviews allow members to demonstrate that they have a testimony and are striving to obey God's commandments and follow His prophets. Priesthood leaders also affirm, through the interview, that the member is worthy."

("Temple Recommends," *General Handbook: Serving in the Church of Jesus Christ of Latter-day Saints*, 26.3.1, ChurchofJesusChrist.org.)

22. See David B. Haight, "Come to the House of the Lord," *Ensign*, May 1992.

23. Marvin J. Ashton, "On Being Worthy," *Ensign,* May 1989.

24. "Strive," Lexico.com.

25. Brigham Young said, "It is not by words, particularly, nor by actions, that men will be judged in the great day of the Lord; but, in connection with words and actions, *the sentiments and intentions of the heart will be taken, and by these* will men be judged [see D&C 137:9]" (*Teachings of the Presidents of the Church: Brigham Young* [1997], 220).

26. Mark 6:5–6.

27. See Kevin W. Pearson, "Faith in the Lord Jesus Christ," *Ensign*, May 2009.

28. See 1 Samuel 15:22.

29. Russell M. Nelson, "Now Is the Time to Prepare," *Ensign*, May 2005.

30. "Faith in Jesus Christ," Gospel Topics, ChurchofJesusChrist.org

31. Doctrine and Covenants 88:63.

32. Doctrine and Covenants 88:63.

33. See Doctrine and Covenants 14:7.

CHAPTER 3

Does God Have a Specific Plan for Me?

As a young convert to the Church, one of the most exciting doc-trines I learned about was the plan of salvation. I recall the day I actually heard that we had lived in a pre-earth life. I was sixteen at the time, and I was walking with a friend to school on La Paz Road in Laguna Hills, California. As we walked and talked, my friend taught me the doctrine.

I explained to him what I had learned from a book that I had just fin-ished reading, the very popular *New York Times* bestselling *Chariots of the Gods?*—a book speculating about how ancient astronauts had assisted early man in populating and developing societies here on earth. At the time, it made sense to me—some kind of outside assistance promoting our exis-tence. Of course! But when this friend taught me about the pre-earth life and God's plan of happiness, I felt my mind fill with light and knowledge and immediately recognized it as true. It trumped any earthly explanation for why we were here and explained where that "outside assistance" was coming from. What had just been revealed to me was a game changer!

As both a missionary and later as a mission president, I quickly real-ized that the plan of salvation is generally a favorite lesson for any mission-ary to teach. For someone interested in the Church, learning the answers to where we came from, why we are here, and where we are going after we die is revolutionary. There are stories of people searching the world over on great adventures trying to find these answers, yet here I was learning about it on a casual walk to school with a friend.

My friend shared with me that our ultimate purpose for existence is to have joy and never-ending happiness.[1] I must say, the walk to school that day—the day I heard about the plan—was remarkable, even miraculous. It sounded right. It sounded familiar. I believed it. It was something I wanted: ultimate joy and never-ending happiness. Where do I sign up?

A Specific Plan for You

That's the big picture, but let's talk more detail—detail that's important for every person to understand. Before you came to this life, God appointed a specific plan for you, your own specific journey on earth.[2] Elder Richard G. Scott taught, "God has a specific plan for your life. He will reveal parts of that plan to you as you look for it with faith and consistent obedience."[3] It is important to understand that we are not just talking about a general plan for everyone that comes to mortality, but also a unique and distinctive plan for each of us as individuals.[4] In fact, God has a specific "mission" for you to fulfill and perform as a part of His plan in your life, and that mission is discoverable and achievable.[5]

> God has a specific "mission" for you to fulfill and perform as a part of His plan in your life, and that mission is discoverable and achievable.

Speaking of your mortal opportunities, President Russell M. Nelson said: "One of the most important things you need to learn in life is to know who you really are. . . . When you begin to catch even a glimpse of how your Heavenly Father sees you and what He is counting on you to do for Him, your life will never be the same."[6] President Nelson's wife, Sister Wendy Nelson, shares: "The only thing that really matters is that you and I are doing exactly what we committed—even covenanted—premortally with our Heavenly Father we would do while we are here on earth. . . . The choice is yours and mine. Will we choose to do whatever it takes to fulfill the wonderful missions for which we were sent to earth? . . . Premortally, you and I committed to do a great work while we are here on earth. And with the Lord's help, we will do it!"[7]

An important note about God's plan for you: the plan is not a minute-by-minute account of what should happen next. It's your life to live and you have decisions to make—that's the way He wants it. However, you are foreordained to accomplish certain important tasks on the earth, as President Nelson teaches. When Adam and Eve came into the Garden, God gave them their agency: "But of the tree of the knowledge of good and evil, thou shalt not eat of it, nevertheless, thou mayest choose for thyself, for it is given unto thee."[8] The Lord told Enoch, "In the Garden of Eden, gave I unto man his agency."[9] Satan seeks to destroy that agency (and has been fairly effective using addictive compulsions to do it for many).[10]

One Church member, Ariel Szuch, captures the differences quite well: "For a lot of my life, I've wondered if I was messing up God's plan for me. I've agonized over making THE RIGHT CHOICE—a common dilemma for someone in my stage of life where big decisions are looming. The one on my mind most often lately is where to go next with my career, but before it's been where to go to college, whom to date, where to live, how to fulfill my calling, and so on. I've wondered if I'm even capable of reaching my potential. It's tempting to think that God has some master plan that He's measuring me against, and if I take one misstep I've missed my chance for happiness forever, or at the very least I'll be doomed to walk around with the nagging feeling that I'm constantly disappointing God.

"But you know what? As I've examined that mindset, I've learned that I need a better understanding of God and what the term 'His plan for me' means."

Ariel continues, "I'm learning that God is much less a divine dictator who demands perfect compliance to a predetermined plan for our individual lives and much more a co-creator with us of the kind of lives we want to live. I'm learning that His plan for me is a lot less like a laser-crossed minefield and a lot more of a journey of coming to know myself and coming to know Him."[11]

Through scripture and what the prophets teach, we know quite a bit about what God's plan for us involves:

First, you were given at least one unique talent or ability, a spiritual gift—probably more.[12] Talents given you are to help shape your life and the things you do here on earth. More to the point, these special spiritual gifts are intended to help you perform your divine mission while here.[13] We are encouraged by the Savior's own teachings in the parable of the talents not to bury those talents but to use them and even multiply them.[14] If not, we may lose them.

Any talent given you is not only given to be a blessing to you but also to bless others, particularly as it relates to building the kingdom of God on earth.[15] This is not a hard concept to believe; we see the expression of these talents all around us every day—people excelling at what they do in so many different fields, occupations, and disciplines. The scriptures tell us that there are an innumerable number of talents that are given to women and men upon the earth.[16]

In a women's session of general conference, President Nelson encouraged members of the Church to understand their spiritual gifts, to use and expand them more than they ever have in their life.[17] There was an urgency and even excitement in his sentiment that these spiritual gifts were needed now in the world more than ever before. When we use these gifts and talents, we should give the best we have to God and His kingdom on earth.[18]

Next, we know that you were appointed to come to earth through a specific lineage of the house of Israel[19] and that you were reserved in the heavens above to come here at this time because of your faithfulness and diligence.[20] In fact, President Nelson said, "You were taught in the spirit world to prepare you for anything and everything you would encounter during this latter part of these latter days (see D&C 138:56)."[21]

President Nelson suggested that one of your primary purposes here is to participate in the gathering of Israel, on both sides of the veil, where "the most important work in the world" is to prepare the earth for the Second Coming of our Lord.[22] Speaking specifically to millennials, President Nelson said: "You are living in the 'eleventh hour.' The Lord has declared that this is the last time He will call laborers into His vineyard to gather the elect from the four quarters of the earth. (See D&C

33:3–6.) And *you* were sent to participate in this gathering. . . . This is part of your identity and your purpose as the seed of Abraham (see Galatians 3:26–29)!"[23]

We also know this: God has designed challenges, trials, and hardships *unique to you* because mortality is also a proving ground.[24] One of the great purposes of this life is to be proven, to see if we will do all that Heavenly Father has taught us to do while out of His presence.[25] This proving is an important part of this phase of our existence. It is most likely that when we are judged at that final day, there will be little regard for what title or position we held in the Church or the world, but the focus will be on how we used our talents in serving those in the Lord's vineyard—were we a good steward and laborer?[26]

Importantly, your patriarchal blessing gives you a glimpse of the Father's plan for you.[27] Here, through an ordained patriarch, prophetic statements are revealed about who you were before this life, your gifts and talents, and your life's work and mission. It's not the complete plan the Lord has laid out, but it is a look at some of what the Lord would have you know about His plan for you. President James E. Faust, in a talk entitled "Patriarchal Blessings," explained, "A person should not expect that the blessing will detail all that will happen to him or her, or be an answer to all questions. The omission of the blessing of a great event in life such as a mission or marriage does not mean it will not happen. My own blessing is short and is limited to perhaps three quarters of one page on one side, yet it has been completely adequate and perfect for me."[28]

What else can you know about God's customized plan for you? For one, His plan for your life encompasses more than just this time in mortality: it all began in the pre-earth life and extends after death into the spirit world, and then on into the eternities. It is an eternal plan. What we have to look forward to really is remarkable. If faithful to the covenants we make both in and out of the temple, we have been promised blessings beyond our comprehension.

His plan for your life encompasses more than just this time in mortality: it all began in the pre-earth life and extends after death into the spirit world, and then on into the eternities.

How far beyond? Consider "thrones, kingdoms, principalities, and powers, dominions."[29] We will live in the presence of God and all things will be present before us, "past, present, and future."[30] We will have never-ending joy and happiness.[31] We will have eternal families and eternal offspring.[32] The blessings that await us are beyond our imaginations and impossible to put into words.[33] C. S. Lewis, the famous Christian writer, suggested that it may be "that the dullest most uninteresting person you can talk to may one day be a creature which, if you saw it now, you would be strongly tempted to worship."[34] The divine destiny that awaits us, if we are willing, is indeed glorious.

The real question is, can we overcome the intense and ever-present appetites, passions, temptations, challenges, trials, blindnesses, and struggles of this brief but very effective mortal probation? Can you believe strongly enough in God's eternal promises to live worthy of them? Our Heavenly Father is perfect in what He does, and He has designed the perfect proving ground for each of us. It's just that simple. And just that tough.

What If I Slip Up and Go Off Plan?

What of mistakes, wrong turns, and errors that would appear to veer you off plan? What about circumstances outside your control that may prevent you from being your best? What if, in your estimation, you've blown it? Is all lost? The Lord's answer: "Of course not!"[35]

Consider these words from Elder Dale G. Renlund: "When we discover that we are off the path, we can stay off, or because of the Atonement of Jesus Christ, we can choose to reverse our steps and get back on. In the scriptures, the process of deciding to change and return to the path is referred to as repentance. Failure to repent means that we choose to disqualify ourselves from the blessings God desires to give. If we are 'not willing to enjoy that which [we] might have received,' we will 'return . . . to [our] own place, to enjoy that which [we] are willing to receive'—our choice, not God's."

He goes on to say, "No matter how long we have been off the path or how far away we have wandered, the moment we decide to change, God helps us return. From God's perspective, through sincere repentance and pressing forward with a steadfastness in Christ, once back on the path, it will be as if we were never off."[36]

Anchoring the message is this great truth from Elder Neil L. Andersen: "Repentance is not the backup plan; it is the plan."[37]

Do you believe this? Can you believe it? If so, how is all this forgiveness and righting-the-ship, so to speak, brought about? Only in and through the Atonement of Jesus Christ.[38] It is by His majestic and merciful gift that we are brought back into the presence of God to be joint heirs with Him.[39] We all need Christ—from the vilest sinner to the most saintly person you know. All fall short. All need a Savior. Forgiveness and purification could not happen without Him. There would be no hope without Christ.[40] But with Him, there is every hope.[41] Weaknesses, mistakes, sins, illnesses, all are overcome through the Atonement of Christ if we are but willing to follow Him.[42]

I mentioned the temple recommend interview in the previous chapter. It's interesting to me that the interview begins with two important questions:

1. Do you have faith in and a testimony of God, the Eternal Father; His Son, Jesus Christ; and the Holy Ghost?
2. Do you have a testimony of the Atonement of Jesus Christ and of His role as your Savior and Redeemer?

It's not a coincidence that the Brethren have instructed priesthood leaders to start the interview here with these first two questions. Everything is built upon these two very important beliefs—your faith in the Godhead and your belief that They love you, have your best interest at heart, and want you to return to be with Them forever. Every commandment, teaching, and doctrine that comes from God is designed to bless you and ultimately bring you joy.[43]

All of your views, feelings, interpretations, understandings, personal biases, and questions should be shaped first by the basic and foundational understanding that it all depends upon this—the love of God for you.[44] If you have this, if you sincerely and honestly feel that love, from and for Him, then you will be able to eventually unlock the answers you seek; answers that will, in turn, compel you to want to receive, even yearn for, the blessings of heaven in your life. If you don't feel that love from God, stay tuned and keep reading. There is more about how you can enjoy that connection with God, feel His love, and understand why He wants that for you above all else.

In the end, it is only this love for and from God that will cause you to want to be subject to His will.

Notes

1. See 2 Nephi 2:25. The Prophet Joseph Smith taught, "Happiness is the object and design of our existence; and will be the end thereof, if we pursue the path that leads to it; and this path is virtue, uprightness, faithfulness, holiness, and keeping all the commandments of God" ("History, 1838–1856, volume D-1 [1 August 1842–1 July 1843] [addenda]," p. 3 [addenda], The Joseph Smith Papers, accessed September 23, 2021, https://www.josephsmith papers.org/paper-summary/history -1838-1856-volume-d-1-1-august -1842-1-july-1843/284).
2. See Doctrine and Covenants 11:8.
3. Richard G. Scott, "How to Live Well Amid Increasing Evil," *Ensign*, May 2004.
4. See Neal A. Maxwell, *Deposition of a Disciple* (Salt Lake City: Deseret Book, 1976), 45.
5. See John H. Groberg, "What Is Your Mission?" BYU devotional, May 1, 1979, https://speeches.byu.edu /talks/john-h-groberg/your-mission/.
6. Russell M. Nelson, "Stand as True Millennials," *Ensign*, Oct. 2016.
7. Wendy Watson Nelson, "Hope of Israel," Worldwide Youth Devotional, June 3, 2018.
8. Moses 3:17.
9. Moses 7:32.
10. See Moses 4:3.
11. "You're Not Messing Up God's Plan for You," ChurchofJesusChrist.org.
12. See Doctrine and Covenants 46:10–11; 1 Corinthians 12:7.
13. See "Real Confidence," *New Era*, Jan. 2007.
14. See Matthew 25:14–30; Doctrine and Covenants 60:13.
15. See "Lesson 10: Building the Kingdom of God," *The Latter-day Saint Woman:*

Basic Manual for Women, Part B, ChurchofJesusChrist.org.

16. See Moroni 10:8–18; Doctrine and Covenants 46:11–33; 1 Corinthians 12:1–12.

17. See Russell M. Nelson, "Sisters' Participation in the Gathering of Israel," *Ensign,* Nov. 2018.

18. President Brigham Young gave this counsel: "If you give anything for the building up of the kingdom of God, *give the best you have.* What is the best thing you have to devote to the Kingdom of God? It is the talents God has given you. . . . Let us devote every qualification we are in possession of to the building up of God's kingdom, and you will accomplish the whole of it."

    Also, "For it is the duty of every man and of every woman to do all that is possible to promote the kingdom of God on the earth." (*Teachings of the Presidents of the Church: Brigham Young,* [1997], 328, 133.)

19 See Deuteronomy 32:8.

20. President Russell M. Nelson stated, "Our Heavenly Father has reserved many of His most noble spirits—perhaps, I might say, His finest team—for this final phase. Those noble spirits—those finest players, those heroes—are *you*!" ("Hope of Israel," President Russell M. Nelson and Sister Wendy W. Nelson, Worldwide Youth Devotional, June 3, 2018.)

21. Russell M. Nelson, "Stand as True Millennials," *Ensign*, Oct. 2016.

22. Russell M. Nelson, "Let God Prevail," *Ensign*, Nov. 2020.

23. Russell M. Nelson, "Stand as True Millennials," *Ensign,* October 2016.

24. "Tests in the school of mortality are a vital element of our eternal progression. . . .He who authored the plan of salvation described the very purpose of our mortal probation using the words *prove, examine,* and *try* in ancient and modern scripture (See Abraham 3:25)." (David A. Bednar, "We Will Prove Them Herewith," *Ensign,* Nov. 2020.)

25. See Abraham 3:25.

26. See Matthew 25:14–30; Doctrine and Covenants 60:13.

27. See "Patriarchal Blessings," Gospel Topics, ChurchofJesusChrist.org.

28. James E. Faust, "Patriarchal Blessings," BYU Devotional, March 30, 1980, https://speeches.byu.edu/talks/james-e-faust/patriarchal-blessings/.

29. Doctrine and Covenants 132:19; 121:29.

30. Doctrine and Covenants 130:7.

31. See Mosiah 2:41.

32. See Doctrine and Covenants 132:19; and *Autobiography of Parley P. Pratt* ed. Parley P. Pratt Jr. 1938, 297–98.

33. See 1 Corinthians 2:9.

34. C. S. Lewis, last paragraph of "The Weight of Glory," in *The Weight of Glory and Other Addresses* (New York: Macmillan, 1949), 14–15.

35. See Romans 8:28. Jeffrey R. Holland taught, "However many chances you think you have missed, however many mistakes you feel you have made . . . , I testify that you have *not* traveled beyond the reach of divine love. It is not possible for you to sink lower than the infinite light of Christ's Atonement shines." (Jeffrey R. Holland, "The Laborers in the Vineyard," *Ensign*, May 2012.)

36. Dale G. Renlund, "Choose You This Day," *Ensign*, Nov. 2018.

37. Neil L. Andersen, "Repentance Is Not a Backup Plan; It Is the Plan," July 3, 2018, *Church News*, https://www.ChurchofJesusChrist.org/church/news/repentance-is-not-a

-backup-plan-it-is-the-plan-says-elder
-andersen?lang=eng.
38. See Articles of Faith 1:3.
39. See Romans 8:17.
40. See Ephesians 2:12.
41. See Ether 12:4.
42. See Alma 7:11-12.
43. See Mosiah 2:41.
44. President Dieter F. Uchtdorf said,
"You are loved. You are dear to your
heavenly parents. The infinite and
eternal Creator of light and life knows
you! He is mindful of you. Yes, God
loves you this very day and always.
He is not waiting to love you until
you have overcome your weaknesses
and bad habits. He loves you today
with a full understanding of your
struggles. . . . He knows everything
about you. He sees you clearly—He
knows you as you really are. And
He loves you—today and always!"
("Living the Gospel Joyful," *Ensign*,
Nov. 2014). See also John 3:16;
Zephaniah 3:17; Psalm 86:15.

CHAPTER 4

Why Do Some Blessings Seem Delayed or Never Come?

A friend I have great respect for, now serving as a patriarch, told me a story I will never forget. He knew a man that I will call Jim, whose wife was greatly respected for her generosity to others. She served unhesitatingly. The problem was that she was hypercritical of and negative about Jim, her own husband. Naturally, it bothered and offended him.

Jim prayed, fasted, and labored over this for years, getting no answers. Seeing no change. He and his wife tried counseling, but the situation didn't improve. Finally, he resolved to apply the Lord's counsel to "pray for them which despitefully use you."[1] Sad to think that this is how he felt about his own wife, but it was the case.

Day after day, week after week, month after month, he prayed, cried, pleaded. He didn't want to lose his marriage. Ultimately, his prayers began to work—not that they changed her, because they didn't—Jim's prayers changed him. Over time, his heart softened. He took less offense. He started to see other qualities that lessened his sensitivity to her nitpicking. He began to see that overall, he actually did have a warm and rewarding marriage.

The lesson: for years it felt like the righteous desired blessings would never come, but they eventually did. Eventually. Was it at times agonizingly tough for Jim to stick with his wife and the Lord? Certainly. Was it worth it? It was to him.

We never really know when the blessings we seek will come. If we did, it wouldn't require faith. It is in exercising faith in God's timing that sufficient spiritual power is built to bring about the desired blessings. We need to remember, "For my thoughts are not your thoughts, neither are your ways my ways, saith the Lord."[2] Heavenly timing may or may not be aligned with our own.[3] Quite frequently, it isn't, which is the very thing that helps us stretch and grow in faith, preparing us for even greater blessings.

It is in exercising faith in God's
timing that sufficient spiritual power is
built to bring about the desired blessings.

It's All About Timing

I had another good friend I happened to be chatting with while writing this book. This friend, who I will call Bradley, is well into his fifties and is an active, faithful member of the Church with an amazing family. He's also been suffering with chronic, frustrating health and financial problems for years, even decades. He said, "I'm at the point of finding a big black Sharpie and lining out half my patriarchal blessing," and that "it's too late for many of the promised blessings to happen," that "my patriarch was one of the best fiction writers of his day," that the Lord "just doesn't care."

Bradley's frustration partly stems from the fact that he has been faithful and diligent throughout his life. So, why would these blessings not come to pass as stated? As promised? I know he is not alone in these feelings. My heart aches for him and for everyone feeling that somehow either the Lord has not followed through on His promises or that they themselves are somehow to blame for seemingly lost blessings. My contention is, in most cases, it really isn't their fault—it's timing.

On this point, the Gospel Topics section of the Church website (a great resource, by the way) reads: "Similarly, the recipient of the [patriarchal] blessing should not assume that everything mentioned in it will be fulfilled in this life. A patriarchal blessing is eternal, and its promises may extend into the eternities. If one is worthy, all promises will be fulfilled in the Lord's due time. Those promises and blessings that are not realized in this life will be fulfilled in the next."[4] While it might seem that some unfulfilled promises were originally intended for this life, it's quite possible that they were meant for the next.

As we talk about delayed blessings, or blessings that never seem to come, I'd like to re-emphasize that my singular goal with this book is to help you really believe that your Eternal Father is there, that you can trust Him, and that He does make good on His promises. As has been said, the challenge usually rests with our view of His timing—if we do our part, the Lord's promises are about "when," not "if."

Remember Old Testament Rachel, Jacob's wife—she agonized over not having children.[5] Elder Spencer J. Condie, then a General Authority Seventy, commented, "With ever-increasing envy and mounting desperation, one day Rachel explosively demanded of Jacob, 'Give me children, or else I die' (Genesis 30:1)." Elder Condie went on: "The Apostle Peter testified that 'the Lord is not slack concerning his promise, as some men count slackness; but is longsuffering' toward us (2 Peter 3:9). In this age of one-hour dry cleaning and one-minute fast-food franchises, it may at times seem to us as though a loving Heavenly Father has misplaced our precious promises, or He has put them on hold or filed them under the wrong name. Such were the feelings of Rachel. . . . But with the passage of time, we encounter four of the most beautiful words in holy writ: '*And God remembered Rachel*' (Genesis 30:22). And she was blessed with the birth of Joseph and later the birth of Benjamin. . . . When heaven's promises sometimes seem afar off, I pray that each of us will embrace these exceeding great and precious promises and never let go. And just as God remembered Rachel, God will remember you."[6]

God is not fickle when it comes to fulfilling promises. Rather, He is strategic, detailed, intentional, logical (in the context of an all-knowing mind), planned, and generous. Everything He does is perfect.[7] And every act He takes toward us, His children, is perfectly designed for our individual happiness and joy.[8] He will fulfill His promises, if we do our part: "Who am I, saith the Lord, that have promised and have not fulfilled? I command and men obey not; I revoke and they receive not the blessing. Then they say in their hearts: This is not the work of the Lord, for his promises are not fulfilled. But wo unto such, for their reward lurketh beneath, and not from above."[9]

Still, when it doesn't happen, it's all too easy to be left asking why the Lord's timing doesn't ever seem to line up with our own—or, more appropriately, why our timing rarely aligns with His.

Elder Jeremy R. Jaggi reminded us, "Sometimes we get impatient when we think we are 'doing everything right' and we still do not receive the blessings we desire. Enoch walked with God for 365 years before he and his people were translated. Three hundred and sixty-five years of striving to do everything right, and then it happened!"[10] Maybe Enoch's timetable would be a good rule of thumb for you and me . . . after three hundred years of waiting on the Lord; we can start to moan a little.

The answers as to why blessings don't come can be found in all the reasons we've discussed here and in previous chapters, most notably: He has a plan for our lives and operates upon principles that govern divine intervention, knowing what is best for us at any given time. Ultimately, we all instinctively know we should want God's will to be done in our life, but as is the case with my friend Bradley above, seemingly unanswered prayers and waning faith can make it hard to believe He's even involved or cares.

There is another reason blessings may be delayed. It happens when we don't follow the patterns revealed by God. When that occurs, it can result in unhappiness, and nearly always in frustration. Take for example the out-of-order pattern of "intimacy before marriage" so widely practiced in the world. Look at what has happened to families and society in general by ignoring God's divine pattern of marriage and chastity: divorce, sexually transmitted diseases, and heartache are all more prevalent.[11] As a result, for many, God's blessings are delayed, postponed, and sometimes even put out of reach. In instances where we break with divine patterns, our actions can be to blame for absent or delayed blessings.

Why "Trust in the Lord"?

Ultimately, understanding why blessings may not be forthcoming comes down to trusting in God, even when that trust is being tested. Solomon, the son of David and king of Israel, was among the wisest men who ever lived—it was a gift given to him by God.[12] The scriptures state, "And God gave Solomon wisdom and understanding exceeding much . . . even as the sand that is on the sea shore."[13] It was this counsel Solomon offered that is relevant: "Trust in the Lord with all thine heart; and lean not unto thine own understanding. In all thy ways acknowledge him, and he shall direct thy paths."[14] This wise counsel to trust, rather than lean on our own understanding, may be considered a blind trust by some. However, when it comes to trusting the Creator of the universe—an all-wise, all-knowing, loving Father in Heaven—that seems to be a safe bet.

Why should we trust so much in God? Because He loves us perfectly.[15] On top of that, remember who He is: God the Father possesses divine traits that make Him uniquely able and willing to bless our lives.

He is omniscient—the divine trait of knowing all things.[16] Imagine this about a personal, loving Heavenly Father: "*He knoweth all things, and there is not anything save he knows it,*"[17] which includes all things past, present, and future.[18] The scriptures expand this understanding: "He comprehendeth all things, and all things are before him, and all things are round about him; and he is above all things, and in all things, and is through all things, and is round about all things; and all things are by him, and of him, even God, forever and ever."[19]

He is omnipresent—the divine trait of being present everywhere through the Spirit.[20] This is significant because it means we can always access Him anytime we need to.[21] He is never too busy doing something else—our prayers are heard—even if we don't feel that they are. God our Father will be with us as we need Him. Of course, our finite minds cannot comprehend how any of this is possible, but understanding that this omnipresence is through the ministry of the Holy Ghost helps.

He is omnipotent—the divine trait of having all power.[22] There is nothing more powerful than God the Father.[23] He governs all creations throughout all eternity.[24] There is no end to His holy influence. Of this, the prophet Joseph Smith taught, "And there are many kingdoms; for there is no space in the which there is no kingdom; and there is no kingdom in which there is no space, either a greater or a lesser kingdom."[25] The Father is truly "God, Almighty,"[26] for there is no power greater than His and He governs all kingdoms that exist.[27] Who better to have on your side? Consider this:

1. God created you and His primary purpose for you is to feel joy.[28]
2. He has a plan for you that, if you follow it, will bring you "never-ending happiness."[29]
3. Like a loving father, He wants *only* what is best for you.[30]
4. He has the power and the will to bring about His plan for you in your life and to bless you beyond measure.[31]
5. Everything He asks you to do—every commandment and law He wants you to obey—is designed to bring about your eternal happiness.[32]
6. You are literally a child of God. His child. His offspring.[33]
7. Putting yourself in God's hands puts you in the most capable and loving hands in the universe![34]

Of course, believing all this takes trust. It takes faith. But what if you don't feel this for or from your Heavenly Father? Feeling love for and from Him is critical. Your relationship with God is the most important relationship you can develop on this earth.

Your relationship with God is the most important relationship you can develop on this earth.

You can begin to improve that relationship by choosing to trust in Him and then patiently accepting His will more than your own. By the way, just like faith or trust, patience is not just a virtue; it's also a choice. Per the dictionary, it is "the capacity to accept or tolerate delay, trouble, or suffering without getting angry or upset."[35] In psychology, "patience is studied as a decision-making problem, involving the choice of either a small reward in the short-term, versus a more valuable reward in the long-term."[36] We empower ourselves when we choose to be patient, and, every time we do, we further develop our capability to exercise greater patience in the future.

If it makes you feel any better, it's probably worth mentioning that it's human nature to not want to wait for blessings. Recently, one of my little grandsons wanted to play with a particularly mesmerizing toy, but his brother was using it. He kept jumping up and down and energetically declaring (i.e., yelling) over and over, "I want it now!" As I watched his dramatic appeal, I wondered to myself how many times I had looked that way to Heavenly Father. I turned to my grandson and said, "You just have to wait until it's your turn."

He looked at me with innocent eyes and said, "Waiting is hard!"

Yes, waiting *is* hard, whether you're three, thirty, or three hundred. But doing hard things is what prepares us for the kingdom of God, where those who seek to be patient and trusting will enjoy thrones, principalities, powers, dominions and exaltations.[37] Elder Dieter F. Uchtdorf taught: "In this age of instant answers—where seemingly absolute and unassailable knowledge is merely a Google search away—we sometimes get frustrated when answers to our most personal, important, and urgent questions are delayed. We lift up our hearts to heaven, and all we seem to get is a frustrating, spinning 'wait cursor.'"

Elder Uchtdorf goes on to say, "Heavenly answers—eternal answers—are priceless. Receiving these answers often requires sacrifice, work, and patience. These answers are worth the wait."[38]

Add to that this apostolic promise from Elder Jeffrey R. Holland: "Some blessings come soon, some come late, and some don't come until heaven; but for those who embrace the gospel of Jesus Christ, they come."[39]

Elder Neal A. Maxwell adds this wise counsel: "Since faith in the timing of the Lord may be tried, let us learn to say not only, 'Thy will be done,' but patiently also, 'Thy timing be done.'"[40]

Trusting heavenly timing and surrendering our will to the will of God

WHY DO SOME BLESSINGS SEEM DELAYED?

are two essential characteristics we must develop to really understand how to claim the promises of heaven and fully appreciate how a loving Father seeks to bless and help us. In the next and final chapter of this section, we will discuss whether you really can count on God to keep His promises to you.

Notes

1. Matthew 5:44.
2. Isaiah 55:8.
3. "The exercise of faith in the Lord Jesus Christ is always subject to the order of heaven, to the goodness and will and wisdom and timing of the Lord. That is why we cannot have true faith in the Lord without also having complete trust in the Lord's will and in the Lord's timing." (Dallin H. Oaks, "Faith in the Lord Jesus Christ," *Ensign*, May 1994.)
4. "Patriarchal Blessings," Gospel Topics, ChurchofJesusChrist.org.
5. See Genesis 29–30.
6. Spencer J. Condie, "Claim the Exceeding Great and Precious Promises," *Ensign*, Nov. 2007.

   Elder John A. Widtsoe, a member of the Quorum of the Twelve Apostles, taught: "It should always be kept in mind that the realization of the promises made *may come in this or the future life*. Men have stumbled at times because promised blessings have not occurred in this life. They have failed to remember that, in the gospel, life with all its activities, continues forever and that the labors of the earth may be continued in heaven. Besides, the Giver of the blessings, the Lord, reserves the right to have them become active in our lives, as suits His divine purpose." (*Evidences and Reconciliations*, 3d ed. [Salt Lake City: Bookcraft, 1943], 72.)

7. See "God the Father," Gospel Topics, ChurchofJesusChrist.org.
8. Joseph Smith assured us, "As God has designed our happiness—and the happiness of all His creatures, He never has—He never will institute an ordinance or give a commandment to His people that is not calculated in its nature to promote that happiness which He has designed, and which will not end in the greatest amount of good and glory to those who become the recipients of His law and ordinances." ("History, 1838–1856, volume D-1 [1 August 1842–1 July 1843] [addenda]," p. 4 [addenda], *The Joseph Smith Papers*, accessed September 23, 2021, https://www.josephsmithpapers .org/paper-summary/history-1838 -1856-volume-d-1-1-august-1842-1 -july-1843/285).
9. Doctrine and Covenants 58:31–33.
10. Jeremy R. Jaggi, "Let Patience Have Her Perfect Work, and Count It All Joy," *Ensign*, Nov. 2020.
11. See "Counterintuitive Trends in the Link Between Premarital Sex and Marital Stability," IFS, June 6, 2016, accessed March 9, 2022, https://ifstud ies.org/blog/counterintuitive-trends-in -the-link-between-premarital-sex-and -marital-stability. See also "The Politics of Chastity," *Des Moines Register*,

November 28, 2014, accessed March 9, 2022, https://www.desmoinesregister.com/story/opinion/columnists/iowa-view/2014/11/29/chastity-politics/19648687/.

12. See 1 Kings 3:8–15.
13. 1 Kings 4:29.
14. Proverbs 3:5–6.
15. See Dieter F. Uchtdorf, "The Love of God," *Ensign*, Nov. 2009.
16. See Matthew 6:8; Alma 18:32; Doctrine and Covenants 6:16.
17. 2 Nephi 9:20.
18. See Doctrine and Covenants 130:7.
19. Doctrine and Covenants 88:41.
20. See Doctrine and Covenants 88:7–13; 41.
21. The Lord has promised, "I am with you alway, even unto the end of the world" (Matthew 28:20).
22. See Alma 26:35.
23. See "God, Godhead," Gospel Topics, ChurchofJesusChrist.org.
24. See Moses 1:3, 33.
25. Doctrine and Covenants 88:37.
26. See Moses 1:3.
27. See Doctrine and Covenants 88:6, 12–13.
28. See 2 Nephi 2:25.
29. Mosiah 2:41.
30. See Matthew 7:7–11.
31. See 1 Corinthians 2:9.
32. See note 8.
33. See "The Family Proclamation," paragraph 2, ChurchofJesusChrist.org.
34. See Proverbs 3:5–6.
35. "Patience," Lexico.com.
36. Al-Ubaydli, Jones, Weel, "Patience, cognitive skill, and coordination in the repeated stag hunt," *Journal of Neuroscience, Psychology, and Economics*, 6 (2): 71–96, 2013.
37. See Doctrine and Covenants 132:19; 121:29.
38. Dieter F. Uchtdorf, Facebook post, January 14, 2018, https://www.facebook.com/dieterf.uchtdorf/posts/640119726158708.
39. Jeffrey R. Holland, "An High Priest of Good Things to Come," *Ensign*, Nov. 1999.
40. Neal A. Maxwell, "Plow in Hope," *Ensign*, May 2001.

CHAPTER 5

Will God Keep His Promises?

Serving as a mission president in the state of Washington (USA) was a great experience. It also proved to be one of the hardest things I have ever done, though among the most rewarding. In my last six months, I found myself aspiring to what many missionaries feel—end strong and give it everything you've got, "leaving it all in the field." Through it all, I worked hard to stay in good shape physically, eating decently and exercising every day. I thought it was going pretty well, but little did I know . . .

One evening, while wrestling with my son, I made what I would consider to be a pretty cool move and pinned him (I should note that he tells the story differently—he was on the high school wrestling team at the time). In the process of making my finely-honed wrestling move, we both heard an audible crack as I felt a slight pain in my back. The pain grew worse over the next few hours until becoming what I can only describe as excruciating. I got to the point where I couldn't make the slightest move without crying out in pain.

The next day, a doctor took some X-rays. His office called a bit later asking both my wife and me to meet him after hours. (Quick tip: being asked to meet a doctor after hours is usually not a good sign.) At that meeting we learned that my T7 vertebra in the middle of my back had been broken. That was the good news. The images also showed a mass in the same location. Further CT scans found that I had masses throughout my body, one the size of a Nerf football in my abdomen. The doctor who read my scans happened to be my home teacher (clearly God knew this was coming) and got me in immediately after the scans were taken.

I was soon diagnosed with Stage 4 Non-Hodgkin's lymphoma cancer. "Shocking" would be an understatement. This one came out of nowhere, as I really didn't have any symptoms to speak of.

The doctors told me that I should leave the mission immediately and begin treatment back home as soon as possible. It was a fast-spreading cancer, and time was of the essence. I had the general impression, along with many others, that this was not just serious but would likely end my life.

Within two days of the diagnosis, Church leaders had us back home in Utah. We soon found ourselves receiving a priesthood blessing with this promise—"if" it was the Lord's desire for me to live, through faith and the power of the priesthood, I would live.

Several months and six chemo treatments later, we found ourselves thinking that things might be turning for the better. Then we were surprised to learn that one of the side effects of the steroids used in my treatment was avascular necrosis, a disease resulting in the collapse of bones around the joints. This affected both my hips and shoulders. At one point, I could not lift either arm more than a few inches.

To solve this problem, I underwent several surgeries for full joint replacements in both shoulders and both hips. I take pride in the fact that I basically had all four of my limbs chopped off and I am still here to talk about it! In total, in the years following my chemo treatments, there were fifteen times I was put under general anesthetic for various reasons.

I share this not to evoke pity or even sympathy, but because something important happened to me throughout all this: the Lord blessed my wife, Gwen, and me and our family abundantly. For me personally, believe it or not, I was somehow fully functional. I worked in my business, wrote several books, orchestrated home renovations, stayed involved with my family, and functioned in busy Church assignments—like serving at the MTC. My family made it through the abrupt adjustment from mission field to home and seemed to have found their way to making the transition work.

It was then miraculous to learn that after all the treatments and two years of careful observation, I was pronounced cured of cancer. Today as

I write this, it's been well over a decade, and I remain physically active in every way. I even play racquetball—artificial joints and all—and regularly win! (Hint: only play people who have never played before.) In all, I have been fully healed and completely restored.

In the 84th section of the Doctrine and Covenants, verse 80, the Lord makes a promise to those who faithfully serve in the mission field: "And any man [or woman] that shall go and preach this gospel of the kingdom, and fail not to continue faithful in all things, shall not be weary in mind, neither darkened, neither in body, limb, nor joint; and a hair of his head shall not fall to the ground unnoticed. And they shall not go hungry, neither athirst."

I experienced this promise in full, including the fact that everyone noticed when every hair of my head was lost! Apparently, it was in accordance with the Lord's plan for me to be blessed through all the treatments with a clear mind and to experience rejuvenated limbs and joints. The promises in that scripture were literally fulfilled in my life to the letter, something for which I will ever be grateful.

I realize this is not how it turns out for everyone, but it is one personal example of how literally the Lord's promises can be fulfilled. God will fulfill His promises in different ways for each of us, according to His plan for us, but fulfill them He will. We should feel confident that His promises to us are literal, as long as we understand that if the blessings haven't yet come, they will one day, "in his own time, and in his own way, and according to his own will."[1] My hope is that you will have increased faith in the promises of the Lord, greater desire to have His promised blessings in your life, and a better understanding of how to seek after those blessings.

We should feel confident that His promises to us
are literal, as long as we understand that if the
blessings haven't yet come, they will one day.

Why Some Blessings Are Not Granted

A question we must ask: why are these blessings not fulfilled for everyone in the same way? Some missionaries do tragically die while serving. A lovely sister missionary from a nearby community recently died while hiking on her preparation day in Europe. A few years ago, a friend's son was permanently paralyzed during a fall while on his mission in Mexico. Even in my home ward, there were men dealing with cancer at the same time I was who lost their battles and returned to their heavenly home.

Why were they not protected and healed? Why do their families need to experience such permanent loss here in mortality? How do we square these types of devastating circumstances with the Lord's scriptural promises? Are such scriptural promises somehow selective?

First, it is comforting to recall the teachings of President Joseph Fielding Smith in regard to the passing of loved ones: "No righteous man [woman] is ever taken before his [her] time. In the case of the faithful Saints, they are simply transferred to other fields of labor. The Lord's work goes on in this life, in the world of spirits, and in the kingdoms of glory where men [women] go after their resurrection."[2]

With those reassuring words, it is important to understand that God's wisdom for what you most need in your life to help bring about your exaltation always *supersedes* the fulfillment of any general scriptural promise of restoration, healing, or blessing. He does not control your life; in fact, He will not.[3] But God will influence it to give you the best chance of preparing to become like Him.

On the one hand, He wants us to understand that He will keep His promises: "I, the Lord, am bound when ye do what I say; but when ye do not what I say, ye have no promise."[4] The Savior was emphatic when He said, "And whatsoever ye shall ask in my name, that will I do, that the Father may be glorified in the Son. If ye shall ask any thing in my name, *I will do it.*"[5] You see, He binds Himself with a solemn vow to keep those promises.

On the other hand, however, is the conditional part of the promise. It seems that God, the Great Physician, has His own guiding ethics. Just like earthly healers in the medical profession who follow the principle of "primum non nocere," or "first, do no harm," God also has a similar heavenly protection clause. All of God's promises are subject to this guiding principle of "do no harm."

Heavenly Father's goal is for us to have eternal life, which is the kind of life that He lives: immortal and glorified, with eternal seed.[6] His objective is to help us be worthy to inherit the highest degree of the celestial kingdom, "to go no more out."[7] He will not do anything—even grant us blessings we are convinced we need and plead for—if it will harm our ability to achieve this ultimate eternal reward.[8]

In fact, He is so focused on helping us achieve this "state of never-ending happiness"[9] that He may withhold blessings, not answer prayers the way we hoped, or even prevent us from obtaining "blessings" that might just happen upon us (winning the lottery is not always in someone's best interest) if they will not further our ability to receive the blessings of eternity.

God balances these two things: the promise and the protection. In other words, His promises to us are always subject to the "do no harm" protection clause: preserving the experience He knows we need in this life to prepare us for the life to come is essential to God's plan for us.

How Blessings Come

In a general conference talk entitled "Abound with Blessings," Elder Dale G. Renlund addresses how the Lord blesses His children: "When you receive any blessing from God, you can conclude that you have complied with an eternal law governing reception of that blessing."[10] Remember, if we want a blessing from God, we need to understand the respective law, the pattern of requirements God has for us that the blessing is predicated upon: "For all who will have a blessing at my hands shall abide the law which was appointed for that blessing, and the conditions thereof, as were instituted from before the foundation of the world."[11] There are divine patterns associated with all of God's laws—things that we must do so the blessings can come.

Elder Renlund continues, "Most blessings that God desires to give us require action on our part—action based on our faith in Jesus Christ. Faith in the Savior is a principle of action and of power. First, we act in faith; then the power comes—according to God's will and timing. *The sequence is crucial.* The required action, though, is always tiny when compared to the blessings we ultimately receive."[12]

A friend who struggles with this (because he feels he has met the requirements but still doesn't see the blessings) suggested that God picks and chooses who to bless based on "how much He likes the person." My friend seems to think that God should be able to make a definitive statement like, "Yes, if you do this, then you get this blessing. Every time. Guaranteed." This friend also asks, "What about the millions of people who don't have any faith, don't want any, or don't need it, yet they are still receiving so-called 'blessings'?"

Really good questions.

Moroni teaches that God is always in the equation whenever something good happens, whether people know or are living God's laws or not: "Wherefore, all things which are good cometh of God; and that which is evil cometh of the devil."[13] The Savior reminded us that here in mortality, "he maketh his sun to rise on the evil and on the good, and sendeth rain on the just and on the unjust."[14] Meaning, there are blessings intended for all of His children, regardless of their faithfulness. President Dallin H. Oaks explains, "The love of God is so universal that His perfect plan bestows many gifts on all of His children, even those who disobey His laws. . . . Many other mortal gifts are not tied to our personal obedience to law."[15]

Foreshadowing our time, Malachi notes that the faithful resented how the nonbelievers prospered, mistakenly putting so much value on the temporal things of the world: "Ye have said, It is vain to serve God: and what profit is it that we have kept his ordinance, and that we have walked mournfully before the Lord of hosts? And now we call the proud happy; yea, they that work wickedness are set up; yea, they that tempt God are even delivered."[16] But Malachi clarifies that this short-term blessing of prosperity was only temporary and that those who kept the ordinances had their names recorded in a book of remembrance. Of these he says, "And they shall be mine, saith the Lord of hosts, in that day when I make up my jewels; and I will spare them, as a man spareth his own son that serveth him. Then shall ye return, and discern between the righteous and the wicked, between him that serveth God and him that serveth him not."[17]

In short, when Christ returns for the second time, the great blessing will be to be claimed by Him and to be called His people—blessings of so much more worth than any material thing we could have gained in this life!

We Activate Blessings in Our Lives

Elder Dale G. Renlund gets to the heart of the matter on how blessings come: "Some contend that blessings are completely earned; we receive them only through our works. Others argue that God has already chosen who He will bless and how—and that these determinations are unchangeable. Both positions are fundamentally flawed. Blessings from heaven are neither earned by frenetically accruing 'good deed coupons' nor by helplessly waiting to see if we win the blessing lottery. . . . No, *the truth is much more nuanced* but more appropriate for the relationship between a loving Heavenly Father and His potential heirs—us. Restored truth reveals that blessings are never earned, but faith-inspired actions on our part, both initial and ongoing, are essential."

He goes on, "That being said, you do not earn a blessing—that notion is false—but you do have to qualify for it. . . . To receive a desired blessing from God, act with faith, striking the metaphorical match on which the heavenly blessing is contingent. . . . Often, *the activation energy needed for blessings* requires more than just looking or asking; ongoing, repeated, faith-filled actions are required."[18]

I should point out that there is no automatic quid pro quo or "this for that" with God. It's not a favor for a favor.[19] While He usually requires effort on our part, there is no "easy button" to order up the blessings we seek; that's *not* how it works. Not how He works. The promised blessings for obeying the Father's will come according to His will, in His own time frame, and in His own way—yet always for our ultimate good. And that's the way we should want it. Putting our trust in an all-knowing, all-powerful, always-present, and all-loving Being is just a smart move. Wanting what He wants, when He thinks we should receive it, and in the way He feels it should come will ultimately provide the positive outcomes we seek, often better than how we could imagine.

What we can be sure of is that His words and promises will "all be ful-filled."[20] And while He generally requires action on our part, we can never put God in debt to us through those actions—the blessings that come are, ultimately, always a gift and never given in exchange just for some effort on our part.[21]

Putting it all together, words we could use to explain how we seek blessings from God are "qualify" or, as Elder Renlund described, "activate." This last word seems the most descriptive—activate: "to make something operative."[22] It means to begin the process of starting, triggering, or ener-gizing something. Obtaining blessings usually involves the activating effort on our part that is associated with our desired blessing.

Obtaining blessings usually involves the activating effort on our part that is associated with our desired blessing.

Speaking to those who feel that promised blessings appear out of reach, Sister Linda S. Reeves, former Second Counselor in the Relief Society General Presidency, shared this experience: "Recently I talked to an old friend who has gone through two divorces due to the addictions and unfaithfulness of her husbands. She and her three children have suf-fered greatly. She pleaded, 'I have tried so hard to live righteously. Why have I had so many trials? What have I done wrong? What does Heavenly Father want me to do? I pray and read my scriptures, help my children, and go to the temple often.' As I listened to this sister, I felt like shouting out, 'You are doing it! You are doing all that Heavenly Father wants and hopes you will do!'"

Sister Reeves added, "Sisters, I do not know why we have the many trials that we have, but it is my personal feeling that the reward is so great, so eternal and everlasting . . . we may feel to say to our merciful, loving Father, 'Was that *all* that was required?' I believe that if we could daily remember and recognize the depth of that love our Heavenly Father and our Savior have for us, we would be willing to do anything to be back in Their presence again, surrounded by Their love eternally. What will it matter, dear sisters, what we suffered here if, in the end, those trials are the very things which qualify us for eternal life and exaltation in the kingdom of God with our Father and Savior?"[23]

Was there any part of you that felt like kicking the cat or screaming into a pillow when Sister Reeves said, "Was that *all* that was required?" It may be hard to say, "Was that all that was required?" when in the throes of deep challenges. But the day will come when we will be presented with unimagined blessings so splendid that we would do anything to obtain them if we could see them now.[24] Indeed, *any* price we pay now for the immensity of blessings that await us will seem small by comparison.

In these first five chapters we have covered some of the most common questions related to God's divine intervention in our lives:

- How do blessings come from God?
- How does God decide which blessings to grant and which to withhold?
- Does God have a specific plan for me?
- Why do some blessings seem delayed or never come?
- Does God keep His promises?

We've also created some context around how to seek after and obtain the blessings of heaven, and the nuances associated with how those blessings come from God.

In the second section, Divine Patterns, we will begin our journey through twenty-five divine patterns selected from the scriptures that are central to our faith in a loving, merciful, and generous God.

Notes

1. Doctrine and Covenants 88:68.
2. Address given at the funeral of Elder Richard L. Evans, November 4, 1971, 1; see also Spencer W. Kimball, *Faith Precedes the Miracle* (Salt Lake City: Deseret Book, 1972), 103, 105.
3. President Wilford Woodruff taught: "By virtue of this agency you and I and all mankind are made responsible beings, responsible for the course we pursue, the lives we live, the deeds we do in the body. It is part of the divine economy not to force any man to heaven, not to coerce the mind but to leave it free to act for itself. [God] lays before His creature man the everlasting gospel, the principles of life and salvation, and then leaves him to choose for himself or to reject for himself, with the definite understanding that he becomes responsible to Him for the results of his acts." (*Teachings of Presidents of the Church: Wilford Woodruff* [2004], 207.)
4. Doctrine and Covenants 82:10.
5. John 14:13–14.
6. See "Becoming Like God," Gospel Topics Essays, ChurchofJesusChrist.org.
7. 3 Nephi 28:40.
8. Richard G. Scott explained, "His invitation, 'Ask, and ye shall receive' (3 Ne. 27:29) does not assure that you will get what you *want*. It does guarantee that, if worthy, you will get what you *need,* as judged by a Father that loves you perfectly, who wants your eternal happiness even more than do you." ("Trust in the Lord," *Ensign*, Nov. 1995.)
9. Mosiah 2:41.
10. Dale G. Renlund, "Abound with Blessings," *Ensign*, May 2019.
11. Doctrine and Covenants 132:5.
12. See note 10.
13. Moroni 7:12.
14. Matthew 5:44–45.
15. Dallin H. Oaks, "Love and Law," *Ensign*, Nov. 2009.
16. Malachi 3:14–15.
17. Malachi 3:16–18.
18. Dale G. Renlund, "Abound with Blessings," *Ensign*, May 2019.
19. "Some misunderstand the promises of God to mean that obedience to Him yields specific outcomes on a fixed schedule. . . . If life doesn't fall out precisely . . . according to an expected timetable, they may feel betrayed by God. But things are not so mechanical in the divine economy. We ought not to think of God's plan as a cosmic vending machine where we (i) select a desired blessing, (ii) insert the required sum of good works, and (iii) the order is promptly delivered. God will indeed honor His covenants and promises to each of us . . . , but not every blessing predicated on obedience to law is shaped, designed and timed according to our expectations. We do our best but must leave to Him the management of blessings, both temporal and spiritual. President Brigham Young explained that his faith was not built on certain outcomes or blessings but on his witness of and relationship with Jesus Christ. He said: 'My faith is not placed upon . . . whether we are blessed or not blessed, but *my faith is placed upon the Lord Jesus Christ, and my knowledge I have received from him.*'" (D. Todd Christofferson, "Our Relationship with God," *Liahona*, May 2022.)
20. Doctrine and Covenants 1:37–38.
21. See Mosiah 2:23–25.
22. "Activate," Lexico.com.
23. Linda S. Reeves, "Worthy of Our Promised Blessings," *Ensign*, Nov. 2015.
24. See 1 Corinthians 2:9.

DIVINE PATTERNS

PART 1

Experiencing God's Power

CHAPTER 6

Motivated by Love:
Loving God and Keeping His Commandments

— JOHN 14:15 —

Consider for a moment all the forces that exist in the universe that cause things to happen. There are the many familiar forces of nature that affect us every day. There are also the forces of man, with laws and armies that can compel desired behavior. But, of all the forces in the world, President Dallin H. Oaks taught, "Love is the most powerful."[1]

I recall the first time I read what, to me, was a sobering doctrine taught by the Apostle Paul: the only motivation that really counts with God is love. "Though I bestow all my goods to feed the poor, and though I give my body to be burned, and have not charity, it profiteth me nothing."[2] That means that it's not enough to just do the right things; we also must do them for the right reason.

Clearly, Paul was teaching that truly loving God and His children is the most important thing we can do—prized by Him above all other earthly sacrifices. Without that love, no other achievement, accomplishment, success, or sacrifice really amounts to all that much. Ultimately, the "why" behind what we do, our motivation, really does matter to the Lord, particularly when it comes to seeking blessings from a generous Heavenly Parent.[3]

The Why

I recall one day when one of my little grandsons was playing in the pool with a prized toy boat, the *Titanic*. He and his brother were taking turns and competing to see who could sink it the fastest. I was surprised when the oldest volunteered to give the ship to his little brother before his turn was over. I thought, *what a good boy!* Then, I realized that he was giving up the ship early in order to get the new toy that was lying on the side of the pool—a toy not yet noticed by his younger brother. At that moment, the good deed lost its luster in the light of understanding his motivation. Of course, once his younger brother realized he had been tricked . . . it wasn't good.

As human behavior would have it, we can do the right thing for the wrong reasons. When that happens, heavenly accounting can see our actions as a minus, not a plus.

The scriptures are filled with divine patterns that describe how we obtain the blessings of God. For example, "Inasmuch as ye shall keep my commandments ye shall prosper in the land."[4] This divine pattern, like all others, tells us *what* we need to do to prosper in the land at the Lord's hand: keep His commandments. What it doesn't tell us, however, is *why* we should do it. The "why" places a condition on receiving the full blessings God is willing to grant, meaning that to receive all He is willing to give, you also have to do it for the right reasons.

This divine pattern, of loving God and keeping His commandments, prioritizes what He expects from His true followers: those who love Him. He wants us to start by obeying His commandments because we love Him—an essential step in everyone's personal quest to "come unto Christ."[5] Everything else follows after that. Everything.

The Savior's Kind of Obedience

The degree to which we love God is often revealed by how obedient we are. Do we pick and choose what we will obey from the menu of commandments? Speaking of this, Elder Robert D. Hales of the Quorum of the Twelve Apostles taught: "At times members may participate in 'selective obedience,' claiming to love God and honor God while picking and choosing which of His commandments and teachings—and the teachings and counsel of His prophets—they will fully follow." He went on, "Spiritually mature obedience is 'the Savior's obedience.' It is motivated by true love for Heavenly Father and His Son."[6]

I have come to believe that most of us have our own short list of "favorite sins"—things we know are not quite right but choose to do anyway because of preference, convenience, laziness, or habit. Because of this, we are all guilty of some form of "selective obedience."

We've learned to coexist with and even accept these "favorite" sins and weaknesses rather than to change them and continue our pursuit of sanctifying and perfecting our lives. In a sense, we let ourselves get away with it, taking ourselves off the hook and thinking that it doesn't really affect us that much, after all. But does it? God would have us root out any imperfection that ultimately affects our ability to have the companionship of the Holy Ghost, no matter how comfortable that undesired habit may be. Our selective obedience doesn't mean we don't love Him. However, the more we do love Him, the more perfected and less selective our obedience becomes.

> The more we do love Him, the more perfected
> and less selective our obedience becomes.

The driving force in our quest to become like the Father and the Son should be the love of God. Loving Him. Loving His ways, His truths. Loving, thinking, and acting how He thinks and acts. Loving righteousness. His directive, "If ye love me, keep my commandments,"[7] also has embedded in it an important truth: that you actually *are* personally capable, with His help, of keeping every commandment He has given or He would not have asked. Of course, this is done only through our Savior and the power of His Atonement—providing the help we all most certainly need as we stumble and fall in our striving to become like Him. The Apostle Paul reminds us, "There hath no temptation taken you but such as is common to man: but God is faithful, who will not suffer you to be tempted above that ye are able; but will with the temptation also make a way to escape, that ye may be able to bear it."[8] The Prophet Joseph taught, "Satan cannot seduce us by his enticements unless we in our hearts consent and yield."[9] Neither God nor Satan can influence us to act unless we allow them to do it.

Nephi testifies that the Lord will never give us a commandment except "he shall prepare a way for them that they may accomplish the thing which he commandeth them."[10] We can do anything God asks of us, if we are willing and if we are motivated by our love for Him and all that He represents. Of course, there is a learning curve when it comes to perfecting our obedience. Fortunately, God has made provision for granting forgiveness as we "practice" our faith in the most literal sense.

I was moved by the story a friend, Diane Wunderli, told in a young single adult stake conference, about her experience preparing to serve a mission with her husband after he was called to serve as mission president. Their call was to Cape Verde, an island nation in the Atlantic Ocean off the coast of Africa, where the ten islands that comprise the country are just larger than the state of Rhode Island in the USA.

Diane's husband, Dave, decided to use Google Maps to view their soon-to-be home. As Dave zoomed in on the satellite photo, they saw a picture of a tiny, remote, desolate island with very few buildings. As Diane looked at the picture on the screen, impressions flooded her mind of her carrying drinking water in buckets, needing to find creative ways to supply and serve rice and beans to all of their missionaries, living on dirt floors and cooking on open fires, as it looked that remote. And with each thought the words came to her mind, "And will you?" She responded each time: "Of course I will!"

As her husband zoomed the picture even closer, she then realized there were no cars, roads, or greenery. And, again, the question came to her mind, "But will you?" Again, each time she responded with, "Of course I will!"

Then, Dave said, "Oh wait . . . I searched the wrong name!"

He then zeroed in on a nearby island that had homes, vegetation, cars, roads—all the signs of civilization she had been hoping for. Diane felt relieved to see that the mission home would be in a place with beauty and some conveniences.

She was then struck by the realization that she actually seemed willing do whatever the Lord needed done. She said, "It was a very sacred experience for me and has carried me through many more difficult experiences on the mission as I have turned to Him. With great love, compassion, and understanding He has whispered again and again . . . 'I know . . . but will you?' That compassion and understanding has strengthened me like nothing else. With great humility, love, and devotion, I continue to respond, 'Of course I will!'"[11]

Diane loved the Lord and was willing to keep His commandments, regardless of how inconvenient it might be. In fact, she was more than willing; she was anxious to obey, even cheerfully. She experienced what Elder Joseph B. Wirthlin described when he said, "When we love the Lord, obedience ceases to be a burden. Obedience becomes a delight."[12]

The engine that powers our obedience is our love for God. The greater our love, the greater our power to keep His commandments.

My wife, Gwen, and I experienced this in a significant way in the first years of our marriage while living in California. We wanted children but were unsuccessful after three years of marriage. Bishop Theo Lassig, who we greatly loved and appreciated, called us in one Sunday. He asked if we would be willing to chaperone a youth conference to be held in Utah. He said that it would take a week of our time and cost 250 dollars each. At the time, I was working a job requiring considerable travel. My immediate thought was that as a new employee, I had only one week of vacation a year, and using that to chaperone a youth conference didn't seem like it would be the rejuvenating shot-in-the-arm I would be looking for. On top of that, money was tight, so finding the budget to pay for the trip would be difficult. However, at the time and throughout our lives, Gwen and I had a very clear guiding principle: *whatever the Lord wants, the Lord gets*. So, we agreed to go and began to prepare.

As part of the trip, we thought we would arrange to visit Gwen's parents, who lived in Utah. In fact, we wanted her father to give us each a blessing, as our great desire was to have children and we wanted to call on priesthood power for help. It had been three years with no hope of success in sight.

The trip from California to Utah was everything we imagined—lots of energetic youth having the time of their lives. It was a great experience to be with them and to support the cause. One evening, we arranged to slip away and visit with Gwen's parents to get the blessing we were seeking. While it's not always the case, in this situation we were blessed that "children would come into our lives and that our desires would be granted." We were thrilled to hear about the promise of this blessing. Driving back to the youth conference, Gwen and I reflected on how grateful we were that the bishop had asked us to chaperone the trip—definitely not the outcome I expected when he made the inspired invitation.

But something else happened from that trip: our blessings were literally doubled that year. Not only were we delighted to see the first of five children come nine months later, but we were blessed in temporal ways as well.

Shortly after returning from Utah, I was sitting in a conference room in a meeting with the small company I worked for. The CEO came into the room and announced that for the first time they would be doing something special in December for everyone—all employees were being given the last week of the year off, in addition to a nice Christmas bonus. Double the vacation and a bonus that was double the cost of the youth trip! Unexpected blessings.

Would these good things have happened if we had not made the choice to be obedient? From our perspective, likely not. In this instance, we believe our obedience was essential for bringing about the blessings that Heavenly Father already intended for us to have; He just needed us to act. Elder Neal A. Maxwell said of choices, "As you submit your wills to God, you are giving Him the only thing you can actually give Him that is really yours to give."[13]

God's Love

God loves all of His children perfectly. All are equal in His eyes. Elder Holland taught, "The first great *truth* of all eternity is that God loves *us* with all of *His* heart, might, mind, and strength. That love is the foundation stone of eternity, and it should be the foundation stone of our daily life."[14] President Thomas S. Monson explained: "That love never changes. . . . It is there for you when you are sad or happy, discouraged or hopeful. God's love is there for you whether or not you feel you deserve [it]. It is simply always there."[15] President Nelson describes the love God has for us as "divine love," a love that is infinite, universal, enduring, and perfect. Correctly understood, this love is not unconditional, as some might think. Rather, President Nelson teaches, the higher levels of love that God has for us is, in fact, are conditional— "the full flower of divine love and our greatest blessings from that love are conditional—predicated upon our obedience to eternal law."[16]

It is difficult to feel personally motivated to obey God if you don't feel His love for you. Feeling God's love isn't a given for everyone. Quite the contrary. There are those who don't really feel it—even when they are seeking to do the right things like faithfully serving in the Church, attending Church meetings, serving others, or worshipping in the temple. Feeling His love for us isn't something that just happens; we must put ourselves in the condition to receive it. And, if that is how we are feeling, "Job One" must be to grow in our love of God. To do that, consider these few essential things.

First, we love those we know. Coming to know Him better through prayer is key to feeling God's love. Since God is love, when we sincerely approach Him, we will begin to see and feel His love for us.[17] Elder Juan A. Uceda taught, "At the very moment we say, 'Father in Heaven,' He hears our prayers and is sensitive to us and our needs."[18] Remembering that He has no favorites[19] and that He loves all of His children perfectly can help you realize that He is there for you, too. Elder David A. Bednar reminds us, "God does not have a list of favorites to which we must hope our names will someday be added."[20] Coupled with prayer, we should look for how the hand of the Lord, His kindness and mercy, is manifest in our life. To know God is to love God.

Second, we love those we serve. One important way to increase your love for God is to serve Him. Of course, we know that "when you are in the service of your fellow beings ye are only in the service of your God."[21] Serving others—watching someone's children, picking up something from the store, assisting in a job search, paying someone a social visit—increases love toward those served and, ultimately, for God Himself.[22]

One familiar story tells of a boy who wanted to give a gift to his teacher, who was returning home to England from a faraway nation. The boy lacked money to buy a gift. The day before the teacher was to leave, the boy brought her a huge seashell. The teacher asked where he had gotten the shell. It was from a bay many miles away. The teacher exclaimed that it was beautiful, but that he shouldn't have gone so far to get her such an exquisite gift. The boy simply said, "The long walk was part of the gift." A profound truth: the greater our service, the deeper we will feel.

Finally, we love those who love us. President Dieter F. Uchtdorf shared, "Since 'God is love,' the closer we approach Him, the more profoundly we experience love. But because a veil separates this mortality from our heavenly home, we must seek in the Spirit that which is imperceptible to mortal eyes."[23] As we seek to spiritually connect with God, we will feel His love in return. "We love him, because he first loved us."[24]

When Jesus was asked, "Which is the great commandment in the law?"[25] He responded by prioritizing all the gospel truths, contained in hundreds of pages of written scripture known at the time, into two succinct ideas: "Thou shalt love the Lord thy God with all thy heart, and with all thy soul, and with all thy mind. This is the first and great commandment. And the second is like unto it, Thou shalt love thy neighbor as thyself."[26]

Our singular and great motivation for all that we do in the gospel should be the love of God—and not half-hearted love, but a love with all our heart, might, mind and strength, greater than our love for anything else on this earth or anyone else we may ever know. This is important to get right. President Uchtdorf stated, "For what we love determines what we seek. What we seek determines what we think and do. What we think and do determines who we are—and who we will become."[27] When we get this right, we will find the personal power needed to exercise our will to keep the commandments, no matter what else is happening around us.

Our singular and great motivation for all that we do in the gospel should be the love of God.

This pattern matters:

1. Love God
2. Love others as yourself

It is most often the case that by loving God first, we find the power and ability to truly love others as ourselves. When we are filled with the love of God, we are blessed with personal power to keep the commandments. We are given an inner strength that can come in *no other way.* Then, no matter how hard the winds of tribulation may be blowing against us, we will forever remain a "true follower" of the Lord Jesus Christ.[28]

Notes

1. See Dallin H. Oaks, "The Gospel Culture," *Ensign,* Mar. 2012.
2. 1 Corinthians 13:3.
3. See Joseph B. Wirthlin, "The Great Commandment," *Ensign,* Nov. 2007.
4. 2 Nephi 1:20.
5. See Jeffrey R. Holland, "Do We Love Him?" *Ensign,* Nov. 2007.
6. Robert D. Hales, "If Ye Love Me, Keep My Commandments," *Ensign,* May 2014.
7. John 14:15.
8. 1 Corinthians 10:13.
9. *Teachings of Presidents of the Church: Joseph Smith* (2007), 214.
10. 1 Nephi 3:7.
11. Personal email from Diane Wunderli

on September 19, 2021; shared with permission.
12. Joseph B. Wirthlin, "The Great Commandment," *Ensign,* Nov. 2007.
13. Neal A. Maxwell, "Remember How Merciful the Lord Hath Been," *Ensign,* May 2004.
14. Jeffrey R. Holland, "Tomorrow the Lord Will Do Wonders among You," *Ensign,* May 2016.
15. Thomas S. Monson, "We Never Walk Alone," *Ensign,* Nov. 2013.
16. Russell M. Nelson taught: "While divine love can be called perfect, infinite, enduring, and universal, it cannot correctly be characterized as *unconditional.* The word does not appear in the scriptures. On the other

67

hand, many verses affirm that the higher levels of love the Father and the Son feel for each of us—and certain divine blessings stemming from that love—are *conditional*. Before citing examples, it is well to recognize various forms of conditional expression in the scriptures. . . . Understanding that divine love and blessings are not truly "unconditional" can defend us against common fallacies such as these: 'Since God's love is unconditional, He will love me regardless . . .'; or 'Since "God is love," He will love me unconditionally, regardless . . .' Does this mean the Lord does not love the sinner? Of course not. Divine love is infinite and universal. The Savior loves both saints and sinners." ("Divine Love," *Ensign*, Feb. 2003.)

17. See 1 John 4:8.

18. Juan A. Uceda, "The Lord Jesus Christ Teaches Us to Pray," *Ensign*, Nov. 2016.
19. See Romans 2:11.
20. David A. Bednar, "The Tender Mercies of the Lord," *Ensign*, May 2005.
21. Mosiah 2:17.
22. See Moroni 7:47. President Marion G. Romney taught, "Service is the very fiber of which an exalted life in the celestial kingdom is made" ("The Celestial Nature of Self-Reliance," *Ensign*, Nov. 1982).
23. Dieter F. Uchtdorf, "The Love of God," *Ensign*, Nov. 2009.
24. 1 John 4:19.
25. Matthew 22:36.
26. Matthew 22:37–39.
27. Dieter F. Uchtdorf, "The Love of God," *Ensign*, Nov. 2009.
28. See Moroni 7:48.

CHAPTER 7

Deliverance from Trials: Trials and Witnesses

— ETHER 12:6 —

Our bodies are really quite amazing. They come with an immune system made up of a very complex and sophisticated network of proteins and cells that defend against infection. Incredibly, "the immune system keeps a record of every germ (microbe) it has ever defeated so it can recognize and destroy the microbe quickly if it enters the body again."[1] We can help our immune system by receiving vaccines that are designed to help us become immune to a particular virus or bacteria. When we say someone is "immune," we are saying that they are "exempt" from that disease.[2]

The Boy in the Plastic Bubble is a film that made famous the story of a little boy, David Vetter, who was born with a compromised immune system. With his body entirely unable to fight infection, his only safety was to live in a completely sterile environment—a plastic bubble. Scientists refer to David's immune system defect (severe combined immunodeficiency, or SCID) as "bubble boy disease." David lived twelve years in this bubble but ultimately succumbed, dying in 1984 at the age of thirteen.[3]

Imagine if you could be made immune to the trials of mortal life, living in a spiritual bubble of sorts, one that would protect you from any pain, suffering, hurt, discouragement, or despair. Sounds pretty good, doesn't it? But how would that affect your ability to learn and grow here in mortality?

At first, this was the case for Adam and Eve. Their Garden of Eden "bubble" provided just such an immunity from the adversities of mortal life. Thankfully, they came to recognize that they were everlastingly limited while in this Edenic condition and chose to leave. Leaving the garden brought upon them all the ups and downs of mortal life, along with the very real blessings that come from earthly experiences.

The Refiner's Fire

As we well know, there is no "pain-free" vaccine available to inoculate us from hardship here in mortality—and for good reason. The refining fire that comes with the trials of life is a primary purpose for our living here—to be tested, tried, and proven. It's how we are prepared to literally inherit "thrones, kingdoms, principalities, and powers, dominions, all heights and depths."[4] It is by heavenly design that our lives are frequented with challenging circumstances that require the exercise of faith, the endurance of suffering, and the expression of choice as we employ our agency and deal with adversity. We shouldn't be surprised when these things come; rather, our curiosity should be piqued if they don't.

There may have been no one better prepared to teach us about how to deal with the trials of life than the last Book of Mormon prophet, Moroni. He was born into a world of degradation and violence where people were "without principle, and past feeling."[5] Moroni witnessed (and participated in) the final cataclysmic battles that resulted in over a quarter million of his people being slain.[6]

One historian writes, "With the loss of his father and his people, Moroni inherited a burden of loneliness virtually unparalleled in human history. By the time of his first entry on the plates, Moroni had already wandered alone for some sixteen years; and another twenty years were still to pass before he finally sealed up the records."[7]

Moroni's initial words are infused with incomprehensible sorrow: "*I am alone.* My father hath been slain in battle, and all my kinsfolk, and I have not friends nor whither to go; and how long the Lord will suffer that I may live I know not. . . . The Lamanites have hunted my people . . . from place to place, even until they are no more. . . . And I even remain alone to write the sad tale of the destruction of my people."[8]

It is this great, prepared prophet who was rightly chosen to connect the past with the present and a modern-day Restoration. This empathetic angel messenger is who appeared to Joseph Smith and taught the fundamental doctrine that the resurrected Lord is our Savior and Deliverer. Moroni was chief in the ranks of mortal men who faced trial and challenge and knew of what he spoke when saying: "And now, I, Moroni, would speak somewhat concerning these things; I would show unto the world that faith is things which are hoped for and not seen; wherefore, dispute not because ye see not, for *ye receive no witness until after the trial of your faith.*"[9]

No witness? No witness of what? That the gospel is true? That the trials we face are part of a divine plan? That God is in it, whatever "it" might be?

God can and will deliver you from whatever *it* is you are facing. In the same way God delivered Nephi and his family to the promised land, He will deliver you "beyond this vale of sorrow into a far better land of promise."[10]

God can and will deliver you from whatever *it* is you are facing.

The scriptures are filled with stories that teach how God is our Deliverer. This was first impressed upon me as a boy, not yet a member of the Church, through a favorite childhood movie, *The Ten Commandments.* Who can forget the story of captive Israel enslaved by their Egyptian taskmasters? For four hundred years the Israelites were enslaved, pushed to their limits, then finally delivered through the miraculous power of God as Jehovah demonstrated His power through the prophet Moses and the ten plagues: blood, frogs, lice, wild animals, pestilence, boils, fiery hail, locusts, darkness, and finally, death of the firstborn.[11] This demonstration of power was probably not only for the Egyptians' sake but also for the Israelites to see that their deliverance was by the hand of God, a signature that will be apparent every time God delivers us—if we have the faith to see it.

One friend, Kim Asay, shared his remarkable story of deliverance, which I share with his permission. Kim was enjoying a successful career in a thriving business. Things were going very well for him. Then suddenly, he found himself unemployed with eight children to feed. Many attempts to start over resulted in failure and great disappointment. As the hardship continued for days, weeks, months, and years, he became angry with God and felt deserted by Him—it was as though Kim had been taken captive by his own personal Egyptian regiment—feeling that his cries for deliverance were left unanswered.

Yet, as he faced the temptation to give up on God and leave the Church, he asked himself, "Where will you go?" Kim realized there was nowhere else to turn to find what he already knew he had—the truth. With that realization, he got to a place where he could humbly repent of his anger and internal rebellion. Within only a couple months of his *mighty change of heart*,[12] he was blessed "beyond [his] wildest imaginations." He soon went on to start what would become a very successful company, one that has blessed both him and his family in marvelous ways. Kim was delivered in a way that he could readily recognize the signature— it could only be the very hand of God.

Remember the pattern: "trials and witnesses." As we experience trials, God is prepared to provide witnesses, all along the way, that He is with us, helping us and intent on delivering us. Those witnesses are most obvious when we are looking for the operation of the divine hand in our lives and the blessings He has given us, however small.[13] Our expressions of gratitude matter to God. They matter to us, as well, allowing us to become our own firsthand witness of the divine hand in our life.

We are all familiar with the biblical story of when the disciples of Jesus found themselves in a ship "in the midst of the sea, tossed with the waves: for the wind was contrary."[14] I didn't fully appreciate what this meant until a friend of mine, a master boater, explained that in a stiff wind, you keep the nose, or bow of the boat, pointed in the direction of the wind to keep the boat from capsizing. As a result, he said that it was fairly easy—especially in the dark—to lose your sense of direction, which could prove deadly in such circumstances.

It was in these dire conditions that the scripture states, "And in the fourth watch of the night Jesus went unto them, walking on the sea."[15] The fourth watch was a scheduling term used by the Romans that referred to the last watch of the night, from 3:00 a.m. to 6:00 a.m. The point: the Lord allowed the disciples to be tossed to and fro upon the waters, toiling all through the night to the early hours of the morning, until it was readily apparent to them that only God could deliver them. To make the point even more definitively, the Savior walked out upon the water to save them.[16] Only God could do what He was doing. He was indeed their Deliverer.

While serving as Young Women General President, Sister Susan W. Tanner testified that the Lord will certainly come to each of us, though we may generally need to be patient: "I know that His tender mercies and His miracles, large and small, are real. They come in His way and on His timetable. Sometimes it is not until we have reached our extremity. *Jesus's disciples on the Sea of Galilee had to toil in rowing against a contrary wind all through the night before Jesus finally came to their aid.* He did not come until the 'fourth watch,' meaning near dawn. Yet He did come. (See Mark 6:45–51.) My testimony is that miracles do come, though sometimes not until the fourth watch."[17]

In the very same way, Jesus Christ is also our Deliverer.[18] He can deliver us from any circumstance, any trial, any hardship—any and every condition in which we find ourselves. There is nothing He cannot deliver us from.[19] Why then, can't it be easier? Why can't it come in that more convenient "first watch" we all hope for? Because deliverance must come after the trial of our faith. Thousands of years of scripture bears witness to the fact: "easy" is just not how God typically does it. He will sometimes show up in the "fourth watch" of the night, after we have exhausted our own abilities and there is no other way we can be saved.

As previously said, God is not just a "God of our gaps" deliverer. He doesn't always wait until the fourth watch but is anxious to actively help throughout our trial, every step of the way. Even still, most of us will have "fourth-watch" trials that will test our faith in the Deliverer to the very core. When that fourth-watch test comes, be assured God will ultimately step in to save you.

> Most of us will have "fourth-watch" trials that
> will test our faith in the Deliverer to the very
> core. When that fourth-watch test comes, be
> assured God will ultimately step in to save you.

With amazing vulnerability and transparency, Elder D. Todd Christofferson, of the Quorum of the Twelve Apostles, detailed his own learning from a significant trial he experienced, "a personal economic challenge that persisted for several years." He said, "It did not come about as a consequence of anyone's wrongdoing or ill will; it was just one of those things that sometimes come into our lives. It ebbed and flowed in seriousness and urgency, but it never went away completely. At times this challenge threatened the welfare of my family and me, and I thought we might be facing financial ruin. I prayed for some miraculous intervention to deliver us. Although I offered that prayer many times with great sincerity and earnest desire, the answer in the end was 'No.' Finally I learned to pray as the Savior did: 'Nevertheless not my will, but thine, be done' (Luke 22:42). I sought the Lord's help with each tiny step along the way to a final resolution."

Elder Christofferson continued: "There were times when I had exhausted all my resources, when I had nowhere or no one to turn to at that moment, when there was simply no other human being I could call on to help meet the exigency before me. With no other recourse, more than once I fell down before my Heavenly Father begging in tears for His help. And He did help. Sometimes it was nothing more than a sense of peace, a feeling of assurance that things would work out. I might not see how or what the path would be, but He gave me to know that, directly or indirectly, He would open a way. Circumstances might change, a new and helpful idea might come to mind, some unanticipated income or other resource might appear at just the right time. Somehow there was a resolution.

"Though I suffered then, as I look back now, *I am grateful that there was not a quick solution to my problem.* The fact that I was forced to turn to God for help almost daily over an extended period of years taught me truly how to pray and get answers to prayer and taught me in a very practical way to have faith in God. I came to know my Savior and my Heavenly Father in a way and to a degree that might not have happened otherwise or that might have taken me much longer to achieve. I learned that daily bread is a precious commodity. I learned that manna today can be as real as the physical manna of biblical history. I learned to trust in the Lord with all my heart. I learned to walk with Him day by day."[20]

Bottom line: Elder Christofferson experienced the "daily bread" blessing that came by relying on the Savior every single day, not just at the end of his trial when he had exhausted every other resource or possibility. God is anxious to assist us with our daily needs, especially as we endure longer-term trials; giving us strength when we are pressed or feel "heavy laden" and in need of rest.[21]

The Witness

Again, what of Moroni's promise of the "witness?"[22] As a verb, the word means to see something take place, to "have knowledge from personal observation or experience." As a noun, *witness* refers to "a person who sees an event," or for something to serve as evidence or proof. [23] The witness promised by Moroni will come in a way you can readily accept as a manifestation from God—from something as simple as a peaceful feeling brought by the Spirit of God, to something as dramatic as seeing heavenly beings.[24]

As with Elder Christofferson, when the Lord does provide the witness of His involvement in your life, He will do it in a way that you can recognize His divine hand. The witness will always include His holy signature—in some way, you will personally know it is of God. Of course, there is always room for doubt when faith is required, but God will provide sufficient evidence for you to believe. You may not immediately recognize it. It may happen in retrospect, as you look back on the circumstance and realize what the Lord has done. But when you do recognize it, you will likely exclaim, "For behold, it is he that has delivered us [me]; yea, that has done this great thing for us [me]."[25]

Here are some questions to ask yourself that will help you more clearly see His hand—His witness:

1. Did the help/answer/blessing come in the "fourth watch"? Is God trying to help me see that it must be Him, as all of my other efforts have failed?

2. Do I feel tried and thoroughly tested? Did the answer come after I felt this way?

3. If I were to explain this to someone who does not live by faith, would they say I was very lucky or that it was a rare coincidence?

4. Do I know, deep within my heart, that it must be God who has brought about this great thing?

5. Was it miraculous to me to receive the blessing how and/or when I did?

Reflecting on these questions will help you recognize the Lord's hand, giving you your own personal witness that comes from faithfully enduring our own personal trials.

I recall reminiscing with one of my sons about an experience our family had in which the Lord clearly delivered us in a time of need years earlier. As we talked, my son said, "Dad, I still pray about that situation."

I was a bit surprised and asked, "Why are you doing that?" It had been at least two years since the situation was resolved.

His humbling response: "For over a year, I prayed every day that the Lord would help. Now, I pray every day and give thanks that the Lord did help."

I was deeply moved by his example. Of all the people who should be continuing to show their gratitude for this deliverance, it should be me, not him. I was reminded of the parable of the ten lepers: "And one of them, when he saw that he was healed, turned back, and *with a loud voice* glorified God, and fell down on his face at his feet, giving him thanks: and he was a Samaritan. And Jesus answering said, 'Were there not ten cleansed? but where are the nine?' 'There are not found that returned to give glory to God, save this stranger.' And he said unto him, 'Arise, go thy way: thy faith hath made thee whole.'"[26]

Taking a page from our son, to this day our deliverance in this situation is remembered in our daily prayers—even though it is many years later. Why? So that the Lord might know *that we know* that we have received the many marvelous witnesses, after so great a trial, that He did intervene and deliver us. We will never forget what He has done for us. And it shall be that way for all who seek Him: "If from thence thou shalt seek the Lord thy God, thou shalt find *him,* if thou seek him with all thy heart and with all thy soul."[27] God is, indeed, watching and helping—anxious to bless you "in every time of trouble."[28]

Notes

1. Department of Health & Human Services. "Immune System." *Better Health Channel*, Department of Health & Human Services, Mar. 30, 2014, www.betterhealth.vic.gov.au/health /conditionsandtreatments/immune -system.
2. "Immune," Lexico.com.
3. Immune Deficiency Foundation, "The Story of David Vetter," accessed July 15, 2021, https://primaryimmune.org /story-david-vetter.
4. Doctrine and Covenants 132:19.
5. Moroni 9:20.
6. See Mormon 8:3.
7. W. Cole Durham, "Moroni," *Ensign*, June 1978.
8. Mormon 8:5, 7, 3.
9. Ether 12:6.
10. Alma 37:45.
11. See Exodus 7–11.
12. See Alma 5:14.
13. President Henry B. Eyring related: "When our children were very small, I started to write down a few things about what happened every day. . . . I wrote down a few lines every day for years. I never missed a day no matter how tired I was or how early I would have to start the next day. Before I would write, I would ponder this question: 'Have I seen the hand of God reaching out to touch us or our children or our family today?' As I kept at it, something began to happen. As I would cast my mind

over the day, I would see evidence of what God had done for one of us that I had not recognized in the busy moments of the day. As that happened, and it happened often, I realized that trying to remember had allowed God to show me what He had done." ("O Remember, Remember," *Ensign*, Nov. 2007.)

14. Matthew 14:24.
15. Matthew 14:25.
16. See Matthew 14:26.
17. Susan W. Tanner, "My Soul Delighteth in the Things of the Lord," *Ensign*, May 2008.
18. See 2 Samuel 22:2; Psalm 40:17; Doctrine and Covenants 138:23.
19. See 1 Nephi 7:12.
20. D. Todd Christofferson, "Give Us This Day Our Daily Bread," BYU devotional, January 9, 2011, https://speeches.byu.edu/talks/d-todd -christofferson/give-us-this-day-our -daily-bread/.
21. Matthew 11:28.
22. See Ether 12:6.
23. "Witness," Lexico.com.
24. "The Spirit does not need to be limited to words; He can communicate Spirit to spirit with a language that is unmistakable because it has no words . . . It is stronger and longer lasting than touching or seeing; we can come to doubt the physical senses, but we cannot doubt when the Holy Spirit speaks to us. It is the surest witness." (D. Todd Christofferson, "Strong Impressions of the Spirit," *New Era*, June 2013.)
25. Alma 57:35.
26. Luke 17:15–19.
27. Deuteronomy 4:29.
28. Doctrine and Covenants 3:8.

CHAPTER 8

Overcoming Doubt:
Doubting Not and Seeing God Act

— MATTHEW 21:21 —

Our favorite family scripture throughout our children's lives was a familiar one: 1 Nephi 3:7. You remember this oft-repeated Book of Mormon story. Lehi had a dream in which he was commanded by the Lord to take his family and flee Jerusalem; it would soon be destroyed. Lehi was then told in another dream to have his sons return to Jerusalem to obtain the brass plates, which contained the spiritual history of his people. Lehi explains to Nephi his older brothers' reaction to the request: "And now, behold thy brothers murmur, saying it is a hard thing which I have required of them; but behold I have not required it of them, but it is a commandment of the Lord."[1] It was undoubtedly a hard thing that was being required and Lehi did not dispute that, but he had faith in *who* was doing the asking.

Nephi's response to the Lord's request was entirely different than his older brothers' and is why our family chose this scripture: "And it came to pass that I, Nephi, said unto my father: I will go and do the things which the Lord hath commanded, for I know that the Lord giveth no commandments unto the children of men, save he shall prepare a way for them that they may accomplish the thing which he commandeth them."[2]

We would often recite this verse aloud as a family and then would ask the children what it meant. Their response: "If the Lord asked us to move a mountain, we could move a mountain!" Of course, that was a trained response, but it seemed to sum up what we wanted them to take away from this scripture: If you don't doubt the Lord or His promises and requests, then the Lord will always prepare a way for it to be done.

This scripture has a parallel in the New Testament. Jesus, speaking to His disciples shortly after the miracle where He commanded the fig tree that bore no fruit to wither and die, taught: "Verily I say unto you, If ye have faith, and *doubt not*, ye shall not only do this which is done to the fig tree, but also if ye shall say unto this mountain, Be thou removed, and be thou cast into the sea; *it shall be done*."[3]

As parents, we knew that our children would likely never need to literally move a physical mountain, but we also knew that they would run up against other types of metaphorical mountains they would need to deal with: adversity, trials, challenges, doubts, fears, even mountains of positive opportunity.

Over the years, I've had many opportunities to work with young men and women preparing to serve full-time missions for the Church. One of these was "Ross." Ross had a great desire to serve the Lord, but he had significant health and lifestyle issues that would affect his ability to thrive as a missionary, where he would be required to ride a bike and walk all day long.

We submitted his mission application, and the request came back that he make significant progress in his health and physical activity. We were encouraged to resubmit his application after Ross had made the necessary changes. Ross was intimidated by the request, and I don't blame him; we both knew that changing his life in such a way would not be easy. Despite that, he believed the request was coming from the Lord and that the person doing the asking was not me as a friend, but the Lord through His appointed servant.

The Monster

I will never forget the day when Ross came to me with his proposal. He said, "I've put a plan together to get ready for my mission. I'm exercising every day, which includes riding my bike up 'the monster,' or, at least trying to." Now, "the monster" he was referring to was a long, steep hill right outside the church building—it was easy to see where it got its name.

Ross added, "When I'm able to make it to the top, I'll be ready to serve my mission!"

Ross would often call me (this was back in the days before texting) and report on his progress. Some days were good; some weren't. He worked on this for several months. I will never forget the day he called to tell me, "I did it! I conquered the monster!"

Between you and me, I couldn't believe it, so I asked, "You mean you made it to the top?"

"Yep, without stopping. I'm ready to go on my mission!"

We met the next day and turned in a letter updating the Missionary Department on Ross's situation, his progress, and what he had been doing to prepare. Shortly after that submission, Ross received his call to serve. He was so excited. He had worked hard to become healthier and was anxious to get out into the mission field.

The takeaway for me: Ross never doubted that the Lord wanted him to become physically prepared to serve a mission. He never doubted that if the Lord was asking, then He would help him accomplish this "hard thing." Ross manifested the same confidence in God that Nephi did, not doubting that he could fulfill the Lord's request and retrieve the brass plates from Laban. In that moment of being called, Ross was Nephi. Neither of them doubted God, and the difficult thing they both had to do got done—undoubtedly with divine assistance.

Now there may be those who would ask, *just how is the Lord responsible for doing any of this?* After all, it was Ross who put in the effort. Ross made smart decisions about what he ate. Ross rode his bike every day. It was Ross who did the work to slay "the monster." Why or how does the Lord get the credit? Certainly, we see people who have no faith in God do similar incredible acts. They don't rely on God, only on themselves. How can anyone really know it's God's doing?

The touching thing is, if you asked Ross, it was *all* the Lord. No doubt. It was through God that Ross found the strength to do something he had never done before. To do the near impossible. He was blessed by his Heavenly Father with the strength to bear his burden because it was something God wanted Ross to achieve.[4] Ross would say that he was given by God the mental, spiritual, and physical motivation to do a very hard thing.

The icing on the cake with Ross was a phone call I received from his mission president several months after Ross entered the mission field. The president wanted to share how effective Ross was as a missionary and leader. The president was gushing over how good it was to have this fine elder in the mission and the positive impact he was having on other missionaries. Amazing.

Looking back, I don't think the Lord was just preparing Ross to serve a mission, He was preparing him to be a great missionary. No doubt Ross helped other missionaries slay their own "monsters" as they looked at difficult mountains they needed to climb in order to do what the Lord was asking. Obviously, the Lord wasn't just building muscles in Ross as he worked to conquer that hill; He was building faith—the kind of faith that would impact many others in Ross's life.

Built within this divine pattern, God has made a great promise: if we don't doubt, it shall be done. Of course, there is always the qualifier: the "*it*" must always be in accord with the Lord's mind, will, and timing. That is when the power to do comes. And, when it *is* something aligned with divine, you can count on God being in it. It's absolute. 100%.

The Savior taught this repeatedly: "For verily I say unto you, That whosoever shall say unto this mountain, Be thou removed, and be thou cast into the sea; *and shall not doubt in his heart, but shall believe that those things which he saith shall come to pass;* he shall have whatsoever he saith."[5]

Recall the episode when Peter walked on the water but briefly lost his faith and nearly went for a swim. Jesus took the occasion to clarify what went wrong: "And immediately Jesus stretched forth his hand, and caught him, and said unto him, O thou of little faith, *wherefore didst thou doubt?*"[6] Setting aside how amazing and miraculous it was that Peter actually did muster the faith to walk on water at all, apparently, our doubting does make a difference and directly affects whether God is able to intervene and help in our lives or not.

Our doubting does make a difference and
directly affects whether God is able to
intervene and help in our lives or not.

Part of the instruction to "doubt not"[7] refers to the inspiration we receive. When that inspiration to act comes, don't doubt it! It's that simple, and that hard.

The importance of this has been underscored in my life time and time again, but a notable experience stands out in which the Lord taught me to

1. Pay attention to promptings when they come. Then,
2. Show my belief by taking action.

I was serving as a stake president at the time. It was a beautiful Saturday morning, and our family was busy doing chores. My job was to hunt the gophers invading our lawn. I was busy trying to figure out how to use those gopher bombs that smoke out the little guys, when suddenly the thought came to my mind to drive to the stake center about twenty-five minutes away. What? Say again? But that was it. No explanation. *Get in the car and go to the stake center.*

By this point in my life, I had learned not to ignore these types of promptings. I also recalled my training and a particular teaching by the Prophet Joseph Smith: "A person may profit by noticing the first intimation of the spirit of revelation; for instance, when you feel pure intelligence flowing into you, it may give you sudden strokes of ideas, so that by noticing it, you may find it fulfilled the same day or soon; (i.e.) those things that were presented unto your minds by the Spirit of God, will come to pass; and thus by learning the Spirit of God and understanding it, you may grow into the principle of revelation, until you become perfect in Christ Jesus."[8]

So, I laid down my gopher bombs, washed my hands, and jumped in the car. When I arrived at the stake center, I could see the parking lot was empty. No one in sight. I was about to drive away—the gophers were waiting—but that strong initial impression deserved a closer look. I parked and got out to walk around. As I did, I heard what sounded like glass breaking in the back of the building.

Feeling a little nervous, I walked to the back and found a van parked with someone rummaging around the large dumpsters. It quickly became apparent that this person was dumping their trash in the church trash bins. Really? That's why I was brought here—to keep people from dumping trash at the church?

I engaged the fellow and faintly recognized him as a less active member of the stake. He mentioned that he was going through a divorce and moving apartments and was trying to get rid of some trash. We talked about what was happening in his life. As we talked, he opened up a bit and indicated that he might be ready to come back to church.

I never said a word about the trash, but we did have a good conversation about his life. As I left the parking lot, I recognized that this brother was why the Lord had led me to the church building. He brought a gopher-hunting stake president twenty-five miles on a Saturday morning to connect with a struggling son, so that son would know he was loved.

Interestingly, this good man eventually became active in the Church again. He got remarried. He became a strong member of his ward. Many years later we found ourselves together at a social event where he reminded me of that day at the stake center and how important our interaction was in his returning to the Church. Not doubting the Lord, His promptings, and His promises often results in blessings not only for ourselves but for others. In this case, we were both blessed in the process.

Not doubting the Lord, His promptings, and
His promises often results in blessings
not only for ourselves but for others.

Remember His Voice

The Book of Mormon is rich with the admonition to "doubt not, but be believing."[9] Helaman reminds us to believe in the inspiration that comes to us and to not doubt the miracles and tender mercies we have seen in our lives. *Was that really God? Was it a coincidence? Am I remembering it correctly?* To "remember" what the Lord has done is one of the most repeated instructions in the Book of Mormon. Helaman recounts the story of Nephi and Lehi (those in Helaman and 3 Nephi, not the originals) and how they were cast into prison and then encircled about by fire to be protected. He underscores the counsel given to all who witnessed the miraculous events: "And there were about three hundred souls who saw and heard these things; and they were bidden (presumably by Nephi and Lehi) to go forth and marvel not, neither should they doubt."[10]

Perhaps the encouragement given for so long in the Church to keep a journal has its origins in this admonition: "That they should remember that it was the Lord that did deliver them."[11]

As we remember the Lord, we should also remember this: following God's divine patterns is always important. Always. Sometimes our expectations may be out of sequence and not consistent with the pattern He has revealed. When that happens, it can lead to frustration or even anger with the Lord. The scriptures are filled with examples of the most faithful people whose faith was tested as they were required to "wait upon the Lord," sometimes for extraordinary periods of time; but ultimately the blessing they were seeking was granted because they didn't doubt God.[12]

Elder Gerald N. Lund, former General Authority and among the most-read authors in Latter-day Saint literature, wrote, "One thing we often forget is that while the Father and the Son will always fulfill Their part of the covenant, if we fulfill ours, They also get to determine all aspects of when Their side of the agreement will be fulfilled. As the Lord Himself put it so succinctly: 'It shall be in his own *time*, and in his own *way*, and according to his own *will*' (D&C 88:68)."[13]

It is this aspect of waiting on the Lord—for His own time, way, and will—that often leaves us open to doubting the Lord. But His promises are sure. He will provide the means to do what He asks of us—every time. But as said, it will be in the manner He deems best: "If ye will turn to the Lord with full purpose of heart, and put your trust in him, and serve him with all diligence of mind, if ye do this, *he will, according to his own will and pleasure,* deliver you out of bondage."[14]

Elder Lund continues, "Because of Their perfections—perfect love, perfect knowledge, perfect power, and so on—Their promises will always be fulfilled if we fulfill ours. But we must always remember to be very careful that we don't start thinking we can tell God how best to answer our prayers, or when they need to be answered.

"If we lose sight of these three important principles [His own time, His own way, according to His own will], we can begin to view God as if He were a divine vending machine. If we put in enough quarters—go to church, pay tithing, say our prayers, read the scriptures . . . then we can punch a button and His obligation will be to make sure the candy drops in our hands."[15]

I feel to end this chapter with my personal testimony that, while putting aside our doubts may not be easy, when we exercise our faith and choose to trust in God, we put ourselves in the position to receive the enabling power of God in our lives so that we can "go and do the things which the Lord has commanded."[16] This divine pattern allows for God to give us the blessings He so greatly wants us to have in our lives.

Notes

1. 1 Nephi 3:5.
2. 1 Nephi 3:7.
3. Matthew 21:21.
4. See Mosiah 24:15. Elder David A. Bednar taught, "I wonder if we fail to fully acknowledge this strengthening aspect of the Atonement in our lives and mistakenly believe we must carry our load all alone—through sheer grit, willpower, and discipline and with our obviously limited capacities" ("Bear Up Their Burdens with Ease," *Ensign*, May 2014).
5. Mark 11:23.
6. Matthew 14:31.
7. Matthew 21:21.
8. *Teachings of Presidents of the Church: Joseph Smith* (2007), 132.
9. Mormon 9:27.
10. Helaman 5:49.
11. Mosiah 25:16.
12. See 2 Nephi 18:17; Isaiah 40:31. Consider these few examples: Simeon

waited into his old age to see "the Lord's Christ" (Luke 2:26); Anna, who "departed not from the temple, but served God with fastings and prayers night and day" (Luke 2:37); Sarah (see Genesis 18:9–15; 21:2), Rebekah (see Genesis 25:21), Rachel (see Genesis 29:31; 30:22); Hannah (see 1 Samuel 1:11, 20), who "waited upon the Lord" to bear children; Enos, who shared the "wrestle which [he] had before God . . . all the day long" (Enos 1:2, 4); and

Joseph Smith, who waited upon the Lord while suffering nearly five cold winter months in Liberty Jail (see Doctrine and Covenants 121).

13. Gerald N. Lund, *The Second Coming of the Lord* (Salt Lake City: Deseret Book, 2020), 33.

14. Mosiah 7:33.

15. Gerald N. Lund, *The Second Coming of the Lord* (Salt Lake City: Deseret Book, 2020), 33.

16. 1 Nephi 3:7.

CHAPTER 9

Seeking Miracles:
Faith and Miracles

— MOSIAH 8:18 —

I will never forget Elder Marcus B. Nash of the Seventy visiting the mission where my wife, Gwen, and I presided. The event was a meeting for new converts being held in conjunction with stake conference. Elder Nash testified with great energy, conviction, and spirit that miracles continue in our day. He taught from Mormon, chapter 9: "And now, O all ye that have imagined up unto yourselves a god who can do no miracles, I would ask of you, have all these things passed, of which I have spoken? Has the end come yet? Behold I say unto you, Nay; and God has not ceased to be a God of miracles."[1]

It *is* a day of miracles. We worship a God of miracles. We can and should seek and pray for miracles in our lives.[2] Indeed, we should expect them, as "signs shall follow them that believe."[3] President Dallin H. Oaks testified, "Many miracles happen *every day* in the work of our Church and in the lives of our members."[4]

The Bible Dictionary states that "miracles were and are a response to faith and its best encouragement. They were never wrought without prayer, felt need, and faith."[5] Miracles are known by different names: "They are called signs. . . powers or mighty works . . . wonders, marvels."[6] The online dictionary adds that a miracle is "a surprising and welcome event that is not explicable by natural or scientific laws . . . a highly improbable or extraordinary event, development, or accomplishment that brings very welcome consequences."[7]

Miracles can be as small as a simple prompting that, when heeded, changes the course of something important. We sometimes refer to these in the Church as "tender mercies."[8] They can also be as big as an actual manifestation of angels or even of God Himself. As I look back on how I became a member of the Church as young man, I can see many little miracles—a divine hand orchestrating a series of small, but important steps.

Miracles or Coincidences?

When I was young, my parents moved into a new family-oriented neighborhood in California that they could barely afford. We soon regularly interacted with members of the Church who "happened" to live on either side of our tract home. My new best buddies on the street were members of the Church. I learned later that their parents had made repeated attempts to take me to church, but my parents had declined every time.

It was one of these same neighbors who would later teach me the gospel in his garage while he worked his hobby reupholstering furniture. He was a great support.

The first time I recall feeling the Spirit of God in my life was as a young boy when my very religious Baptist aunt took me to her church. There, in those meetings, I felt a warm, peaceful feeling that God loved me and that I needed to love Him. It was the same Spirit that I recognized the first time I attended The Church of Jesus Christ of Latter-day Saints.

Around the same time, I was drawn to backpacking and the outdoors, where my eyes were opened to the grandeur of God, which led to a wilderness survival class with a high school counselor, Doc Wallace, who "coincidentally" was also a Church member. "Doc" would become my friend and tutor in the gospel and was instrumental in anchoring my faith and helping me navigate my early spiritual development.

If that wasn't enough, my soon-to-be-bishop, Garth Rogers, was my math teacher. I would even find myself in his classroom at lunch studying the gospel, along with other math students who needed a little help.

The point is, God saw to it that I was surrounded by those who would bring me safely into the kingdom of God. Looking back, it is miraculous that these people were placed in my life at just the right time for just the right purpose—all brought about by parents not of the faith who moved to a home that didn't make sense.

Sometimes, the manifestation of the miracle isn't immediate but develops over time—not becoming obvious until we put the entire picture together. That was certainly true for me. In fact, taken alone, any of these experiences might not seem miraculous, but combined, they paint a clear picture of a divine hand guiding my life. While I had to do my part and respond to promptings and opportunity, Heavenly Father did the heavy lifting in bringing these blessings about. He is willing to perform miracles—tender mercies in my life and yours—but most often we have to do our part and exercise our faith by taking the activating action that will unleash His power.

He is willing to perform miracles—tender mercies in my life and yours—but most often we have to do our part and exercise our faith by taking the activating action that will unleash His power.

As a young recently returned missionary, I was attending a local junior college near my parents' home in Southern California. I had been accepted into BYU's evening program at the time but had decided not to go. However, after an interview with my bishop where he encouraged me to take the next step in my life, I changed my mind last-minute. (Thank you, Bishop!)

With less than a week before school, no Utah friends I knew of, and no place to stay, it was a total act of faith. The upside, though, is that I did believe this was what Heavenly Father wanted me to do and I somehow just knew things would work out—that miracles, the little miracles I most needed then, were bound to happen if I was doing His will.

I loaded up my little '72 Opel with everything I owned, duct taped plastic in the driver's window because it was stuck open, used a gum wrapper to hold up the rearview mirror, and turned toward Utah. I had no idea what I would do when I got there.

It was early evening when I arrived in Provo after a very long day of driving. I stopped at the intersection of Center Street and 900 East, again, with no idea what to do next. As I thought to myself, *okay, now what?* I glanced over to the southeastern corner of the intersection and noticed what appeared to be a small apartment complex. The strong impression came: "Go there!"

I pulled into the parking lot and found the manager's door of what was then Fairmount Square. At first, no answer. But with repeated attempts, the manager finally came to the door and asked what I needed. I explained my situation and she began to laugh. "You really plan ahead. School starts next week!" After the heckling, she said, "Well, I do have one bed left. If you go down and meet the roommates and they agree, you can have it."

As I walked to the apartment, I thought, *roommates?* At that moment I realized I really hadn't given any thought as to who I might be living with and began to wonder how that would work out.

Once again, I found myself knocking on a strange door. What was I getting myself into? To my shock and surprise, when the door opened, I came face-to-face with three former missionary friends from the Georgia Atlanta Mission. We had served in the same mission district together and knew each other well. They were equally surprised to see me and asked what I was doing there. I explained that I needed a place to stay. They quickly responded, "You found it!"

For me, this met every definition of a miracle—truly a "surprising and welcome," though "highly improbable extraordinary event." Think of it: the Lord took me from California, 650 miles to Utah, to one door, one bed, and three friends. The world might call it a remarkable, a one-in-a-million coincidence. To the faithful, it was a divine manifestation of God's love done in a miraculous way.

Hard to believe? Doesn't happen these days? Doesn't happen to you? I can assure you it does happen today, and it can happen for you—if you faithfully follow the patterns and principles from the scriptures we've been discussing in this book. Recall Moroni's words: "And if there were miracles wrought then, why has God ceased to be a God of miracles and yet be an unchangeable Being? And behold, I say unto you he changeth not; if so he would cease to be God; and he ceaseth not to be God, and is a God of miracles. *And the reason why he ceaseth to do miracles among the children of men is because that they dwindle in unbelief, and depart from the right way, and know not the God in whom they should trust.* Behold, I say unto you that whoso believeth in Christ, doubting nothing, whatsoever he shall ask the Father in the name of Christ it shall be granted him; and this promise is unto all, even unto the ends of the earth."[9]

The miracles we seek, and should seek in our lives, often come because we first have faith. Of course, there are those times when God delivers miracles without our prior action: consider Saul (who became Paul the Apostle) on the road to Damascus, where the resurrected Jesus visits him to stop his persecution of the Saints and call him to the work.[10] Though one might argue this was a miracle in answer to the prayers of the people being persecuted, it nevertheless was not brought about by faithful action on Saul's part. God intervened in Saul's life not because of his faith, but because God's (and the Savior's) greater purposes for Saul and the Church required it.

The Book of Mormon prophet Ammon taught that "God has provided a means that man, through faith, might work mighty miracles; therefore he becometh a great benefit to his fellow beings."[11] Usually, that faith is more than just a state of mind; it is turned into action and demonstrated in some notable way (like packing up the car and driving 650 miles). The Lord most often requires our action, based on faith, to show ourselves and Him that our faith is real. As we do, we access God's power in our life, which will almost always be seen as miraculous to us.

Sheri Dew describes four foundational principles related to God's power: "First, God wants a powerful people. Second, He gives His power to those who are faithful. Third, we have a sacred obligation to seek after the power of God and then to use that power as He directs. Fourth, when we have the power of God with us, nothing is impossible."[12] The power of God is available for us in our lives to not only bless others but to be a blessing to us, as well. Sister Dew describes some of the places this power can be found: 1) the word of God, 2) the gift of the Holy Ghost, 3) the priesthood, 4) the house of the Lord, and 5) the Atonement of Jesus Christ. All of these allow us to access the power of God.

"We have a sacred obligation to seek after the power of God and then to use that power as He directs."

—Sheri Dew

President Spencer W. Kimball was the first prophet that I experienced as a convert to the Church. He was a walking miracle. While he suffered at least two heart attacks as an Apostle, he also had a serious encounter with throat cancer, twice, that resulted in surgery that took one of his vocal cords and half of the other. Many thought he would never be able to talk again.

Over time, he did learn to speak in a hoarse whisper, able to continue his ministry as an Apostle, and then prophet, all with the Lord's blessing and help. His raspy voice the rest of his life was a reminder to all of the miracle of speech that was given to him.

Every time I heard that voice, I recognized we were, in that moment, witnessing a miracle.[13] President Kimball taught, "In faith we plant the seed, and soon we see the miracle of the blossoming. *Men have often misunderstood and have reversed the process. They would have the harvest before the planting, the reward before the service, the miracle before the faith.* Even the most demanding labor unions would hardly ask the wages before the labor. But many of us would have the vigor without the observance of the health laws, prosperity through the opened windows of heaven without the payment of our tithes. We would have the close communion with our Father without fasting and praying; we would have rain in due season and peace in the land without observing the Sabbath and keeping the other commandments of the Lord. We would pluck the rose before planting the roots; we would harvest the grain before sowing and cultivating."[14]

Here, President Kimball is teaching that there is a pattern to follow for receiving the blessings we want. While it is true that sometimes it happens out of order—miracles before the expression of faith (i.e., God being His amazingly merciful self), it is most often true that faith *precedes* the miracle, at least in some small degree. A heavenly pattern that requires "a principle of action and power"—the faith—which brings forth the fruit of divine action—the miracle.[15] Life's experience teaches even the youngest among us that we don't generally harvest before the planting!

Selective Perception

On one occasion, I was home teaching some good friends when their daughter entered the room listening to music. Her dad asked what she was doing, and she replied, "I'm listening to Weezer."

I asked, "What is Weezer?" (I imagined some elderly folks sitting around having trouble breathing). She said they were a chart-topping band and that "everyone knows who Weezer is!" We laughed, I felt old, and I went on not thinking any more about it.

On my way home from the visit, however, I noticed a sticker on the car in front of me—a Weezer bumper sticker. As I continued my drive, I saw a Weezer concert poster in the window of a store. When I got home, I asked my own daughters about them, and they said, "Dad, we listen to 'em all the time."

Somehow now, Weezer was everywhere!

What had happened? Before the visit, I had never heard of them. After the visit, they were everywhere I looked. This experience teaches a good lesson about human behavior. *We see what we look for.* It's called selective perception—the tendency to take more notice of things that interest you.[16] When it comes to seeing miracles in our lives and the lives of others, I am quite certain that if you look for them, you will find them.

I recall hearing of a mission president who started asking his missionaries, "What miracle did you see today?" Every time he interacted with them, he would ask the question—phone calls, chance meetings, interviews—any occasion that brought them together, he would ask, "What miracle did you see today?"

Over time, the missionaries couldn't wait to share their stories with him. They started looking and began finding ("seek and ye shall find") examples of the Lord's hand working in miraculous ways. The lesson: if we faithfully seek the Lord's blessings, then we will see the miracles He is willing to perform for us. Sometimes, He will even help us know what miracles we should seek.

Daniel W. Jones was a Latter-day Saint pioneer who was in a party of men that aided in the rescue of the handcart companies stranded in the harsh Wyoming winter. After the rescue party found the survivors, Daniel, along with a number of other young men, volunteered to remain at Devil's Gate, a major landmark on the Oregon/Mormon Trail, to safeguard the company's possessions.[17] They had few provisions and had to survive on what they could hunt or scavenge. Daniel records, "Game soon became so scarce that we could kill nothing. . . . Finally that was all gone, nothing now but hides were left. We made a trial of them. A lot was cooked and eaten without any seasoning and it made the whole company sick. Many were so turned against the stuff that it made them sick to think of it."

Daniel continues: "Things looked dark, for nothing remained but the poor raw hides taken from starved cattle. We asked the Lord to direct us what to do. . . . Finally I was impressed how to fix the stuff and gave the company advice, telling them how to cook it."

Daniel then provided a number of relatively complicated steps for scraping, boiling, scalding, boiling again, and washing the hides to eat. He says, "This was considerable trouble, but we had little else to do and it was better than starving."

Daniel concludes, "We asked the Lord to bless our stomachs and adapt them to this food . . . now all seemed to relish the feast. . . . We enjoyed this sumptuous fare for about six weeks, and never had the gout."[18]

Of this event, Elder David A. Bednar observes, "Dear brothers and sisters, I know what I would have prayed for in those circumstances. I would have prayed for something else to eat. 'Heavenly Father, please send me a quail or a buffalo.' It never would have occurred to me to pray that my stomach would be strengthened and adapted to what we already had.

What did Daniel W. Jones know? He knew about the enabling power of the Atonement of Jesus Christ. He did not pray that his circumstances would be changed. He prayed that he would be strengthened to deal with his circumstances."[19]

Daniel Jones's experience is a great lesson in faith and miracles: when we exercise our faith, then we are in the best position to see the Lord bring about the miracles He most certainly wants us to enjoy. Those miracles will come. They must. It is His promise. And through faith we can see His hand throughout the trial, just as Daniel did—ranging in size from small tender mercies to significant divine interventions that change everything. And when these miracles do come, it will be "in his own time, and in his own way, and according to his own will."[20] But come they will, from a generous and loving Father in Heaven.

Notes

1. Mormon 9:15.
2. "Suggestion number 4: *Seek and expect* miracles. . . . The Lord will bless *you* with miracles *if* you believe in Him, 'doubting nothing.' Do the spiritual work to seek miracles." (Russell M. Nelson, "The Power of Spiritual Momentum," *Liahona*, May 2022.)
3. Doctrine and Covenants 84:65.
4. Dallin H. Oaks, "Miracles," *Ensign*, June 2001.
5. Bible Dictionary, "Miracles."
6. Bible Dictionary, "Miracles."
7. "Miracle," Lexico.com.
8. See David A. Bednar, "The Tender Mercies of the Lord," *Ensign*, May 2005.
9. Mormon 9:19–21.
10. See Acts 9:1–22.
11. Mosiah 8:18.
12. Sheri L. Dew, "You Were Born to Lead, You Were Born for Glory," BYU devotional, December 9, 2003, https://speeches.byu.edu/talks/sheri-l-dew/born-lead-born-glory/.
13. "Spencer W. Kimball: He Did Not Give Up," *Liahona*, Mar. 1994.
14. Spencer W. Kimball, *Faith Precedes the Miracle* (Salt Lake City: Deseret Book, 1972), 4.
15. See "Faith in Jesus Christ," Gospel Topics, ChurchofJesusChrist.org
16. "Selective perception," APA Dictionary of Psychology, accessed July 16, 2021, https://dictionary.apa.org/selective-perception.
17. Daniel W. Jones, *Forty Years Among the Indians* (Salt Lake City: Juvenile Instructor, 1890), 70–71.
18. Jones, *Forty Years Among the Indians* (Salt Lake City: Juvenile Instructor, 1890), 81–82.
19. David A. Bednar, "In the Strength of the Lord," BYU devotional, October 23, 2001, https://speeches.byu.edu/talks/david-a-bednar/strength-lord/.
20. Doctrine and Covenants 88:68.

DIVINE PATTERNS

PART 2

Adopting a Fresh Perspective
about God and Yourself

CHAPTER 10

Approaching God: Broken Hearts, Contrite Spirits, and Forgiveness

— 2 NEPHI 2:7 —

Earlier in the book, I mentioned the two full shoulder replacements that I needed as a result of my cancer treatment. Those surgeries were separated by about a year—first the right shoulder, then the left. Sometime after the first replacement I recall getting the definite news that the other shoulder would need to be replaced as well. It was discouraging news, particularly since the Tony Stark "Iron Man" parts hadn't been invented yet!

One of the ways I processed the news was to go to the temple and seek comfort. I recall sitting in the endowment session, feeling a little sorry for myself—I knew how hard recovery was from this surgery from firsthand, or should I say, first shoulder, experience. It involved six hours a day for six weeks straight in a machine that lifted my arm in the air and brought it gently back down—with my other hand furiously typing on my laptop, trying to keep business, church, and family life going. Now, I'm not complaining—I am grateful for that little invention and the full mobility it helped me have today, but it nonetheless wasn't any fun. The idea of doing that again didn't have any appeal.

As I sat in the temple session contemplating my situation, I received what I recognized to be the voice of the Lord to me personally. It was a simple statement of pure revelation. In my mind, I heard the words, *"This is not a problem, this is a solution."* These few words were profound and immediately caused me to think differently about what was happening. Even though the road ahead would be painful and take a lot of work, the ultimate result would be blessings. Indeed, that is what happened: full mobility, with almost no limits to what I could do (minus the Iron Man power thrusters!).

This is a good way to think about the principle of repentance, as well: it's not a problem, it's a solution! In fact, your understanding, your belief in the importance of personal repentance needs to be firmly rooted in the idea that this is a positive, powerful step toward solutions—not rooted in problems, but rooted in the hope of a better future. Having this testimony of this key gospel principle of repentance is essential. Why? Because repentance is how we obtain forgiveness. Forgiveness is how we come unto Christ. Without repentance, there is no forgiveness—that is the principle contained within this divine pattern.

> Your belief in the importance of personal repentance needs to be firmly rooted in the idea that this is a positive, powerful step toward solutions—not rooted in problems, but rooted in the hope of a better future.

Elder D. Todd Christofferson taught, "*Repenting is what we do to claim the gracious gift of forgiveness* that a just Father in Heaven can offer us because His Beloved Son atoned for our sins."[1]

After All We Can Do

Nephi taught, "For we know that it is by grace that we are saved, after all we can do."[2] Pondering this scripture, one is led to ask, "What does, 'after all we can do' mean?" Does it mean we need to perform some heroic deed? Sell all we have and give it to the poor? How about being perfectly obedient? To gain our salvation, must we do some very great thing?

King Lamoni's father, who proclaimed, "I will give away all my sins to know thee,"[3] had a son who also became king. He took on the new name of Anti-Nephi-Lehi.[4] His people were the people of Ammon, who were the parents of the two thousand stripling warriors who followed Helaman.[5]

Prior to the people of Ammon's conversion, the Anti-Nephi-Lehies were engaged in rebellion against the converted Nephites, fighting wars and shedding the blood of their fellow men.[6] Once converted through the teaching of Ammon and his brethren and threatened with imminent attack by their enemies, their king, Anti-Nephi-Lehi, proclaimed, "Since God hath taken away our stains, and our swords have become bright, then let us stain our swords no more with the blood of our brethren . . . for perhaps, if we should stain our swords again they can no more be washed bright through the blood of the Son of our great God, which shall be shed for the atonement of our sins."[7]

Anti-Nephi-Lehi then states: "And I also thank my God, yea, my great God, that he hath granted unto us that we might repent of these things, and also that he hath forgiven us of those our many sins and murders which we have committed, and taken away the guilt from our hearts, through the merits of his Son. And now behold, my brethren, *since it has been all that we could do, (as we were the most lost of all mankind) to repent of all our sins* and the many murders which we have committed, and to get God to take them away from our hearts, *for it was all we could do to repent sufficiently before God* that he would take away our stain."[8] Here, we see that *all they could do* was repent and rely on the mercy and grace of Christ for forgiveness. There was no other heroic act or deed that could help; the only thing they could do to have any chance of reconciling with God and any hope of improving their prospects in the hereafter was repent. And so it is with us.

Taken in its most complete and full definition, repentance means not just trying to make right a wrong, but also faithfully forsaking our misguided ways, bad habits, and favorite sins and committing to strive to keep all the commandments more faithfully for the rest of our lives. Even after all that, our repentance does not "earn" our forgiveness—it is granted by the grace of God through the atoning power of the Savior.[9]

President Dieter F. Uchtdorf clarified: "We are not saved 'because' of all that we can do. Have any of us done *all* that we can do? Does God wait until we've expended every effort before He will intervene in our lives with

His saving grace? Many people feel discouraged because they constantly fall short. They know firsthand that 'the spirit indeed is willing, but the flesh is weak.' They raise their voices with Nephi in proclaiming, 'My soul grieveth because of mine iniquities.'

"I am certain Nephi knew that the Savior's grace *allows* and *enables* us to overcome sin. This is why Nephi labored so diligently to persuade his children and brethren 'to believe in Christ, and to be reconciled to God.' After all, *that is* what we can do! And *that is* our task in mortality!"[10]

A Sacrifice Is Required

Throughout the scriptures, the Lord speaks of an essential ingredient that *must* be present in the repentance process—an "*absolute requisite*."[11] Without it, our efforts to repent fall short and don't lead to the desired gift of forgiveness. That is the ingredient of a "broken heart and contrite spirit."[12] Alma explains: "But God did call on men, in the name of his Son, (this being the plan of redemption which was laid) saying: If ye will repent, *and harden not your hearts*, then will I have mercy upon you, through mine Only Begotten Son; Therefore, whosoever repenteth, and hardeneth not his heart, he shall have claim on mercy through mine Only Begotten Son, unto a remission of his sins; and these shall enter into my rest."[13]

When we repent, a personal sacrifice is required. That sacrifice is our own hardened hearts. Jacob, Nephi's younger brother, taught, "Behold, he offereth himself a sacrifice for sin, to answer the ends of the law, unto all those who have a broken heart and a contrite spirit; and unto none else can the ends of the law be answered."[14] Having a broken heart and contrite spirit is the essence of repentance.

What does it mean to have a broken heart? One example many of us can relate to is having your heart broken at the end of a romantic relationship. Remember how that felt? Ouch! It was an inescapable pain that hung on for longer than you ever thought possible. It was humbling. There may have even been a moment when you would have done anything to change the outcome—be granted a "do-over."

When you recognize that you have offended God and likely others through your actions and words, you should also feel brokenhearted—it might even feel a bit like that devastating romantic disappointment. This may not happen all at once, but as you come unto Christ and draw nearer to Him, you will have a sense of growing regret that you have offended God and jeopardized your standing before Him. And oh, how you would then wish for a do-over, making it as though it had never occurred.

Of course, a close companion to a broken heart and contrite spirit is godly sorrow. Elder Neil L. Andersen, in his book *The Divine Gift of Forgiveness* (a must-read on this topic that is thorough and authoritative) defines godly sorrow: "To feel profound sadness and remorse for behavior that added pain and suffering to the Savior, as our soul removes any denial or excuse."[15] He continues, "Those who have a broken heart and a contrite spirit are willing to do anything and everything that God asks of them, without resistance or resentment."[16] Notably, Elder Bruce D. Porter taught that this broken heart also "serves as a divine shield against temptation" in the future.[17]

What of a contrite spirit? The Hebrew rendering of the word in many scriptures is defined as "crushed" or "dust."[18] Meaning, when we are contrite, we have developed a willingness to totally submit to God's will, having crushed the instincts of the natural man and completely rooted them out. In such a state, having recognized that we are less than the dust of the earth,[19] we are ready and want to be obedient to God. Those who are truly contrite no longer resist the things of the Spirit but embrace them and choose that God should be their guide.[20]

One caution: A checklist approach to repenting will likely cause someone to miss the whole point—repentance isn't accomplished by just going through a list of steps you need to take; rather, it's a process that requires a sincerity of heart that produces a willingness to do whatever God may require to be pronounced clean.[21] Elder Neil L. Andersen explains how teaching the principle in the mission field can sometimes be misconstrued: "Sometimes, missionaries will teach repentance with a check-the-box approach—rather than teaching a process as the scriptures teach of doing 'all . . . in the name of the Son, . . . repent[ing] and call[ing] upon

God in the name of the Son forevermore' (Moses 5:8). . . . Missionaries will sometimes overly teach that beginning to pray, keep the commandments, and come to church are the steps of repentance, and they are—but they will under-teach the need to call upon the Father for the atoning grace of His Son."[22]

One of the miracles of the gospel is how quickly God will be there to help once you begin to repent. Alma taught, "If ye will repent and harden not your hearts, *immediately* shall the great plan of redemption be brought about unto you."[23] Equally comforting are these words from Elder Jeffrey R. Holland: "Please remember tomorrow, and all the days after that, that the Lord blesses those who *want* to improve, who accept the need for commandments and *try* to keep them, who cherish Christlike virtues and *strive* to the best of their ability to acquire them. If you stumble in that pursuit, so does everyone; the Savior is there to help you keep going. If you fall, summon His strength. Call out like Alma, 'O Jesus . . . have mercy on me.' He will help you get back up. He will help you repent, repair, fix whatever you have to fix, and keep going. Soon enough you will have the success you seek."[24]

The verbs Elder Holland uses are *want*, *try*, and *strive*. Unlike many things in life, our effort, as opposed to only the results, counts for something. God cares about our intent, what we were trying—hoping—to do. It matters to Him that we are *trying* and *striving*, in addition to *doing* and *being*. He has made provision for our stumbles with His foreknowledge of all things.[25]

God has made provision for our stumbles
with His foreknowledge of all things.

Does Seeking Forgiveness Really Matter?

Forgiveness is the grand prize. It's what we all should be seeking. With forgiveness come all the other blessings of the gospel that have been promised. The Savior taught this important principle when He addressed a man stricken with palsy (paralysis and uncontrolled body movements). Upon meeting him, Jesus pronounced, "Son, be of good cheer; thy sins be forgiven thee."[26] This man was given a blessing greater than being healed, but this greater promise of forgiveness only infuriated the scribes even more. The Savior then addressed them and asked, "For whether is easier, to say, Thy sins be forgiven thee; or to say, Arise, and walk?"[27] The greater blessing is always forgiveness.

Sister Linda S. Reeves, then Second Counselor in the Relief Society General Presidency, taught: "To me, the greatest miracles in life are not the parting of the Red Sea, the moving of mountains, or even the healing of the body. The greatest miracle happens when we humbly approach our Father in Heaven in prayer, fervently plead to be forgiven, and then are cleansed of those sins through the atoning sacrifice of our Savior."[28]

Miraculously, the Atonement of Jesus Christ saves from both sin and death, from mistakes and sickness. The Atonement is infinite, perfect, and complete in every way, including bringing perfect forgiveness to those who truly repent. Indeed, among the greatest blessings we should seek is that of forgiveness—a blessing more important than almost any other we may desire. It is only through the forgiveness of our sins that we will return to live with our Father in Heaven and His Son in the celestial world.[29] It should be our personal quest, infused with a bit of zeal, to obtain forgiveness from God. We should want that blessing more than anything else.

And, when God does forgive, it is perfectly done. President Boyd K. Packer offers this comfort—a statement taken from Elder Renlund's personal notes made during a training meeting: "The Atonement leaves no tracks, no traces. What it fixes is fixed. . . . It just heals, and what it heals stays healed. The Atonement, which can reclaim each one of us, bears no scars. That means that no matter what we have done or where we have been or how something happened, if we truly repent, [the Savior] has promised that He would atone. And when He atoned, that settled that. . . . The Atonement . . . can wash clean every stain no matter how difficult or how long or how many times repeated."[30]

Key to applying the divine pattern of repentance is to come before God with a broken heart and contrite spirit. As we do this, while meeting the other "conditions of repentance," through the grace of God, we *will* receive the gift of forgiveness and the everlasting joy that comes with it.[31]

Notes

1. D. Todd Christofferson, "Why We Need Jesus Christ," *Ensign*, Dec. 2020.
2. 2 Nephi 25:23.
3. Alma 22:18.
4. See Alma 24:3.
5. See "Anti-Nephi-Lehies," Guide to the Scriptures, ChurchofJesusChrist.org.
6. See Alma 24:9.
7. Alma 24:12–13.
8. Alma 24:10–11. "A just and loving God has provided for every man to be judged according to the level of law he has been given, and 'where there is not law given there is no punishment. . . . Thus, in some cases, repentance for murder may be available." (Dennis L. Largey, ed., *Book of Mormon Reference Companion* [Salt Lake City: Deseret Book, 2003], 576.)
9. Elder Neil L. Andersen said, "We must remember, however, that the divine gift of forgiveness can never be earned; it can only be received. Yes, commandments must be obeyed and ordinances observed to receive forgiveness, but personal effort, no matter how great, pales in comparison to the cost of redemption. In fact, there is no comparison." ("The Gift of Forgiveness," *Liahona*, Feb. 2021.)
10. Dieter F. Uchtdorf, "The Gift of Grace," *Ensign*, May 2015.
11. See Richard G. Scott, "Jesus Christ, Our Redeemer," *Ensign*, May 1997.
12. Doctrine and Covenants 59:8.
13. Alma 12:33–34.
14. 2 Nephi 2:6–7.
15. Neil L. Andersen, *The Divine Gift of Forgiveness* (Salt Lake City: Deseret Book, 2019), 149.
16. Neil L. Andersen, *The Divine Gift of Forgiveness* (Salt Lake City: Deseret Book, 2019), 154.
17. Bruce D. Porter, "A Broken Heart and a Contrite Spirit," *Ensign*, Nov. 2007.
18. Francis Brown et al., *The Brown-Driver-Briggs Hebrew and English Lexicon* (Peabody, MA: Hendrickson Publishers, 2015), 193–94.
19. See Helaman 12:7.
20. See Helaman 12:6.
21. See Linda S. Reeves, "The Great Plan of Redemption," *Liahona*, Nov. 2016.
22. Neil L. Andersen, Mission Leadership Seminar at the Provo Missionary Training Center, June 25, 2018, *Church News*, July 3, 2018, https://www.ChurchofJesusChrist.org/church/news/repentance-is-not-a-backup-plan-it-is-the-plan-says-elder-andersen?lang=eng.
23. Alma 34:31.
24. Jeffrey R. Holland, "Tomorrow the Lord Will Do Wonders among You," *Ensign*, May 2016.
25. See "Foreknowledge of God," *Encyclopedia of Mormonism* (New York: Macmillan, 1992), 521.
26. Matthew 9:2.
27. Matthew 9:5.
28. Linda S. Reeves, "The Great Plan of Redemption," *Ensign*, Nov. 2016.
29. See 3 Nephi 9:13–14.
30. Dale G. Renlund, "Repentance: A Joyful Choice," *Ensign*, Nov. 2016.
31. See Alma 42:13.

CHAPTER 11

Obtaining Forgiveness: Confessing and
Forsaking and Remembered No More

— DOCTRINE AND COVENANTS 58:42–43 —

Brigham Young once taught, "When we learn it is wrong, then it is our duty to refrain from that wrong immediately and forever."[1] That's certainly how I felt as a young man preparing to be baptized a member of the Church. I wanted to make sure that I had taken care of anything and everything I needed to in order to truly be forgiven and receive the gift of the Holy Ghost.

On the list of things to resolve was something from my junior year in high school. I'd had a biology class that was taught by Dr. Shennum, a favorite teacher on campus. In his class, he required that you complete a big project that was turned in at the end of the semester—a project accounting for a large portion of your grade. I remember being pretty excited about it. I worked hard and invested myself more than I typically would at that age. However, part of the project included a telephone survey. After a few phone calls I could tell that no one was going to talk to me, so the assignment would be really difficult to complete. Not knowing what else to do, I faked it! Yep—I created make-believe survey results and turned in my project.

When the time came to get our projects back, Dr. Shennum stopped by my desk and said, "I'm going to keep this one." He announced to everyone standing around, "Every year I select one or two standout projects that go in my binder as examples of excellent work. Roger, I've selected your project this year. Nice job." Wow! That had never happened to me before. My grades in high school were not stellar, so this was a big deal.

The problem . . . a couple of years later as I prepared for baptism, it bothered me that I had a report sitting in a "binder of excellent work" somewhere that I had cheated on. I knew I needed to take care of it somehow.

With a little sleuthing, I was able to find Dr. Shennum's home address. I wanted to talk with him and let him know what I'd done. When I pulled up to his house, I recognized him standing in the front yard watering his grass and talking to a neighbor. My first thought was, *this is not going to be easy*, and the temptation came to hit the gas and just keep driving. But I was determined to get this handled, so I got out of my car.

I recall the conversation going something like this:

"Hey, Dr. Shennum."

"Hi, who are you?" he replied.

"I'm one of your old students from high school, Roger Connors. I had your biology class about three years ago."

"Oh, yes, I think I recognize you. What can I do for you?"

I simply asked, "Can I talk with you for a minute?"

He smiled and said, "Sure."

"I mean, privately."

"Oh, well this is my neighbor and good friend, you can talk in front of him."

I thought, *great, it's hard enough to come and confess to him, now I need to do it in front of a neighbor?*

Somehow, I persisted. "Okay, well, you remember that report you have everyone do at the end of the year? You picked mine and put it in your example binder?"

"Oh yeah, I remember your report now. It was good. Great, even."

Now, feeling even more uncomfortable, I said, "Well, I need to tell you that I worked hard on that report—"

"But . . . ?"

I went on to explain about making up the telephone poll results in the back of the report.

He asked me if the rest of the report was legitimate.

I told him it was.

He then asked me why I was coming to see him now, after all these years.

I explained that I was being baptized into The Church of Jesus Christ of Latter-day Saints and that I wanted to clear my conscience. Feel clean. Forgiven by God.

Dr. Shennum was shocked. "Well, I've never experienced this before. Tell you what, how 'bout I keep the report in the binder and just remove the telephone survey from the back?"

I recall hesitating for a moment until he said, "Thanks, Roger, for letting me know."

I think he wasn't quite sure how to process the crazy kid with the overactive conscience, but he did a nice job going along with it. I thanked both him and the neighbor, who I imagine didn't realize his morning visit with a friend would be so entertaining, and drove away as quickly as I could.

Confess

Clearly, it wasn't easy to confess what I had done, but I believed the scriptural promise in this divine pattern: "Behold, he who has repented of his sins, the same is forgiven, and I, the Lord, remember them no more. By this ye may know if a man repenteth of his sins—behold, he will confess them and forsake them."[2] What accompanied my confession was a sense of peace that I had done all that I felt I could do to make restitution and repair any problem my actions had caused—to clear my conscience so that I could call upon the Lord unhindered, relying on His mercy that He would accept what little offering I could make. Confession is one of the signs of true repentance and one of the absolute requirements of forgiveness. It's also not easy.

Confession is one of the signs of true repentance and one of the absolute requirements of forgiveness.

Confession needs to be complete—what's the point of a halfway confession?—even if it's in front of the next-door neighbor! Elder Richard G. Scott said, "You always need to confess your sins to the Lord. If they are serious transgressions, such as [sexual] immorality, they need to be confessed to a bishop or stake president. Please understand that confession is not repentance. It is an essential step but is not of itself adequate. Partial confession by mentioning lesser mistakes will not help you resolve a more serious, undisclosed transgression. Essential to forgiveness is a willingness to fully disclose to the Lord and, where necessary, His priesthood judge, *all* that you have done."[3]

There are three confessions that we customarily make:

- To the Lord (always).
- To the person we have wronged (whenever possible).
- To our priesthood leader (if the sin is serious enough).

Just after the Sermon on the Mount, Jesus taught a sobering doctrine. It was another moment of real talk and plain truth from the Master Teacher: "For there is nothing covered, that shall not be revealed; neither hid, that shall not be known. Therefore whatsoever ye have spoken in darkness shall be heard in the light; and that which ye have spoken in the ear in closets shall be proclaimed upon the housetops."[4] The Savior is helping us understand that, while our God is full of love and mercy, He also must operate according to the laws of justice.[5] We must be clean to be with Him, and becoming clean requires that we confess and forsake our sins.[6] No matter how uncomfortable the process may be at times, it's more than worth it.

The divine promise is clear: if you apply the pattern of confessing and forsaking, as well as all the other "conditions of repentance" taught in the scriptures (e.g., a broken heart and contrite spirit), *then* your sins are remembered no more by God. The slate is wiped clean. You are given a fresh start, "fellow citizens with the Saints and of the household of God,"[7] communing with others who have likewise received the grace of God and the forgiveness of their sins. This isn't a step-by-step procedure but a sincere process that takes time and requires a true change of heart.

Forsake

The prophet Alma declared the importance of forsaking sins as part of the repentance process in his counsel to his youngest son, Corianton: "Now my son, I would that ye should repent and *forsake your sins,* and go no more after the lusts of your eyes, but *cross yourself in all these things;* for except ye do this ye can in nowise inherit the kingdom of God."[8] While we do not commonly use the phrase "cross yourself" today, in the 1828 Webster's dictionary from the Prophet Joseph's time, it means "to erase, to cancel, to counteract, to stop, to preclude."[9] Appropriate words that would seem to apply any time we are engaged in an effort to forsake sin.

There may not be a better scriptural example of the effort required to forsake sin than the Book of Mormon account of the Anti-Nephi-Lehies, the people of Ammon, who we talked about in the last chapter. To show their commitment to forsake their sins and avoid the temptation to repeat them, the king offered this solution: "And now, my brethren, if our brethren seek to destroy us, behold, we will hide away our swords, yea, even we will bury them deep in the earth, that they may be kept bright, as a testimony that we have never used them."[10] Of course, burying them *deep* within the earth meant that when the time of temptation came, it would not be easy to retrieve their swords and repeat their sins. To forsake means to renounce, abandon, and give up. To forsake, in the scriptural context of repentance, means to give it up *forever.*[11]

There is a great lesson in this story. If we are to truly forsake, we must remove ourselves completely from temptation's path. It might include getting a new job, putting the TV in another room, or not using the Internet or social media for a period of time—whatever it takes to show the Lord that we are serious and to protect ourselves from being easily tempted.

> If we are to truly forsake, we must remove
> ourselves completely from temptation's path.

Do Not Delay

Real repentance requires great spiritual, emotional, and sometimes physical effort. For example, someone courageously working to overcome compulsive pornography use must deal with the very real challenge of the effects that prolonged exposure to pornography have on the brain.[12] Of course, we know that pornography violates the law of chastity and is highly addictive.[13] But President M. Russell Ballard of the Quorum of the Twelve Apostles offers hope and encouragement: "If you are involved in it, if you are entrapped in this practice, get spiritual help now. You can overcome pornography with the Savior's assistance. Do not wait."[14] A very hopeful message from a prophet of God: this challenge can be overcome through the power of the Atonement of Jesus Christ. The Church offers a powerful and positive Addiction Recovery Program to assist those who need help in overcoming these compulsive habits—an approach that has proven very effective in the lives of many members of the Church.

President Henry B. Eyring once quoted President Spencer W. Kimball, saying: "'One of the most serious human defects in all ages is procrastination.'" President Eyring then continued, "'Now' can seem so difficult, and 'later' appear so much easier. The truth is that today is always a better day to repent than any tomorrow. . . . The very faith we need to repent is weakened by delay. The choice to continue in sin diminishes our faith and lessens our right to claim the Holy Ghost as our companion and comforter."[15]

Why is today a better day to repent than tomorrow? Just like starting an exercise program, the longer you delay, the harder it becomes to get off the couch and start moving. Wait too long and the task soon seems impossible. In the end, there is a price we pay when we delay—the cost of missed opportunity and unnecessary pain and heartache. Don't put off to tomorrow what is best done today.

God Can Make It Right

When we feel discouraged about our sins, we can find hope in knowing that God, an omniscient being, knows everything that will happen in our life. The Lord taught Abraham, "My name is Jehovah, and I know the end from the beginning; therefore my hand shall be over thee."[16] And, His hand will be over you too. With God's foreknowledge He knows what mistakes you and I will make and has prepared everything needed for us to overcome those mistakes.

Remember the 116 manuscript pages that were lost by Joseph Smith and Martin Harris? Knowing they would eventually disobey, leading to the loss of the pages, the Lord not only forgave them but compensated for the error thousands of years before.[17] If He can do that for Joseph and Martin, He can do that for each of us. Is it that hard to believe that the Lord has actually made preparations to help us recover from our mistakes so that we can get back on the straight and narrow, reengaging with the plan that He has for our lives? Indeed, His "wisdom is greater than the cunning of the devil,"[18] who sets traps and looks for ways to cause us to stumble and fall—a devil who certainly doesn't want you or me to truly repent.

With the encouragement to change comes this important counsel from Elder Dieter F. Uchtdorf: "Satan will try to make us believe that our sins are not forgiven because *we* can [still] remember them. Satan is a liar; he tries to blur our vision and lead us away from the path of repentance and forgiveness. God did not promise that *we* would not remember our sins. Remembering will help us avoid making the same mistakes again. But if we stay true and faithful, the memory of our sins will be softened over time. This will be part of the needed healing and sanctification process."[19] Ultimately, it is a blessing for us to not completely forget our sins—a safeguard to help us not repeat them.

I learned some time ago that it takes courage to be a patient in a hospital, undergoing procedures that you are not familiar with, wondering how much it will hurt. Trusting in the doctors that they know what they are doing and care. When we seek spiritual healing, through repentance, it's much the same. It takes courage. Faith. Trust. All traits amply rewarded as we become right with God and are blessed with a clear conscience and companionship of the Holy Ghost.

I close this chapter with this compelling testimony and witness from Elder Andersen, an Apostle of the Lord: "When a sin has been confessed and forsaken, we go forward, trusting in the power of the Savior's Atonement. As the Lord's servant, I give you my humble assurance that as you truly forsake your sins, you will be forgiven."[20]

Notes

1. *Teachings of Presidents of the Church: Brigham Young* (1997), 61.
2. Doctrine and Covenants 58:42–43.
3. Richard G. Scott, "Finding Forgiveness," *Ensign*, May 1995. See also Neil L. Andersen, *The Divine Gift of Forgiveness* (Salt Lake City: Deseret Book, 2019), 204–5, for wise counsel on how to approach confessing to others.
4. Luke 12:2–5.
5. See "Justice," Gospel Topics, ChurchofJesusChrist.org.
6. See 1 Nephi 10:21; Moses 6:57; Alma 11:37; Alma 40:26; 1 Nephi 15:34; 3 Nephi 27:19; Doctrine and Covenants 42:41; 1 Corinthians 6:9-10; Revelation 21:27.
7. Richard G. Scott taught, "If you have repented from serious transgression and mistakenly believe that you will always be a second-class citizen in the kingdom of God, learn that is not true" ("The Path to Peace and Joy," *Ensign*, November 2000). See also Alma 42:13; Romans 3:23; 5:12; Ephesians 2:19.
8. Alma 39:9.
9. "Cross," American Dictionary of the English Language, accessed June 16, 2021, http://webstersdictionary1828.com/Dictionary/cross.
10. Alma 24:16.
11. "Forsake," Lexico.com.
12. Kendra J. Muller, "Pornography's Effect on the Brain: A Review of Modifications in the Prefrontal Cortex," accessed June 16, 2021, https://scholarsarchive.byu.edu/cgi/viewcontent.cgi?article=1029&context=intuition.
13. See Dallin H. Oaks, "Pornography," *Ensign*, May 2005.
14. M. Russell Ballard, "The Lord Needs You Now!" *Ensign*, Sept. 2015.
15. Henry B. Eyring, "Do Not Delay," *Ensign*, Nov. 1999.
16. Abraham 2:8.
17. See "Lost Manuscript of the Book of Mormon," Church History Topics, ChurchofJesusChrist.org.
18. Doctrine and Covenants 10:43.
19. Dieter F. Uchtdorf, "Point of Safe Return," *Ensign*, May 2007.
20. Neil L. Andersen, *The Divine Gift of Forgiveness* (Salt Lake City: Deseret Book, 2019), 214.

CHAPTER 12

Renewing Covenants: Worthily Partaking of the Sacrament and Becoming Unspotted from the World

— DOCTRINE AND COVENANTS 59:8–9 —

As a young man in my early teens, not yet a member of the Church, I worked a paper route in a retirement community called Leisure World, in Laguna Hills, California. It was about a four-mile bike ride from my home to the actual route where I would deliver the papers. Every week, rain, earthquake, or shine, I made the daily commute to get the papers delivered. But the Sunday morning newspaper was the heaviest and hardest.

On the weekdays, I could pick up my newspapers each afternoon. But the Sunday morning paper would come at 3:00 a.m., and I was expected to show up around that time to get the papers, roll or fold them, then get them delivered—all before 5:00 a.m.

The four-mile route to my destination snaked through what was then undeveloped fields—open spaces for miles. I remember one part of the road dipping down where the temperature would noticeably change, and living near the coast, it was often socked in with fog. I always dreaded that part of the road; it was colder, darker, and scarier.

One day, the early Sunday morning fog was particularly thick. As I dropped down into the "dip," I realized that it had become completely socked in: I literally could not see more than a foot in front of me. I was faced with the dilemma to either turn back and wait it out or press on and hope there were no oncoming cars. Problem was, I couldn't even tell if I was on the road without looking straight down at my feet. When I did, I noticed the double yellow lines marking the middle of the road directly beneath me.

That's when the idea hit: I could just point my bike's headlight straight down at the front tire, watch the road directly under me, and simply stay in the space between the double yellow lines in the middle of the road through the fog to get to the other side of the dip! Probably not a parent-approved solution, but it made sense to me at the time.

I recall never looking up, as there was nothing to see. Instead, my attention was focused on keeping my front bike tire in the middle of those yellow center lines and getting through the dip as quickly as I could. I knew I could trust those lines—they would not, could not, and did not lead me astray.

Renewing Our Covenants: A Fresh Start

I've often thought back to this experience as an analogy for what our effort should be like in following what President Russell M. Nelson refers to as "the covenant path."[1] What is the covenant path? Elder D. Todd Christofferson answers, "It is the one path that leads to the celestial kingdom of God. We embark upon the path at the gate of baptism and then 'press forward with a steadfastness in Christ, having a perfect brightness of hope, and a love of God and of all men [the two great commandments] . . . to the end.' In the course of the covenant path (which, by the way, extends beyond mortality), we receive all the ordinances and covenants pertaining to salvation and exaltation."[2]

These ordinances include baptism, confirmation, Melchizedek Priesthood ordination (for men), temple endowment, and temple sealing. We make sacred covenants with God when we receive these ordinances.[3] President Nelson taught that "making and keeping covenants will open the door to every spiritual blessing and privilege available."[4]

Walking the covenant path is a little bit like keeping your front bike tire in that space between the double yellow lines. When the fogs of life begin to settle, you can trust the covenant path to guide you safely through to your intended destination: one of never-ending happiness, everlasting joy, and eternal bliss (yes, the scriptures do actually use that term, "eternal bliss!").[5] However, it takes great intention, concentration, and effort to continually stay within the space between the lines. Get distracted, you'll likely veer off course and potentially meet a metaphoric oncoming Mack Truck!

Sister Rosemary M. Wixom, while General Primary President, said, "A covenant is . . . so personal that it is given to us individually, and often our very own name is said in conjunction with the ordinance that accompanies the covenant."[6]

Sister Silvia H. Allred, then a member of the Relief Society General Presidency, taught that the covenants we make in the temple ordinances "*become our credentials for admission into God's presence.*"[7]

When we partake of the sacrament, we renew our baptismal covenants

- to be willing to take upon ourselves the name of Jesus Christ;
- to always remember Him;
- to keep His commandments.[8]

The word *renew* means to "give fresh life or strength to; repeat; reestablish" and even "to resume after an interruption."[9] In this sense, we recommit to do those things we promised to do when we were baptized. God offers us a fresh start on a continual basis, knowing that we will need to reaffirm our commitments as we work to overcome the natural man in each of us.[10]

Here's something to think about. Various Church leaders have taught that we renew not only our baptismal covenants when taking the sacrament, *but all the covenants* we have made with the Lord during our journey along the covenant path.[11] I have personally found it helpful to review all the covenants I have made with Heavenly Father each week: baptism, priesthood, and temple.[12] This is a personal choice, but one that may provide some benefit to you as well as you reflect on the covenant relationship you have with God.

The Weekly Pardon: Remaining Unspotted from the World

When we are baptized worthily, we receive a remission of our sins.[13] The word *remission* means "the cancellation of a debt, charge, or penalty." In some cultures, it also means a "reduction of a prison sentence," or, in other words, a pardon.[14] The word of the Lord came to the prophet Jeremiah: "And *I will cleanse them from all their iniquity, whereby they have sinned against me; and I will pardon [forgive or excuse, release from the consequences of an offense, implicitly from blame] all their iniquities.*"[15] In essence, we become unspotted from the world.

It is essential for baptized members to consistently partake of the sacrament. By following this divine pattern, we engage in a process that allows us to retain a remission of the sins we have committed, not just prior to our baptism, but also for all the sins committed since our baptism. Elder Lynn G. Robbins of the Seventy clarifies: "In this lifetime curriculum of repentance, the sacrament is the Lord's designated way of providing continual access to His forgiveness. *If we partake with a broken heart and a contrite spirit, He proffers us weekly pardon* as we progress from failure to failure along the covenant path."[16]

"If we partake with a broken heart and a contrite spirit, He proffers us weekly pardon as we progress . . . along the covenant path."

—Elder Lynn G. Robbins

In return for renewing our covenants with God, He promises us the companionship of the Holy Ghost. But, to have His Spirit, we must be clean from sin. Therein lies the other great blessing of the sacrament and the role this ordinance plays in helping us remain clean. Carefully approached, this ordinance provides, as it were, a fresh start for each of us. President Dallin H. Oaks teaches, "No one lives without sin after his or her baptism . . . without some provision for further cleansing, each of us is lost. How grateful we are that the Lord has provided a process for each baptized member of His Church to be cleansed from the soil of sin. The sacrament is an essential part of that process.

"We are commanded to repent of our sins, to come to the Lord with a broken heart and a contrite spirit, and to partake of the sacrament. When we renew our baptismal covenants this way, *the Lord renews the cleansing effect of our baptism.* We are made clean and can always have His Spirit to be with us."[17]

Of course, the sacrament, by itself, does not bring forgiveness.[18] There is no forgiveness of sins without a broken heart and contrite spirit, where we truly seek to repent. Elder Melvin J. Ballard, a member of the Quorum of the Twelve Apostles (and President M. Russell Ballard's grandfather), taught, "Who is there among us that does not wound his spirit by word, thought, or deed, from Sabbath to Sabbath? We do things for which we are sorry and desire to be forgiven. . . . The method to obtain forgiveness is . . . to repent of our sins, to go to those against whom we have sinned or transgressed and obtain their forgiveness and then repair to the sacrament table where, if we have sincerely repented and put ourselves in proper condition, we shall be forgiven, and spiritual healing will come to our souls."[19]

The pattern is clear: worthily partaking of the sacrament allows us to become unspotted from the world. As we properly prepare ourselves through the process of repentance, the sacrament offers both the cleansing of sins and the promise of the companionship of the Holy Ghost—compelling reasons to never skip a Sunday or miss the opportunity to partake of the sacrament.

Worthily Partaking

God does not expect us to be perfect to be worthy to partake of the sacrament. And yet, the scriptures have many admonitions that we should not partake of the sacrament unworthily. In 3 Nephi, the Savior Himself said, "Ye shall not suffer any one knowingly to partake of my flesh and blood unworthily, when ye shall minister it; For whoso eateth and drinketh my flesh and blood unworthily eateth and drinketh damnation to his soul."[20] The Apostle Paul counseled: "Let a man examine himself, and so let him eat of that bread and drink of that cup."[21]

Priesthood leaders (specifically the bishop) have a sacred responsibility to administer the sacrament only to those who are worthy to receive it. This scriptural injunction comes directly from the Savior: "And now behold, this is the commandment which I give unto you, that ye shall not suffer any one knowingly to partake of my flesh and blood unworthily, when ye shall minister it."[22] A bishop may counsel someone to refrain from partaking of the sacrament for a period of time to assist them in the process of repentance. Each individual case will be different. There may even be those situations where someone is encouraged to take the sacrament and someone else is not even though they are in very similar circumstances. There may be many factors that are different, however, including the extent to which the two individuals have a broken heart and contrite spirit.[23] Bishops and stake presidents, the two common judges in every Church member's life, are encouraged to be guided by the Spirit and use flexibility in determining how to proceed in each situation—no two situations are the same.[24]

Each of us has the responsibility to recognize that we are not worthy to partake of the sacrament when we are involved in serious sin that requires confession to the bishop (think of those things related to the temple recommend questions). In those cases, we refrain from partaking of the sacrament and counsel with the bishop on how to proceed with the repentance process, anxiously looking forward to the time when we are once again worthy to partake of the sacred emblems.

Consider this well-thought-out response found in the Church magazine the *New Era* in answer to the question, *When should I not partake of the sacrament?* Speaking of those things that we do not clearly need to talk to the bishop about: "What about matters that do not necessarily require confession [to the bishop]? Here we must look into our own souls. Are we aware of our sins, and are we trying to overcome them? Are we truly repentant? Are our hearts filled with hatred or anger or bitterness toward another, or do we feel at peace? Are we living more righteously this week than last? Do we truly appreciate what the Savior did for us? These are some of the questions we might ask ourselves before we take the sacrament. . . .

"The Sunday School Gospel Doctrine manual . . . contain[ed] this worthwhile statement: 'If a person finds himself unworthy and does not repent, he should attend sacrament meeting but have the courage not to partake of the sacrament. Those present who see another not partaking should not speculate about the reasons. We should all accept that one can allow the sacrament to pass by if he does not feel he should partake. One should neither miss sacrament meeting if he is not worthy to partake, nor partake because he feels social pressure.'"[25]

What We Reflect on During the Sacrament

In addition to thinking about the covenants we are renewing during the sacrament, we should strive to make the ordinance a "truly spiritual experience, a holy communion, a renewal for [our] soul,"[26] by remembering Him. Here are some things you could consider thinking about during the sacrament:

- Ponder and remember with gratitude the life, ministry, and Atonement of Jesus Christ.[27]
- Consider the Savior's redeeming and enabling power that comes through the Atonement.[28]
- Renew your covenants by reflecting on them and reminding yourself what they are.[29]
- Think about the changes you are making in your personal life to become more like the Savior.[30]
- Reflect on the Savior's love and mercy for us.[31]

Of course, there are many other ways to remember Him during the sacrament. Making the sacrament a moment of personal worship of the Savior is key.

Former Young Women General President Sister Ardeth G. Kapp taught: "We must come to *the sacrament altar hungry*, with a spiritual hunger and thirst for righteousness. It is a time for self-evaluation, a time to rectify our course, if necessary, to decide to make right our lives. It is a time and place for us to judge ourselves, to come to better understand the magnitude of that sacred, divine gift, the atonement, and the reality of being allowed to have his Spirit with us always to direct every act of our lives."[32]

The sacrifice of a broken heart and contrite spirit that we bring to metaphorically place on the sacramental table, or altar, each week requires sincere thought and personal reflection. In our quest to be like the Savior, we should consider offering up those things that keep us from purifying our lives—making promises to be and do better. Elder Neal A. Maxwell of the Quorum of the Twelve Apostles drove the point home when he said: "Real, personal sacrifice never was placing an animal on the altar. Instead, it is a willingness to put the animal in us upon the altar and letting it be consumed!"[33]

For a Latter-day Saint, the weekly sacrament is an important part of our personal improvement plan, in which we evaluate, discover, and commit to do those things that make us better disciples, knowing that forgiveness can be obtained for our slips and falls.

> The weekly sacrament is an important part of our personal improvement plan, in which we evaluate, discover, and commit to do those things that make us better disciples, knowing that forgiveness can be obtained for our slips and falls.

We still live the law of sacrifice today, though it has changed from Old Testament Biblical times: "Thou shalt offer a sacrifice unto the Lord thy God in righteousness."[34] Consider these teachings from President M. Russell Ballard: "After the Savior's ultimate sacrifice, two adjustments were made in the practice of [the law of sacrifice]. First, the ordinance of the sacrament replaced the ordinance of sacrifice; and second, this change moved the focus of the sacrifice from a person's animal to the person himself. In a sense, the sacrifice changed from the *offering* to the *offerer*. . . . Instead of the Lord requiring our animals or grain, now He wants us to give up all that is ungodly. . . . When we overcome our own selfish desires and put God first in our lives and covenant to serve Him regardless of the cost, we are then living the law of sacrifice."[35]

We worthily partake of the sacrament when we apply these teachings and come to the sacrament table—a type of sacrificial altar—prepared to do better and be better. Doing so is a weekly exercise that keeps us unspotted from the world as we walk the covenant path—a "strait and narrow path" that leads to eternal life.[36] It is there that we center ourselves between the yellow lines on our life's journey back to the Father, providing a direct course to a "far better land of promise."[37]

Notes

1. See Russell M. and Wendy W. Nelson, "Keep on the Covenant Path!" *New Era*, March 2019.
2. D. Todd Christofferson, "Why the Covenant Path," *Ensign*, May 2021.
3. *General Handbook: Serving in The Church of Jesus Christ of Latter-Day Saints*, 18.1, ChurchofJesusChrist.org.
4. Russell M. Nelson, "As We Go Forward Together," *Ensign*, Apr. 2018.
5. See Alma 37:44. See also Mosiah 2:41; Moses 7:53.
6. Rosemary M. Wixom, "The Covenant Path," BYU devotional, March 12, 2013, https://speeches.byu.edu/talks/rosemary-m-wixom/the-covenant-path/.
7. Silvia H. Allred, "Holy Temples, Sacred Covenants," *Ensign*, Nov. 2008.
8. See "The Sacrament," Gospel Principles, ChurchofJesusChrist.org.
9. "Renew," Lexico.com.
10. See Mosiah 3:19.
11. Elder L. Tom Perry of the Quorum of the Twelve Apostles taught: "The purpose of partaking of the sacrament is, of course, to renew the covenants we have made with the Lord. Elder Delbert L. Stapley instructed us in this when he said about covenants:

'. . . By partaking of the Sacrament we renew *all covenants* entered into with the Lord and pledge ourselves to take upon us the name of his Son, to always remember him and keep his commandments.'" ("As Now We Take the Sacrament," *Ensign*, May 2006.) See also "What Covenants Do We Renew When We Partake of the Sacrament?" *Ensign*, Mar. 1995.
12. "We make covenants with our Heavenly Father when we participate in the ordinances of the gospel" ("How Can I Deepen My Understanding of Covenants?" Sunday School: Come Follow Me, https://www.ChurchofJesusChrist.org/study/youth/learn/ss/ordinances-covenants/learn?lang=eng).
13. See "Remission of Sins," Guide to the Scriptures, ChurchofJesusChrist.org.
14. "Remission," Lexico.com.
15. Jeremiah 33:8; Isaiah 55:7. God will "abundantly pardon."
16. Lynn G. Robbins, "Until Seventy Times Seven," *Ensign*, May 2018. See also Boyd K. Packer, *Mine Errand from the Lord* (Salt Lake City: Deseret Book, 2008), 196.

17. See Dallin H. Oaks, "Renewing Our Covenants," *Friend*, Aug. 1999.

18. Elder David A Bednar taught, "The ordinance of the sacrament is a holy and repeated invitation to repent sincerely and to be renewed spiritually. The act of partaking of the sacrament, in and of itself, does not remit sins. But as we prepare conscientiously and participate in this holy ordinance with a broken heart and a contrite spirit, then the promise is that we may *always* have the Spirit of the Lord to be with us. And by the sanctifying power of the Holy Ghost as our constant companion, we can *always* retain a remission of our sins." ("Always Retain a Remission of Your Sins," *Ensign*, May 2016.)

19. Melvin J. Ballard, in Melvin R. Ballard, *Melvin J. Ballard: Crusader for Righteousness* (Salt Lake City: Bookcraft, 1966), 132–33.

20. 3 Nephi 18:28–29.

21. 1 Corinthians 11:28.

22. 3 Nephi 18:28.

23. See "Confession," *General Handbook: Serving in The Church of Jesus Christ of Latter-day Saints, 32.4.1*, ChurchofJesusChrist.org.

24. See "The Role of Judges in Israel," *General Handbook: Serving in The Church of Jesus Christ of Latter-day Saints*, 32.3, ChurchofJesusChrist.org.

25. "When Should I Not Take the Sacrament?" *New Era*, November 2017. This article also states, "It's important to remember that '*you do not need to be perfect in order to partake of the sacrament, but you should have a spirit of humility and repentance in your heart*' (*True to the Faith* [2004], 148). In most cases not involving serious sins, if you've reflected on your conduct and humbly and sincerely desire to repent and follow the Savior, you should partake of the sacrament. You can then experience the cleansing effect of this ordinance and renew your covenant to take upon yourself the name of Jesus Christ and keep His commandments. If you have any questions, talk to your bishop."

Also, Bruce R. McConkie taught, "The worthiness to be baptized and the worthiness to partake of the sacrament are one and the same. [See Mormon 9:29] Recipients of each of these ordinances must meet the same identical standards. . . . The preparation is the same for each ordinance; the covenant is the same; and the rewards are the same. ("The Sacrament of the Lord's Supper," *A New Witness for the Articles of Faith* (Salt Lake City: Deseret Book, 1985), 297.)

26. Jeffrey R. Holland, *Christ and the New Covenant: The Messianic Message of the Book of Mormon* (Salt Lake City: Deseret Book, 1997), 283.

27. See "Sacrament," Gospel Topics, ChurchofJesusChrist.org.

28. See Cheryl A. Esplin, "The Sacrament—A Renewal for the Soul," *Ensign*, Nov. 2014.

29. See "Sacrament," Gospel Topics, ChurchofJesusChrist.org.

30. See "What Am I Supposed to Think about During the Sacrament?" *New Era*, June 2014.

31. See "The Sacrament—A Renewal for the Soul," *Ensign*, Nov. 2014.

32. Ardeth G. Kapp, "Taking Upon Us His Name," *New Era*, Apr. 1982.

33. Neal A. Maxwell, "Deny Yourselves of All Ungodliness," *Ensign*, May 1995.

34. Doctrine and Covenants 59:8.

35. M. Russell Ballard, "The Law of Sacrifice," *Ensign*, Oct. 1998.

36. 2 Nephi 31:18; 9:41.

37. Alma 37:45.

CHAPTER 13

Staying Forgiven:
Forgiveness and Being Forgiven

— DOCTRINE AND COVENANTS 82:1 —

We have all heard the saying, "Before you judge others, walk a mile in their shoes." That expression took on new meaning one Saturday morning as I was rushing to a church meeting. I had no idea that I was moments away from an experience that would teach me a great insight about the Savior—*who* He really is and *what* He really did.

At the time, we had a shed with a single-car, four-section garage door that we had to pull down manually. As the door comes down, four panels separate while rolling along a track. The panels then come back together as the door closes.

The way I had always done it was to grab the open edge of the panel around the height of my eyes and pull down to create momentum, allowing gravity to do the rest with the door. It had always worked in the past. But I was in a hurry and not paying attention this time.

When I grabbed the panel to shut the door and began to pull it down, I didn't move my fingers out of the way in time and the panel above closed against the panel below, with the fingers of both hands stuck between the panels. Can you say ouch?! Gravity had taken over, and the two panels had completely closed on my fingertips, locking them between the panels!

Then, it happened . . .

The pain began to register in my brain. It was excruciating. If you have ever smashed your finger with a hammer or jammed it in a door, take that and multiply by some number you would use in an algebraic equation, and you would be getting close to how it felt!

With my fingertips still stuck in the door, the only thing I could do was try to lift the door back up with my smashed fingers. As I pushed up on the door, the weight made the previously excruciating pain even worse—if that were possible. After a few tries and near desperation, the door finally rose high enough that the panels began to follow the curve of the track and separate, freeing all of my fingers.

My heart was now throbbing in my hands. I couldn't believe how bad it hurt. Since I'd done this to both hands it was difficult for me to try to doctor myself, so I did the only thing a grown man could . . . I ran in the house screaming for my wife. Gwen tried to help by icing my hands, but that didn't work. All she could really do was watch me as I moaned. My fingers continued to throb for the next few hours, but the major pain began to subside, and I survived.

Now I'm not sharing this because I want you to "feel my pain" or even muse over how clumsy I was, but because I learned something significant from the experience.

This is where part two of the story comes in.

A few days later, my oldest son, Michael, probably eight at the time, was running out the front door to play with friends. In his haste (must take after his father), he grabbed the door and swung it closed behind him. When he did, he somehow slammed the door shut—right on the fingers of one of his hands. This was followed by a look of bewilderment and shrieks of pain. I immediately knew what had happened.

I ran to the door and opened it, worried that I might find some missing digits, but everything was intact.

And then, it happened for him. The same excruciating pain that I was familiar with from only a week before. I knew exactly what he was feeling, what he was going through. Why? Because it had just happened to me. I knew that ice would not help and that there was nothing anyone could do except wait it out.

I gathered him up in my arms with my still-healing hands and told him it would get better. I coached him with confidence about what would happen next and assured him that the pain would eventually go away.

It was my reflection on this situation with my son that soon led me to deeper insight about the Savior. With my son, I knew exactly how he was feeling and what he was going through: well-earned empathy. While I could not stop Michael's pain, I could console him with fatherly love and help him through it. I had a pretty good sense of what, and what not, to do.

The Savior Requires Us to Forgive

This is exactly who the Savior really is and what He really does: someone who can perfectly empathize with us because He has felt exactly what we have felt. Not because He experienced *something like* we did (like me with my son), but because He—in some way we don't yet comprehend—experienced *the very same pain* that we personally experience: "And he cometh into the world that he may save all men if they will hearken unto his voice; for behold, he suffereth the pains of all men, yea, the pains of every living creature, both men, women, and children, who belong to the family of Adam."[1]

Elder David A. Bednar speaks of this perfect empathy our Savior has for us: "The Savior has suffered not just for our iniquities but also for the inequality, the unfairness, the pain, the anguish, and the emotional distresses that so frequently beset us. There is no physical pain, no anguish of soul, no suffering of spirit, no infirmity or weakness that you or I ever experience during our mortal journey that the Savior did not experience first.

"You and I in a moment of weakness may cry out, 'No one understands. No one knows.' No human being, perhaps, knows. But the Son of God perfectly knows and understands, for He felt and bore our burdens before we ever did. And because He paid the ultimate price and bore that burden, He has perfect empathy and can extend to us His arm of mercy in so many phases of our life. He can reach out, touch, succor . . . and strengthen us to be more than we could ever be and help us to do that which we could never do through relying only upon our own power."[2]

"There is . . . no infirmity or weakness that
you or I ever experience during our mortal
journey that the Savior did not experience first."

—Elder David A. Bednar

The Savior has literally walked in our shoes—experiencing exactly what we experience, feeling exactly what we feel. In fact, He felt more intensely any heartache or joy that we experience in this life.[3] Because of this, He knows what He asks of us when he says, "I, the Lord, will forgive whom I will forgive, but of you it is required to forgive all men."[4] With this perfect empathy and understanding, the Savior requires each one of us, regardless of how harrowing the experience, to also forgive any who have offended or harmed us in any way, large or small, "until seventy times seven."[5]

In this divine pattern, God makes plain that our ultimate forgiveness is actually dependent upon the forgiveness we offer to others: "Inasmuch as you have forgiven one another your trespasses, even so I, the Lord, forgive you."[6] In the end, the Savior teaches that we should not expect the forgiveness we are unwilling to give. It's not necessarily sequential—we don't have to go find someone to forgive to be forgiven. But as we repeatedly learn to and, in fact, offer forgiveness to others, we too can gain the forgiveness we hope to have (and we will probably appreciate that gift of forgiveness even more, knowing firsthand the spiritual effort it takes to forgive others).

God knows how difficult this may be for us to do, as He has perfect empathy for how we feel—even in the most complex of situations. It is the Savior's perfect empathy—knowing exactly how we feel and why we feel it—that can help us obey such a sweeping divine command with the faith to follow.

There is another feature of forgiving others that makes it compelling: "For, if ye forgive men their trespasses your heavenly Father will also forgive you."[7] It should be a comfort and strength to know that whatever measure of forgiveness we offer to others, that is the same measure of forgiveness that will be offered to us. On this subject the Prophet Joseph said, "The nearer we get to our Heavenly Father, the more we are disposed to look with compassion on perishing souls; we feel that we want to take them upon our shoulders, and cast their sins behind our backs. If you would have God have mercy on you, have mercy on one another."[8]

What Does It Really Mean to Forgive?

When we forgive others, does that mean relationships should be reconciled, trust immediately restored, memories erased? In other words, are we to act as though the wrong, however big, never occurred? Elder Neil L. Andersen taught: "Our faith in the Atonement of Jesus Christ not only includes faith in the Savior's ability to pay for our sins, but also His ability to heal our wounds when others have sinned against us. . . . Forgiveness is not excusing accountability or failing to protect ourselves, our families, and other innocent victims. Forgiveness is not continuing in a relationship with someone who is not trustworthy. Forgiveness is not condoning injustice. Forgiveness is not dismissing the hurt or disgust we feel because of the actions of others. Forgiveness is not forgetting but remembering in peace."[9]

One friend who served as a priesthood leader shares the story of attending a special training meeting with Elder Richard G. Scott of the Quorum of the Twelve Apostles. He said that Elder Scott responded to questions (particularly questions that had to do with forgiveness) with this main idea: "This is one you need to take up with the Lord," or "This is one you really need to fast and pray about." The lesson: The road to forgiving others differs for every individual.[10]

Forgiving others comes a little easier when we understand these comforting doctrines: "Through the Savior and His Atonement, all that is unfair, all that is evil and despicable, will be overcome."[11] It will "be made right through the Atonement of Jesus Christ."[12] And, "every trial and experience you have passed through is necessary for your salvation."[13]

One case in point is the ordeal that young Elizabeth Smart endured. Elizabeth, as a fourteen-year-old Latter-day Saint girl, was abducted at knifepoint from her bedroom in her family's house in Salt Lake City, Utah. For the next nine months, Elizabeth was sexually abused daily and was under the threat of death if she ever attempted escape. She was eventually rescued by police officers working off a tip from fellow citizens.[14]

Sister Smart has gone on from this horrible ordeal to a very successful and happy life. Reflecting on her nine months of abuse as a young teenager she said, "I realized that forgiveness is not for the other person, it's for yourself. Life is so worthwhile, that no matter what has happened to you, no matter what your background is, no matter what your past is, each of us deserve to be happy. Bad things do happen, but that doesn't mean that they need to define us or to destroy our life. . . . I hope that whatever you are faced with, whatever you deal with, you just remember that you are who you decide to be. You are the captain of your destiny."[15]

"Bad things do happen, but that doesn't mean that they need to define us or to destroy our life."

—Elizabeth Smart

When you forgive others, you free yourself from the hold that not forgiving has over you. It's an empowering step, as Elizabeth so powerfully describes, and one that God wants you to take. He is the Judge, and there could be none better.[16] He frees you from worrying about what judgment should be made, taking that upon Himself. In all our weakness and blindness, what kind of impartial judge would we make anyway? God sees all, knows all, hears all, and loves perfectly. Only He truly knows what is in the mind of man, what circumstances and hidden challenges are behind the acts of another.[17] So relax. Take a breath. Let God be the Judge. And find peace.

Please understand, I get that this is not easy. Far from it. When I was in college at BYU, I regularly drove to Utah Lake and took walks when I needed to think, forgive, or when life was just getting too hard. I would find a place to park off the road and then pick a tree way off in the distance. Before I began my walk to the tree, I remembered the deal I had made with myself: on the way to the tree it was okay to vent, moan, and whine, talking to God about how challenging life was. I could grumble at will about the unfairness of whatever it was I was working through.

The key ground rule, however, was this: when I arrived at the tree, I then had to change my point of view on the walk back. I had to look for my blessings, take accountability for whatever applied, and adopt a positive, faithful outlook on next steps and life in general. This took a lot of discipline but was actually quite therapeutic. (I must admit that there were more than a few times when I had to pick a tree that was a lot farther away from the car than usual.) The upside of this little exercise was that when I returned to the car and headed for my apartment, I felt ready to get back in the game—ready for life.

Whatever your method, it's worth it to take the steps needed to forgive others in your life so you can feel forgiven yourself and find peace. The law of Moses allowed "an eye for an eye, and a tooth for a tooth,"[18] but the higher law introduced by the Savior required more of us: "Ye have heard that it hath been said, Thou shalt love thy neighbour, and hate thine enemy. But I say unto you, Love your enemies, bless them that curse you, do good to them that hate you, and pray for them which despitefully use you, and persecute you."[19]

Here, Jesus teaches that if we know someone has been offended by us in some way, we should take the accountability to reach out and attempt to resolve the situation and not wait for them to come to us.[20] The disciple of Christ takes extra steps to assist the Redeemer in His anointed mission to "to bind up the broken-hearted, to proclaim liberty to the captives, and the opening of the prison to them that were bound."[21] President Russell M. Nelson offers this powerful promise: "A . . . gift the Savior offers you is the ability to forgive. . . . It is usually easy to forgive one who sincerely and humbly seeks your forgiveness. But the Savior will grant you the ability to forgive anyone who has mistreated you in any way. Then their hurtful acts can no longer canker your soul."[22]

Harboring feelings of ill will toward others takes its toll on you, both physically and spiritually.[23] This may be one reason why the Savior teaches us to love our enemies and to pray for them. Pray for your enemies? This was such different doctrine when I heard it the first time as a convert to the Church. Yet, it is *more* than aspirational; it is how the Savior would have us lead our day-to-day lives.

We might withhold forgiveness because we feel that others have not earned it and don't deserve it. Regardless, the Savior still commands us to forgive—not because of *their* merit, but because of *His* merit. He knows that we simply punish ourselves when an unforgiving heart blinds us and hardens us, sometimes to the point of spiritual collapse. Ultimately, the unforgiving become angrier than ever, closing themselves off from light and love.

President Russell M. Nelson challenged each member of the Church to take this important step: "I invite you to seek an end to a personal conflict that has weighed you down. Could there be a more fitting act of gratitude to Jesus Christ for His Atonement? If forgiveness presently seems impossible, plead for power through the atoning blood of Jesus Christ to help you. As you do so, I promise personal peace and a burst of spiritual momentum." That "burst" of momentum included these additional promises: "the ability to move forward on the covenant path with increased momentum, despite whatever obstacles you face," "greater strength to resist temptation," and "more peace of mind, freedom from fear, and greater unity in your families."[24]

Again, what greater promise can we gain from God than the forgiveness of our sins? Is there a greater blessing we can seek from Him? Is it better to be healed of sickness, disability, or even to be raised from the dead? Is it better to gain prosperity, to have food, clothing, and shelter? While these are important and pressing needs, the greatest miracle that God can perform in our lives is the miracle of forgiveness—to be pronounced clean and accepted by God. When that happens, we are firmly on the path to gaining our exaltation and eternal life.

Notes

1. 2 Nephi 9:21. See also Alma 7:12; Mosiah 3:7.
2. David A. Bednar, "The Atonement and the Journey of Mortality," *Ensign*, Apr. 2012.
3. See Robert L. Backman, "Jesus the Christ," *Ensign*, Nov. 1991. See also Alma 7:12; Mosiah 3:7.
4. Doctrine and Covenants 64:10.
5. Matthew 18:21–22.
6. Doctrine and Covenants 82:1.
7. 3 Nephi 13:14–15.
8. "Minutes and Discourse, 9 June 1842," p. [62], *The Joseph Smith Papers*, accessed February 9, 2020, https://www .josephsmithpapers.org/paper -summary/minutes-and-discourse -9-june-1842/2.
9. Neil L. Andersen, *The Divine Gift of Forgiveness* (Salt Lake City: Deseret Book, 2019), 226, 225.
10. From personal notes of Kent Wood, taken at a meeting featuring Elder Richard G. Scott as keynote speaker.
11. Neil L. Andersen, *The Divine Gift of Forgiveness* (Salt Lake City: Deseret Book, 2019), 226.
12. "The Plan of Salvation: The Atonement of Jesus Christ," *Preach My Gospel* (2018), 52.
13. *Teachings of Presidents of the Church: Brigham Young* (1997), 262.
14. Deseret News, "Elizabeth Smart Found Alive in Sandy," Mar. 13, 2003, https://www.deseret.com /2003/3/13/19781761/elizabeth -smart-found-alive-in-sandy.
15. "Kidnapped but Not Powerless! An Inspiring Speech by Elizabeth Smart," https://www.youtube .com/watch?v=vYVAQk8WG -Q and https://www.deseret.com /2003/3/13/19781761/elizabeth -smart-found-alive-in-sandy.
16. Dallin H. Oaks said, "The Lord's way of final judgment will be to apply His perfect knowledge of the law a person has received and to judge on the basis of that person's circumstances, motives, and actions throughout his or her entire life (see Luke 12:47-48; John 15:22; 2 Ne 9:25)" ("'Judge Not' and Judging," *Ensign*, Aug. 1999).
17. "Each of us will stand to be judged of Him according to our works *and the desires of our hearts*" ("The Living Christ: The Testimony of the Apostles," ChurchofJesusChrist.org).
18. Matthew 5:38.
19. Matthew 5:43–44.
20. See 3 Nephi 12:22–24.
21. Doctrine and Covenants 138:42. See also Jeffrey R. Holland, "The Ministry of Reconciliation," *Ensign*, Nov. 2018.
22. Russell M. Nelson, "Four Gifts That Jesus Christ Offers to You," Christmas Devotional, December 2, 2018.
23. Johns Hopkins Medicine, "Forgiveness: Your Health Depends on It," https:// www.hopkinsmedicine.org/health /wellness-and-prevention/forgiveness -your-health-depends-on-it.
24. Russell M. Nelson, "The Power of Spiritual Momentum," *Liahona*, May 2022. President Nelson also taught, "We have never needed *positive* spiritual momentum more than we do now, to counteract the speed with which evil and the darker signs of the times are intensifying. Positive spiritual momentum will keep us moving forward amid the fear and uncertainty created by pandemics, tsunamis, volcanic eruptions, and armed hostilities. Spiritual momentum can help us withstand the relentless, wicked attacks of the adversary and thwart his efforts to erode our personal spiritual foundation."

DIVINE PATTERNS

PART 3

Walking the Covenant Path

CHAPTER 14

*Becoming a Disciple: Thy Will, My Will,
and God Performing His Perfect Work*

— MARK 14:36 —

I can't think of a better way to start a chapter on this particular divine pattern than with a statement I often shared with missionaries: "You can get what you want, or you can have something better."

Learning how to prioritize God's will over our own and disciplining our desires is key to putting off the natural man in order to "become a saint through the atonement of Christ the Lord, and becometh as a child, submissive, meek, humble, patient, full of love, willing to submit to all things which the Lord seeth fit to inflict upon him."[1] Elder Richard G. Scott said it well: "Your agency, the right to make choices, *is not given so that you can get what you want.* This divine gift is provided so that you will *choose what your Father in Heaven wants for you.* That way He can lead you to become all that He intends you to be."[2]

One young single adult friend of mine came face-to-face with needing to accept God's will despite his own desires. This happened right around the time I was writing this book. I share his story with permission because it illustrates what we all experience as the Lord guides and shapes us.

Hollis Hunt had long wanted to become student body president at Brigham Young University.[3] He was motivated to serve his fellow students and was particularly driven to create a stronger sense of belonging at the university. Hollis was on a mission to foster a more inclusive campus and felt inspired in his effort. He certainly involved the Lord in the process and felt this was something God wanted him to do.

He worked tirelessly during the campaign, reaching out to students to share his message and enlist their vote. He attended events, endured sunburnt-filled days of canvasing campus, and talked to everyone he could—including his Father in Heaven. This was something Hollis had dreamed about doing, and now he had the opportunity to do it!

After the election Hollis explained, "We all gathered in the room anxiously waiting for the results. Everyone was confident, happy, and ready to hear the news. The announcement was made that over 10,000 votes had been submitted! You could hear people gasp while repeating the number, '10,000?' Then, we were told that in the 145-year history of the university, there had never been an election this close: the winner had won by a total of just three votes. Three votes! My heart began to pound. I couldn't believe that after all that effort, it came down to just three people.

"Then, the winner was announced . . . and it wasn't me. I had just lost by three votes. The other side of the room erupted in cheering, while me and my team were all stunned in disbelief.

"I thought I could have just talked to four more people; tried just a little harder; done just a little better. I was dumbfounded. If I had lost by 300, 400, 500 votes, it wouldn't sting so much: but just three votes out of 10,000 meant the difference between achieving my goal and failing."

Hollis continues, "I wore my heart on my sleeve and put everything I had into the election . . . Before the election, I had sort of planned out the next phase of my life—expecting to win. After I lost . . . my whole life was turned upside down."

Then Hollis's powerful self-reflection: "When unfortunate things have happened in my life, I was sometimes too quick to say, 'Why?' Sometimes I would question why I would be going through something . . . when I felt like I had done my best. As I look back on my life, I can see why certain things happened. In the moment of what I thought were 'negative' experiences, I was frustrated. In reality, those experiences had been shaping me into who I am today. I needed to try and understand my experiences rather than putting an automatic label of self-pity and discouragement on them. I knew when I turned to God, He was with me through it all. Any so-called 'failures' reminded me of how much I needed to depend on Him."

Hollis came to see that God had an even better plan for him. Since the election, he has founded his own business while still in school—a business called Treehouse Talks, where he can continue his personal mission of elevating the conversation while connecting peers in a diverse community where "there is room for everyone." He was also offered a sought-after full-time job in a humanitarian field related to his interests. Hollis said, "The company would not have started if I had won. The experience gave me the momentum I needed to have all of these other things happen." In the end, you can either have what you want or you can have something better. God always has something better in mind for us.

We can all relate to Hollis—a time when you really wanted something, something important that you worked hard for, but it didn't happen. Maybe it almost seemed that the Lord had other plans in mind and wasn't going to "make" this one work. But of course, it's always easier to accept His will when everything works out the way we hoped. Learning to submit our will to His comes through experiences like the one Hollis had—you won't get good at it unless you have the opportunity to practice.

Recall what we know about the pre-earth life, when the Father asked the question, "Whom shall I send?" In reality, the Father knew who He would be sending: the "whom" could only be Jesus, who was the Chosen from the beginning.[4] One of the key purposes in asking the question was to allow the Savior to make the choice to serve in that capacity. That is why He was the first to volunteer His response, "Here am I, send me."[5] In the book of Moses, we learn something more, "But, behold, my Beloved Son, which was my Beloved and Chosen from the beginning, said unto me—Father, thy will be done, and the glory be thine forever."[6] In His initial response, the Savior revealed a defining characteristic—He sought only the Father's will. Every time.[7]

Christ Showed the Way

The divine pattern, *thy will before my will*, is a preeminent concept the Savior taught throughout His earthly ministry: "For I came down from heaven, not to do mine own will, but the will of him that sent me."[8] The Apostle Paul taught us that the will of God is "good, and acceptable, and perfect."[9]

The divine pattern, *thy will before my will*, is the preeminent pattern the Savior set throughout His earthly ministry.

Again, in the garden, Jesus prayed under the most trying of conditions, "O my Father, if it be possible, let this cup pass from me: nevertheless *not as I will, but as thou wilt*."[10] God expects His disciples to follow this pattern that the Savior set. Consider Mary's response to the angel Gabriel: "Behold the handmaid of the Lord; *be it unto me according to thy word*."[11] Mary showed a servant's heart aligned with God—a willingness to accept whatever the Lord would send her way.

President Brigham Young wrote in a letter to Orson Spencer, a faithful convert to the Church, "As the Lord's will is my will all the time, as he dictates so I will perform."[12] Teaching ourselves to want what He wants is a worthwhile task. While it may be hard, it puts us even closer on the path to becoming like Him. The Prophet Joseph Smith prayed: "Help thy servants to say, *with thy grace assisting them*: Thy will be done, O Lord, and not ours."[13] The Lord promised that if we do His will, before our own, we "shall overcome" and gain eternal life.[14]

You may be familiar with the story of President Gordon B. Hinckley when he was a young missionary in Preston England. He was struggling and wrote his father a letter, confessing that he felt like he was wasting his time serving. As the story goes, "a little while later, Elder Hinckley received a reply from his dad. It said, 'Dear Gordon, I have your recent letter. I have only one suggestion: forget yourself and go to work.'"

Young Elder Hinckley then said, "With my father's letter in hand, I went into our bedroom in the house at 15 Wadham Road, where we lived, and got on my knees and made a pledge with the Lord. I covenanted that

I would try to forget myself and lose myself in His service."[15] Of course, from that point on in Gordon's life, we see him submit his will to the Lord's, allowing God's plan to unfold for him.

But there is another part of the story, a part that only few know about. A good sister we know shared that her grandfather entered into the same mission as Elder Hinckley shortly after his time of struggle. She explained that it wasn't just Gordon Hinckley who was feeling discouraged, but also her grandfather. While Elder Hinckley chose to stay in London after his father's letter and remained faithful to the covenant path through his life (as many of us personally witnessed in his role as a Church leader), this other elder chose to let discouragement prevail and left the mission early, returned home, and followed a different course. Rather than submit his will to God and stay on the covenant path, he remained less active the remainder of his life.[16] Now, missionaries come home early all the time, often due to factors beyond their control. What matters most is what happens next—do we turn toward God or away from Him? Do we prioritize our will or do we submit to His?

In this story, two similar paths, two different choices: one chose to submit his will to God and follow the covenant path, the other chose to follow after his own will. The Savior's example is one for us to follow: "And he said, Abba, Father, all things *are* possible unto thee; take away this cup from me: nevertheless not what I will, but what thou wilt."[17] When we apply this divine pattern of "thy will before my will," then we allow God to perform the perfect work that He has planned, setting in motion the many blessings He intends for both ourselves and others of His children.

By the way, this granddaughter in our stake went on to relate how, later in life, her grandfather confessed that a life of poor decisions had brought about many painful consequences, and upon his deathbed he cried out, "Lord, have mercy on my soul!"

Learn to Prefer His Will Over Your Own

It's one thing to be willing to *accept* God's will, but quite another to *prefer* His will over your own.

Not too many years ago, I had an experience that helped deepen my own understanding of this principle. My wife and I had the blessing of owning several properties in California. We were at that stage of life where we had accumulated these "assets": places that had been built some time ago that we were able to purchase at relatively bargain prices. Real estate and home renovation had become a hobby of mine, and these places were all candidates for an upgrade.

We had since moved to another state and now needed to sell them so we could take the next step in our lives. We really couldn't move forward until they were sold, so we were anxious to get it done. A sluggish real estate market at the time proved challenging. More than a year passed with no real success. In fact, we encountered a number of people who pretended to be interested, stringing us along, but had no real intention of following through. We even had to defend against a few fraudulent attempts to steal the homes from us. Needless to say, we were ready to be done and anxious to move on.

Even with a full-time property manager, we were continually being hounded by problems with the aging properties. Many had been neglected for some time, so they were particularly susceptible to water problems—leaks, old plumbing, roof issues. In fact, anytime I heard it was going to rain in Southern California, I would brace myself, knowing it would likely result in some kind of problem.

In one case, a condo near the beach developed a pinhole leak in the hot water line below the kitchen sink that eventually damaged not only our property but all of the neighbors' properties in the building. I got to the point of instant knots in my stomach anytime the phone rang, just knowing it would be yet another problem and another airplane trip.

As time went on, properties that had started out feeling like smart investments began feeling like curses. We prayed and fasted and fasted and prayed. We vigilantly monitored the sales processes. Tried creative ideas and approaches to marketing. Nothing worked. Nothing sold. The longer time went on, the more aggravating the entire situation became, and my sense of relying on the Lord's timing was once again tested.

After more than a year and a half, my prayers to importune the Lord to immediately sell the properties slowly gave way to His timing—changing from a daily pleading for my will to be done to a meek surrender to whatever the Lord's mind might be—a deep commitment to want His will to be done. I became willing to submit to whatever experience He wanted us to have—even if it meant that we continue dealing with these circumstances for the foreseeable future, putting everything else we had wanted to do on hold. I had always ended my prayers with "Thy will be done," but now I really came to mean it in a deeper way.

Only then did we begin to see the purpose in the Lord's timing. One by one, it became apparent the role each property was playing in our lives. One son lived at one of the properties and met his lovely wife while attending the YSA branch there. Another son and his wife were able to stay at another property that facilitated the launch of his career. A daughter was able to stay at a home during an important phase of an out-of-state adoption. Then and only then, after each property had served its purpose, did inspiration come and legitimate buyers emerge. In many cases, just weeks following the fulfillment of the purpose and, notably, after years of effort.

God knows us better than we know ourselves. Elder Dale G. Renlund testified, "He has known you for a long time and He has loved you for as long as He has known you."[18] President Ezra Taft Benson declared when referring to Deity, "They know us best and love us most and will not leave one thing undone for our eternal welfare."[19] God knew exactly the right circumstances that I needed to deepen my desire to want the will of the Father to be done in my life, in all things. That feeling has been lasting for me. It might have been fleeting had He lifted the burden too soon. It was long enough for me to develop a deep and abiding trust that His will was and always will be best.

Again, "You can have what you want or you can have something better." It could have happened my way, but the blessings that came from the experience would likely not have been realized. My wife and I have learned that the Lord's way is *always better*.

You can have what you want or you
can have something better.

Elder Neal A. Maxwell of the Quorum of the Twelve Apostles so elo-quently encouraged us, "Don't wait too long to find the altar or to begin to place the gift of your wills upon it! No need to wait for a receipt; the Lord has His own special ways of acknowledging."[20]

Be Grateful

It's one thing to submit your will to God, but another to do it with a grateful heart. It may seem a high bar to not only want His will before your own but then to also expect to be grateful for it. We often go through various stages before we fully accept the fact that God's will *is* the better way:

- First, we resist.
- Next, we surrender.
- Then, we embrace.

Believing that He has your best interest at heart, has a plan for you, and wants to do nothing but bless you so that you can live the life He is living is inspiring and empowering. Focusing on this can take you from a sense of "I might as well accept it; there's nothing else I can do" (surren-der) to "Be it unto me according to thy word"[21] (embrace).

President Russell M. Nelson said, "I have concluded that counting our blessings is far better than recounting our problems. No matter our situation, showing gratitude for our privileges is a unique, fast-acting, and long-lasting spiritual prescription. . . . Simply stated, 'In every thing give thanks' (1 Thessalonians 5:18)."[22]

I end this chapter with a profound sense of appreciation to the Lord for the masterful way that He continues to teach me this divine pattern. He is anxious for each of us to learn to put Him first—in everything and all the time—particularly when it comes to what we want. This is how we will overcome the world in our own lives. President Ezra Taft Benson said it well:

The great test of life is obedience to God. . . .

The great task of life is to learn the will of the Lord and then do it.

The great commandment of life is to love the Lord.[23]

Notes

1. Mosiah 3:19.
2. Richard G. Scott, "Finding Joy in Life," *Ensign*, May 1996.
3. See Hollis's video on The Church of Jesus Christ of Latter-day Saints YouTube Channel: https://www.youtube.com/watch?v=axiRz-rZ9uQ.
4. "However, even though Heavenly Father asked 'Whom shall I send?' it was not because He did not know whom to send to earth to be the Savior and Redeemer of mankind. He always knew whom He would send. . . . By asking this question, our Heavenly Father allowed His Firstborn Son to offer Himself 'of his own voluntary will' (Leviticus 1:3)." ("Lesson 24: Abraham 3," Old Testament Seminary Teacher Material, ChurchofJesusChrist.org.)
5. Abraham 3:27.
6. Moses 4:2.
7. See John 5:10, 30; 8:28.
8. John 6:38; see also John 5:30; 3 Nephi 11:11; 27:13.
9. Romans 12:2.
10. Matthew 26:39.
11. Luke 1:38.
12. *Millennial Star*, Vol. 10, 115.
13. Doctrine and Covenants 109:44.
14. Doctrine and Covenants 63:20.
15. "Sweet Is the Work: Gordon B. Hinckley, 15th President of the Church," *New Era*, May 1995.
16. Personal conversation, September 2021; shared with permission.
17. Mark 14:36.
18. Dale G. Renlund, "The Blessing of the Restoration for You," *New Era*, Feb. 2020.
19. *Teachings of Presidents of the Church: Ezra Taft Benson* (2014), 41.
20. Neal A. Maxwell, "Remember How Merciful the Lord Hath Been," *Ensign*, May 2004.
21. Luke 1:38.
22. Russell M. Nelson, "The Story behind My Global Prayer of Gratitude," blog post, November 20, 2020, ChurchofJesusChrist.org.
23. Ezra Taft Benson, "The Great Commandment—Love the Lord," *Ensign*, May 1988.

CHAPTER 15

Relying on God: Keeping the Commandments and Prospering in the Land

— 2 NEPHI 1:20 —

Many years ago, I attended a neighboring ward for the day. It proved to be an interesting priesthood lesson. The instructor began with this statement: "Anyone who is faithful in the Church should be making a six-figure income or more, without exception." I almost blew a gasket! Normally when visiting another ward, I would be more hesitant to jump into the fray, but I raised my hand and shared that I disagreed and made what I considered to be obvious points. The teacher, however, was adamant in his stance and insisted he was correct.

Yes, we prosper and are blessed when we keep the commandments, and that may include material success. But we must be careful about the expectation that "prospering" primarily means material riches. Elder Quentin L. Cook clarifies, "Along with having the Spirit, sacred teachings of the Church establish *having sufficient for our needs as the best measure of temporal prosperity.* Lucifer's paradigm shift here is to elevate the seeking of great wealth and the acquisition of highly visible luxury products. Some seem absolutely driven to achieve the lifestyle of the rich and famous. Excess wealth is not promised to faithful members, nor does it usually bring happiness."[1]

Wealth is clearly not a good barometer for righteousness, and righteousness is not a guarantee for wealth. The Lord asks, "What is property unto me?"[2] God's view is eternal, and His promise is everlasting: "If ye seek the riches which it is the will of the Father to give unto you, ye shall be the richest of all people, for ye shall have the riches of eternity."[3] What are the riches of eternity? "Eye hath not seen, nor ear heard, neither have entered into the heart of man, the things which God hath prepared for them that love him."[4] In other words, we cannot even imagine how wondrous the blessings to come will be. While the world may define prosperity in terms of material success, the Lord's view is much broader and prioritizes spiritual blessings.

When we apply this divine pattern and keep His commandments, we have the absolute assurance from God that we shall "prosper" in the land. In fact, this is one of the most repeated promises in Book of Mormon: "And he hath said that: *Inasmuch as ye shall keep my commandments ye shall prosper in the land*; but inasmuch as ye will not keep my commandments ye shall be cut off from my presence."[5] Of course, the Brethren have clarified for a worldwide Church that "land" means whatever land you may live in; if you keep the commandments, you shall prosper in *the* land of your residence.[6]

While it is true that in a few cases in the Book of Mormon the word *prosper* is being used in conjunction with material blessings or monetary wealth, it is most often used in reference to blessings that are not material— blessings granted to the Church and its members, including living in peace and safety, protection from enemies, a growing posterity, and all manner of spiritual blessings. Elder Quentin L. Cook affirms, "Prospering and being wealthy are not necessarily synonymous. A much better gospel definition of prospering in the land is having sufficient for our needs while having the abundant blessing of the Spirit in our lives. When we provide for our families and love and serve the Savior, we will enjoy the reward of having the Spirit and prospering in the land."[7]

Our daughter Katie experienced this blessing in a rather dramatic way. Katie is one of those children whose deepest desire is to keep God's commandments. She and her husband, Ben, prioritize living as the Lord would have them live, doing the best they can to follow Him.

Katie has always looked forward to having her own family. In fact, she wanted nothing more in life. However, she and Ben experienced infertility for five years after they were married. The implications of their inability to have children weighed heavily on them. Fervent prayers, earnest fasting, and priesthood blessings were all part of the process that had not yet yielded any fruit. The most invasive IVF treatments failed, leaving them with less than a five percent chance of ever getting pregnant. IVF involved shots, mood swings, multiple medications with side effects, and a fair amount of discomfort. Repeated priesthood blessings reinforced the promise of children, as did Katie's patriarchal blessing, but none brought the results they sought.

The doctors' counsel eventually called for them to move on and explore adoption.

Adoption was hard for Katie to hear, as it was another hurdle with many unknowns. In addition, she felt she had been as diligent and faithful as possible. Like the prodigal son's brother, she reflected on her love of God: "These many years do I serve thee, neither transgressed I at any time thy commandment."[8] Yet, the promise and hope of children remained unanswered. She wondered, "Many of my friends are having families—why not me?" Natural questions when promised blessings seem to go unanswered.

Putting these feelings aside, Katie and Ben did decide to pursue adoption. They made sure all the T's were crossed and I's dotted—preparing their home, filling out the intensive applications, and qualifying for approval. They were anxious to begin their family and hopeful that an expectant mom would find them and be willing to place her child with them.

Six nail-biting months later, they were successfully matched with an expectant mother from Katie's hometown a few states away. This was such exciting news for them and our entire family. The birth went well, and a new son was welcomed into their home. Then, out of the blue, just two and a half months later, a member of their ward knew someone who was looking for an adoptive family for their child—and they wanted Katie and Ben to be the parents!

Even though they had their hands full with a newborn, they knew this chance may never come again. Eight days later their second adopted son was born, and their little family began to grow. Then, when the boys were two months and five months old, the unthinkable happened—Katie found out she was pregnant with a little daughter. A miracle! Although it was overwhelming at times with three little ones under a year old, they were delighted with the joys of building a growing family.

If you asked Katie and Ben today, they would certainly say they have "prospered" as a family. The blessing they most wanted, to have children, was granted in wonderful and miraculous ways. And in their waiting, they gained spiritual knowledge and experience that has strengthened them— all of which were blessings that, for them, far outweighed financial wealth and material gain.

While it doesn't happen this way for everyone in this situation, it is what the Lord had planned for them. Everyone can be assured that God is hearing their pleas and prayers and is anxious to grant them, if those desires are in accordance with His plan to bless their lives.[9]

You Shall Prosper in the Land

Sometimes you see others prospering when you are not. That can be frustrating, particularly when you are doing the best you can to live the gospel. Such apparent inequities can naturally cause one to want answers from God:

- Why don't the promised blessings of prosperity always come the way I would expect?
- Why do other people seem to prosper when I don't?
- Why were Katie and Ben's prayers answered when mine never are?

The answers are not the same for everyone—we each have different paths, different tests, and different plans that God has intended for us. However, some of these important questions can be answered by better understanding exactly what the Lord has promised.

It's likely that most of us enjoy the blessings of prosperity in greater abundance than we think we do; we just need to better understand how the Lord intends to prosper us. Again, Elder Quentin Cook teaches, "Let me assure you that prospering in the land is not defined by the size of your bank account. *It has a much fuller meaning than that. . . .* Accordingly, having the Spirit in our lives is the primary ingredient in prospering in the land."[10]

Elder L. Whitney Clayton's summarizing statement seems appropriate: "God's prosperity is the power to press forward despite the problems of life."[11]

"God's prosperity is the power to press forward despite the problems of life."

—Elder L. Whitney Clayton

It will certainly be the case that we will look back upon this life and realize that the treasures of the earth do not compare, even remotely, to the treasures of heaven. This is not what the world teaches, but it is what God is trying to help us understand.[12]

Do Not Covet Your Own Property

Martin Harris was one of the Three Witnesses of the Book of Mormon and an early supporter of the Restoration of the gospel. The Lord called upon Martin, and the use of his property, to help fund the first publication of the Book of Mormon. The history states, "To pay the printer for the first 5,000 copies of the Book of Mormon, Martin Harris mortgaged his home and farm for $3,000. By some estimates . . . if you compare Martin's wealth to the local economy at that time, his gift would be about $1.6 million today.

"To help repay the mortgage on Martin's farm, Joseph Smith gave him the right to sell copies of the book. The books did not sell as well as they had hoped however, and Martin struggled to repay the loan. In a revelation given through Joseph Smith, the Lord told Martin: 'I command thee that *thou shalt not covet thine own property*, but impart it freely to the printing of the Book of Mormon, which contains the truth and the word of God.' (Doctrine and Covenants 19:26, 34–35.) Obeying this commandment, Martin sold 151 acres of his property to pay the debt."[13]

But how can someone covet their own property?[14] That idea is usually reserved for eyeing the neighbor's new car. Recall that to "covet" means to "yearn to possess."[15] When it comes to the law of consecration, it's important for us to remember that everything we have is a gift from God and ultimately belongs to Him—even the air we breathe. In fact, the Book of Mormon teaches that we are unprofitable servants—meaning, no matter how hard we work at it, we can never get ahead of what the Lord has done for us.[16]

This isn't a negative. Being in debt to God is not only a reality; it's a blessing. It means that He has done some wonderful things for us, His children. Consider just a few we likely take for granted:

- Creating the earth and our physical bodies.
- Granting us time in mortality to grow and learn.
- Preparing a Savior to redeem and save us from our sins, mistakes, and weakness.
- Providing us the companionship of the Holy Ghost.
- Granting us the guarantee of immortality and possibility of eternal life.
- And, as a bonus, it is hard to imagine more forgiving, kind, and generous benefactors than our Heavenly Father and His Son, Jesus Christ.

A Path to Prosperity—The Law of Tithing and the Sabbath Day

Two of God's laws are especially connected to this divine pattern: tithing and the Sabbath day. Living both laws helps to pave the path to enjoying both the temporal and spiritual dimensions of prospering in the land.

First, the law of the tithe. President N. Eldon Tanner, then a counselor in the First Presidency, taught: "The payment of tithing is a commandment, a commandment with a promise. *If we obey this commandment, we are promised that we will 'prosper in the land.'* This prosperity consists of more than material goods—it may include enjoying good health and vigor of mind. It includes family solidarity and spiritual increase."[17] It has been said that we don't pay tithing with money, we pay it with faith—faith that God will deliver on His promises.[18]

Notice that in the scriptures, this commandment is given with a promise: "Bring ye all the tithes into the storehouse, that there may be meat in mine house, and prove me now herewith, saith the Lord of hosts, if I will not open you the windows of heaven, and pour you out a blessing, that *there shall* not *be room* enough *to receive it.*"[19] God wants to bless us as we pay our tithes. However, those blessings are often personal and unique. Elder Robert D. Hales of the Quorum of the Twelve taught: "The temporal and spiritual blessings of tithing are *specifically tailored to us and our families*, according to the Lord's will."[20]

Second, the law of the Sabbath. The Lord has promised great spiritual and temporal blessings when we keep the Sabbath day holy.[21] In brief, the blessings are reassuring: "Inasmuch as ye do this [honor the Sabbath], the fulness of the earth is yours . . . the good things which come of the earth, whether for food or for raiment, or for houses, or for barns, or for orchards, or for gardens, or for vineyards."[22] Comforting promises God gives to those who are willing to honor the Sabbath day and follow Him.

As we seek the blessings of heaven by doing our best to obey God's laws, He will bless us with power to obtain the blessings that He intends for us to have. Of course, acknowledging the tender mercies and miracles that come along the way is just as important as applying the divine patterns He gives us. In the same way that I as a father love to bless my children by helping them any way I can (especially the grandchildren!), Heavenly Father loves to bless and prosper His children; only He does it perfectly, and always with an eye to helping us achieve the most prized blessings of all.

He Will Provide Help for Us

Elder Dean L. Larsen reassures us with his witness: "We have the sure promise of the Lord that he will prosper us in every way necessary for our well-being. That is my faith and my testimony. But it is a conditional promise. May we qualify for its fulfillment in our lives and in our time is my earnest prayer."[23] Here, Elder Larsen points out that we must do our part to obtain the blessings of heaven.

I recall an occasion when one of my sons was asked to memorize a hymn as a young man to earn his Duty to God award. When I asked which hymn he learned, he replied, "God Save the King" And then he said, "Dad, it's the shortest hymn in the book!" I thought, *What a clever boy!* But in truth, there are no shortcuts with God. When we do *our part*, it should be our best part, our best effort. That's what we can do to seek the promises of heaven and begin the process that brings about desired blessings in our lives.

King Benjamin, in the book of Mosiah, teaches the *absolute guarantee* that the Lord will prosper those who obey the commandments: "And behold, *all that he requires of you is to keep his commandments*; and he has promised you that if ye would keep his commandments ye should prosper in the land; and *he never doth vary from that which he hath said*."[24]

The Lord has promised that He will help us in our times of need, but He requires that we do our part: work to be self-reliant,[25] live providently,[26] care for the poor among us,[27] and strive to keep His commandments. His promises are sure—He *will* help us obtain what we and our families need. When we keep His commandments, we *will* prosper in the land, in all the most important ways. Guaranteed.

Notes

1. Quentin L. Cook, "A Banquet of Consequences: The Cumulative Result of All Choices," BYU devotional, February 7, 2017, https://speeches.byu.edu/talks/quentin-l-cook/banquet-consequences-cumulative-result-choices/.
2. Doctrine and Covenants 117:4.
3. Doctrine and Covenants 38:39.
4. 1 Corinthians 2:9.
5. 2 Nephi 1:20; see also 26:3–6.
6. For example, see L. Whitney Clayton, "The Promised Land," BYU Commencement address, August 12, 2010, https://speeches.byu.edu/talks/l-whitney-clayton/promised-land/.
7. Quentin L. Cook, "Reaping the Rewards of Righteousness," *Ensign*, July 2015.
8. Luke 15:29.
9. Jeffery R. Holland said: "Remember that God is on your side. He is not an angry, vicious God trying to trip you. He is for you—not against you. He is your Father. He is anxious to do everything possible to bless you. He hears your prayers and desires to make your life all that it can be."

("Holding on to Hope," May 22, 2021, ChurchofJesusChrist.org.)

10. Quentin L. Cook, "Reaping the Rewards of Righteousness," *Ensign*, July 2015.

11. L. Whitney Clayton, "The Finest Homes," *Ensign*, May 2020.

12. See 2 Nephi 9:30; Matthew 6:19–21; 3 Nephi 13:18–21; Helaman 8:25.

13. "Martin Harris, The Great Benefactor," Church History, ChurchofJesusChrist.org.

14. See Mosiah 4:22.

15. "Covet," Lexico.com.

16. See Mosiah 2:21.

17. N. Eldon Tanner, "Constancy Amid Changes," *Ensign*, Nov. 1979.

18. See Robert D. Hales, "The Divine Law of Tithing," *Ensign*, Dec. 1986.

19. Malachi 3:10.

20. Robert D. Hales, "Tithing: A Test of Faith with Eternal Blessings," *Ensign*, Nov. 2002.

21. See "Keeping the Sabbath Day Holy," Duties and Blessings of the Priesthood: Basic Manual for Priesthood Holders, Part B, ChurchofJesusChrist.org. See also Doctrine and Covenants 59:9–20.

22. Doctrine and Covenants 59:16–20.

23. Dean L. Larsen, "The Lord Will Prosper the Righteous," *Ensign*, Nov. 1992.

24. Mosiah 2:22.

25. "The Lord has declared, 'It is my purpose to provide for my saints' (D&C 104:15). This revelation is a promise from the Lord that He will provide temporal blessings and open the door of self-reliance, which is the ability for us to provide the necessities of life for ourselves and our family members. . . . Please be assured that you are a child of our Father in Heaven. He loves you and will never forsake you. He knows you and is ready to extend to you the spiritual and temporal blessings of self-reliance." (*Leader's Guide for the Self-Reliance Initiative,* First Presidency Message, https://www.ChurchofJesusChrist.org/bc/content/ldsorg/topics/self-reliance/leader-guide-new-eng.pdf?lang=eng&download=true.)

See also Alma 34:17–27 and *The Gospel and the Productive Life Teacher Manual Religion 150,* 21.

26. See "Prepare by Living Providently and Paying Tithes and Offerings," *Ensign*, Dec. 2003.

27. See Mosiah 4:11–25.

CHAPTER 16

Practicing Holiness: Virtuous Thoughts and Confidence in the Presence of God

— DOCTRINE AND COVENANTS 121:45 —

My wife, Gwen, and I didn't know we would need a miracle one particular Saturday morning. As a young father, I was out mowing my yard early, trying to get ahead of the day. I enjoyed mowing, as it gave me time to think. I was a bit lost in my thoughts when I turned the corner of the house with the mower and looked up to the second story window, surprised to see all four of my young children waving at me as I passed by. I recall thinking that it was different to see them all in the window, but happily returned the wave and continued to enjoy my mowing.

A couple minutes later, it dawned on me that my little children—the oldest was four—had been standing in the open window of the second-story bedroom! None of them were tall enough to reach that high! How did they do it? I immediately raced in the house and up the stairs.

When I got to the room, I saw a very creative, albeit devious platform they had built—stacked tables, chairs, whatever they could find. As it happened, the windows were left open because of the warm summer morning, and when I inspected, I found that I could push the screen fully out. It had been torn all the way across the bottom and up either side. Apparently, the weight of the children pushing on the screen had ripped it open.

I realized that all of my children could have easily fallen out and gotten terribly hurt, perhaps fatally. I immediately dismantled the journey-man's quality scaffolding and breathed a sigh of relief that God was protecting our family that day.

But that wasn't the miracle I wanted to share, though a miracle none-theless.

The first miracle happened an hour before. Earlier that morning, about 7:30 a.m., the full-time missionaries in our area had called and asked if they could come by to copy some agendas for a meeting. They showed up about thirty minutes later. After they copied their documents, they did what effective missionaries do and asked if they could share a brief message with the family.

After they finished, I called on one of the elders to offer a closing prayer. He asked me if he could also leave a blessing on our home. Who could turn that down! Then, the miracle. In that blessing, he said some-thing unexpected. He offered a blessing specifically on our children and particularly emphasized their safety and well-being. I don't recall the exact words, but it left a distinct impression on my mind. This wasn't your typical closing prayer, but a special blessing of protection for our family. After they left, I went back to mowing the lawn, reflecting on what had just happened.

Soon after was when I noticed the children in the window.

The miracle I wish to emphasize might seem small to someone else, but it was enormous to Gwen and me. The miracle was in the confidence this missionary showed in listening to the Spirit of the Lord and pro-nouncing a blessing of protection on our children. Sure, they made the copies they needed to, but those missionaries were inspired to bless our children with safety—that's why they came that morning.

Confidence before God

No question in my mind, the missionaries were in tune with our Heavenly Father and were directed in their activities that day. They were clearly applying the divine pattern taught in this well-known scripture: "Let thy bowels also be full of charity towards all men, and to the house-hold of faith, and *let virtue garnish thy thoughts unceasingly; then shall thy confidence wax strong in the presence of God.*"[1]

Ensuring that you are garnishing your thoughts with virtue "unceas-ingly" in today's media-indulged society requires diligent effort. Twenty years ago, President Gordon B. Hinckley actually compared the day in which we live to the times of Sodom and Gomorrah: "We live in a season of wickedness, pornography, immorality. All of the sins of Sodom and Gomorrah haunt our society. Our young people have never faced a greater challenge. We have never seen more clearly the lecherous face of evil."[2] Imagine what he might say about our society and culture today—it certainly hasn't gotten any better. In just that short period of time we have witnessed the advent of pornography, taking just one aspect of this culture he describes, sweeping the world like an ever-increasing plague—some studies suggest that thirty-five percent of all Internet downloads in the world are related to pornography and over half of all divorces include one party having an obsessive interest in pornographic websites.[3]

It is no longer enough to mount a good *offense*, like daily scripture study, prayer, church and temple attendance, etc.; you also need to have a world-class *defense*. Protecting yourself against immoral influences that saturate our daily lives is essential, as is having the will to "look away"— not glancing, not watching, not checking.[4] As we learn to train our minds and hearts toward virtuous thoughts, we will be blessed with greater confidence in the presence of God. But what does this really mean?

It is no longer enough to mount a good *offense*;
you also need to have a world-class *defense*.

One answer: the promised confidence is knowing that when we call upon the Lord, He will be there to help us. "Then shalt thou call, and the Lord shall answer; thou shalt cry, and he shall say, Here I am."[5] Elder L. Tom Perry of the Quorum of the Twelve Apostles stated, "It is our privilege to have the Holy Ghost, a member of the Godhead, as our constant companion, to edify and inspire us. . . . We should prepare ourselves through obedience to God's commandments, *that our confidence will wax strong when we call upon the Lord, that His Spirit might magnify us. . . . When we have the Spirit to direct us, we are capable of . . . great power.*"[6]

Our ability to confidently call upon God, represent Him, and use His priesthood power (as either men or women) is directly related to our success in living a virtuous life (i.e., having high moral standards). When we "practice" virtue, we can be assured that the Spirit of God will feel at home in our presence.

Priesthood and the Power of God

Sister Elaine S. Dalton illustrates the connection between virtue and priesthood power in an example from the life of the Savior: "When the woman in the streets of Jerusalem reached out and touched the hem of the Savior's garment, she knew she would be healed. Why? Because she recognized His purity and His power. The Savior Himself said, 'I perceive that *virtue* is gone out of me' (Luke 8:46; emphasis added; see also Mark 5:30; Luke 6:19). The kind of virtue to which He was referring is power, priesthood power, which always accompanies Latter-day Saint[s] who are pure and practice 'virtue and holiness before [the Lord]' (D&C 38:24)."[7]

Of course, priesthood power is available to *both* women and men. Sister Sheri L. Dew, who served as a counselor in the Relief Society General Presidency, clarified the point: "Sisters, some will try to persuade you that because you are not ordained to the priesthood, you have been shortchanged. They are simply wrong, and they do not understand the gospel of Jesus Christ. The blessings of the priesthood are available to every righteous man *and* woman."[8]

There has been much written and taught lately about women and the priesthood. Suffice it to say, there is real clarity that priesthood *power* and priesthood *authority* are both something that men and women can enjoy. Women function with priesthood authority when they are acting in their appointed office or calling, just as the brethren do. That authority is delegated by those who hold priesthood keys for that specific assignment. Women also receive priesthood power.[9]

President Russell M. Nelson taught: "The heavens are just as open to women who are endowed with God's power flowing from their priesthood covenants as they are to men who bear the priesthood. I pray that truth will register upon each of your hearts because I believe it will change your life. Sisters, you have the right to draw liberally upon the Savior's power to help your family and others you love."[10]

Practice Virtue and Holiness

We are instructed by God that we "must practice virtue and holiness before [Him] continually."[11] Of course, the term "practice" can mean both the actual application of the principle as well as working on becoming more proficient in the thing we want to master. In either case, it is an active pursuit of these qualities we are encouraged to seek.

Practicing virtue. Sister Elaine Dalton, former Young Women General President, taught that virtue "encompasses chastity and moral purity. Virtue begins in the heart and in the mind. It is nurtured in the home. It is the accumulation of thousands of small decisions and actions. *Virtue* is a word we don't hear often in today's society, but the Latin root word *virtus* means strength. Virtuous women and men possess a quiet dignity and inner strength. They are confident because they are worthy to receive and be guided by the Holy Ghost."[12]

Practicing holiness. As we become more holy, we are sanctified and set apart from the world and become more dedicated to the Lord's purposes in our lives. Becoming holy is becoming like God and His Son. One of Christ's names is Holy.[13] He is the Son of Man of Holiness.[14] He is the Holy One, signifying that he is a holy, pure, sanctified person, one who was and is without sin, who had no need for repentance, and who stands perfect in all things. "I am the Lord, your Holy One, the creator of Israel, your King."[15] When we speak of holiness, we speak of being like the Savior.

This is the quest that each of us should desire and pursue to be prepared to live with God forever. The Lord has commanded: "Be ye holy; for I am holy."[16] In fact, President Russell M. Nelson underscored the importance of becoming a holy people: "Those who enter the temple are also to bear the attribute of holiness. It may be easier to ascribe holiness to a building than it is to a people. We can acquire holiness only by enduring and persistent personal effort. . . . As temples are prepared for our members, our members need to prepare for the temple."[17]

God's Standard of Sexual Purity

We practice holiness when we live the moral standards that God has revealed to men and women on earth today. Through the temple recommend questions, General Handbook, conference talks, lesson manuals, and other official publications, Church leaders clarify these standards—authoritative direction in this area that we can rely on.

I will draw heavily upon this counsel in the next few pages—no need for personal opinion here. Church leaders have said much on this subject that is important for us to understand.

Chief among them in clearly defining sexual purity is the booklet *For the Strength of Youth.* The booklet is endorsed by the First Presidency and comes with this promise: "We promise that as you keep the covenants you have made and these standards, you will be blessed with the companionship of the Holy Ghost, your faith and testimony will grow stronger, and you will enjoy increasing happiness."[18]

"As you keep the covenants you have made and these standards, you will be blessed with the companionship of the Holy Ghost, your faith and testimony will grow stronger, and you will enjoy increasing happiness."

—For the Strength of Youth

Here is an excerpt from the passage on sexual purity from *For the Strength of Youth.* It is as clear a statement as anyone can find on what the Lord expects in this area: "The Lord's standard regarding sexual purity is clear and unchanging. Do not have any sexual relations before marriage, and be completely faithful to your spouse after marriage. Do not allow the media, your peers, or others to persuade you that sexual intimacy before marriage is acceptable. It is not. In God's sight, sexual sins are extremely serious. They defile the sacred power God has given us to create life. The prophet Alma taught that sexual sins are more serious than any other sins except murder or denying the Holy Ghost (see Alma 39:5).

"Never do anything that could lead to sexual transgression. Treat others with respect, not as objects used to satisfy lustful and selfish desires. Before marriage, do not participate in passionate kissing, lie on top of another person, or touch the private, sacred parts of another person's body, with or without clothing. Do not do anything else that arouses sexual feelings. Do not arouse those emotions in your own body. Pay attention to the promptings of the Spirit so that you can be clean and virtuous. The Spirit of the Lord will withdraw from one who is in sexual transgression."[19]

This counsel is as unchanging as the law of chastity itself. It doesn't matter where you live or when you lived or how old you are, these are standards that do not vary with the changing moral norms of modern culture. God wants us to be clean—that won't change.[20]

Preach My Gospel offers this additional guidance: "People who experience same-sex attraction should also keep the law of chastity and keep covenants with God. Experiencing same-sex attraction or identifying as gay, lesbian, or bisexual is not a sin and does not prohibit one from participating in the Church, holding callings, or attending the temple. Baptismal candidates are to live the law of chastity, which prohibits any sexual relations outside of a legal marriage between one man and one woman. They are not to participate in abortions or homosexual relations. Because God loves all His children and reaches out to them in love through Jesus Christ (see Romans 5:8), those who have committed sexual sin can repent, be forgiven, and live after the manner of happiness (see 2 Nephi 5:27)."[21]

Elder David A. Bednar's comments reinforce this divine pattern: "The Church of Jesus Christ of Latter-day Saints has a single, undeviating standard of sexual morality: intimate relations are proper only between a man and a woman in the marriage relationship prescribed in God's plan. Such relations are not merely a curiosity to be explored, an appetite to be satisfied, or a type of recreation or entertainment to be pursued selfishly. They are not a conquest to be achieved or simply an act to be performed."[22]

On the subject of pornography, President Gordon B. Hinckley gave this stark warning: "Pornography, with its sleazy filth, sweeps over the earth like a horrible, engulfing tide. It is poison. Do not watch it or read it. It will destroy you if you do. It will take from you your self-respect. It will rob you of a sense of the beauties of life. It will tear you down and pull you into a slough of evil thoughts and possibly of evil actions. Stay away from it. Shun it as you would a foul disease, for it is just as deadly."[23]

Though some of the above counsel can be hard to hear and even harder to follow, it's critical to trust that God's ultimate plan for each of us is to achieve a state of "never-ending happiness" and "fulness of joy."[24] With that incomprehensible happiness and joy in mind, making a commitment to follow His standards, no matter what, will provide the confidence that He lives and loves us and will be there for us when we need Him. An interrelated pattern that continues to strengthen us throughout our lives: as we continue to become more and more virtuous, our confidence in the Lord continually increases. A confidence that begins with the simplest of thoughts. The importance of which is captured in this well-known saying:

Sow a thought and you reap an action;
Sow an act and you reap a habit;
Sow a habit and you reap a character;
Sow a character and you reap a destiny.

Notes

1. Doctrine and Covenants 121:45–46.
2. Gordon B. Hinckley, "Living in the Fulness of Times," *Ensign*, Nov. 2001.
3. See "Internet Pornography by the Numbers; A Significant Threat to Society," https://www.webroot.com /us/en/resources/tips-articles/internet -pornography-by-the-numbers.
4. See Genesis 19:26.
5. Isaiah 58:9.
6. L. Tom Perry, "Teach Them the Word of God with All Diligence," *Ensign*, May 1999.
7. Elaine S. Dalton, "Zion Is the Pure in Heart," BYU devotional, September 13, 2009, https://speeches.byu.edu /talks/elaine-s-dalton/zion-pure-in -heart/.
8. Sheri L. Dew, "It Is Not Good for Man or Woman to Be Alone," *Ensign*, Nov. 2001. See also Dallin H. Oaks, "The

Keys and Authority of the Priesthood," *Ensign*, May 2014.

9. See Relief Society General Presidency, "Endowed with Priesthood Power," BYU Women's Conference, May 2, 2019, https://womensconference.byu.edu/sites/womensconference.ce.byu.edu/files/relief_society_general_presidency_-_2019.05.02_-_endowed_with_priesthood_power.pdf.

10. Russell M. Nelson, "Spiritual Treasures," *Ensign*, Nov. 2019.

11. Doctrine and Covenants 46:33.

12. Elaine S. Dalton, "A Return to Virtue," *Ensign*, Nov. 2008.

13. See Isaiah 57:15.

14. See Moses 6:57.

15. Isaiah 43:15.

16. 1 Peter 1:16.

17. Russell M. Nelson, "Personal Preparation for Temple Blessings," *Ensign*, May 2001.

18. "Message to the Youth from the First Presidency," *For the Strength of Youth,* ChurchofJesusChrist.org.

19. "Sexual Purity," *For the Strength of Youth*, ChurchofJesusChrist.org.

20. See Doctrine and Covenants 42:41.

21. "Lesson 4: The Commandments," *Preach My Gospel* (2018), 81. See also President M. Russell Ballard's comments on this topic: https://newsroom.ChurchofJesusChrist.org/article/same-sex-attraction.

22. David A. Bednar, "We Believe in Being Chaste," *Ensign*, May 2013.

23. Gordon B. Hinckley, "Some Thoughts on Temples, Retention of Converts, and Missionary Service," *Ensign*, Nov. 1997.

24. See Alma 28:12; 3 Nephi 28:10; Doctrine and Covenants 93:33.

CHAPTER 17

*Taking Accountability: Cheerfully Doing
All Things and His Arm Is Revealed*

— DOCTRINE AND COVENANTS 123:17 —

The prophet Joseph Smith was held captive in the squalor of Liberty Jail for five months. While there, several attempts were made on his life, from poisoning to mob attacks. In spite of all this (and so much more), the prophet recorded this revelatory instruction now found in the 123rd section of the Doctrine and Covenants: "Therefore, dearly beloved brethren, let us cheerfully do all things that lie in our power; and then may we stand still, with the utmost assurance, to see the salvation of God, and for his arm to be revealed."[1]

With this simple yet profound statement, Joseph was inspired to capture a truth that can have a life-changing impact on our emotional, mental, spiritual, and often even physical state of mind and well-being.

What does it mean to "see the salvation of God and for His arm to be revealed"? It means that we can have the utmost assurance that, when we do all we can in that moment—whatever we are able to conceive of doing given our challenges, obstacles and difficulties—the Lord *will* intervene. He will take action and help us. Of course, as we have established by now, it will be in His own due time and according to His infinite wisdom.[2]

Speaking to the Prophet Joseph about the loss of the book of Lehi, the 116 manuscript pages he reluctantly gave to Martin Harris, the Lord said, "For, behold, you should not have feared man more than God . . . *he would have extended his arm and supported you against all the fiery darts of the adversary; and he would have been with you in every time of trouble.*"[3] Every time of trouble? What a great literal promise from God! With that promise, we can feel empowered to fight off any feelings of discouragement or despair.

On this point, Elder Jeffrey R. Holland powerfully taught: "I wish at the outset to make a distinction F. Scott Fitzgerald once made, that 'trouble has no necessary connection with discouragement—discouragement has a germ of its own, as different from trouble as arthritis is different from a stiff joint' (*The Crack-Up,* 1945). Troubles we all have, but the 'germ' of discouragement, to use Fitzgerald's word, is not in the trouble, it is in us. Or to be more precise, I believe it is in Satan, the Prince of Darkness, the Father of Lies. And he would have it be in us. It's frequently a small germ . . . but it will work and it will grow and it will spread. In fact it can become almost a habit, a way of living and thinking, and there the greatest damage is done. Then it takes an increasingly severe toll on our spirit, for it erodes the deepest religious commitments we can make—those of faith, and hope, and charity. We turn inward and look downward, and these greatest of Christlike virtues are damaged or at very least impaired. We become unhappy and soon make others unhappy, and before long Lucifer laughs."[4]

In the end, the scriptural counsel is clear: don't let your circumstances control you or your attitude, no matter how bad things may be. Remember, He will be with you in every time of trouble.

> The scriptural counsel is clear: don't let your circumstances control you or your attitude, no matter how bad things may be. Remember, He will be with you in every time of trouble.

When the Lord promises His *arm will be revealed*, that has specific scriptural meaning:

- "His greatness, his mighty hand, and his stretched out arm."[5]

- "He hath done marvellous things: his right hand, and his holy arm, hath gotten him the victory."[6]
- "And brought out Israel . . . with a strong hand, and with a stretched out arm."[7]
- "And they were led by the power of his arm, through the wilderness."[8]
- "If he had not extended his arm in the preservation of our fathers they must have fallen into the hands of the Lamanites and become victims to their hatred."[9]
- "And we see that his arm is extended to all people who will repent and believe on his name."[10]

Finally, "But behold, he did deliver them because they did humble themselves before him; and because they cried mightily unto him he did deliver them out of bondage; *and thus doth the Lord work with his power* **in all cases** *among the children of men, extending the arm of mercy towards them that put their trust in him.*"[11] The promise: the powerful, merciful, delivering arm of the Lord will be revealed on your behalf.

Act, Not Acted Upon

When you are faced with hardship, difficulty, disappointment or even disaster, you can respond in one of two ways. Consider this profound Book of Mormon scripture that clarifies the two paths: "And the Messiah cometh in the fulness of time, that he may redeem the children of men from the fall. And because that they are redeemed from the fall they have become free forever, knowing good from evil; *to act for themselves and not to be acted upon.*"[12]

It is given to us in this mortal life to either act or be acted upon. These are the only two real choices we have when faced with tribulation or challenge. Either:

- allow yourself to feel victimized by your circumstances, which leads to inaction, confusion, and an erosion of faith and trust in the Lord; or,
- rise above those circumstances and act, by choosing to do everything

in your power to address the problem with a firm hope, *meaning an actual expectation*, that the arm of the Lord will be revealed in your behalf.

Of course, there is always the exception that someone is so traumatized by a situation that they are unable to rationalize these two choices. In those cases, they need to heal before they can really get going and begin to navigate this truth. For the rest of us not experiencing such an extreme situation, the choice to act and not be acted upon is a powerful one that God wants us to make.

President Henry B. Eyring taught this profound but sometimes difficult to accept principle: "A second truth about our accountability is to know that we are not the helpless victims of our circumstances. The world tries to tell us that the opposite is true: imperfections in our parents or our faulty genetic inheritance are presented to us as absolving us of personal responsibility. But difficult as circumstances may be, they do not relieve us of accountability for our actions or our inactions. Nephi was right. God gives no commandments to the children of men save He prepares a way for them to obey."[13]

Throughout my professional career, I have written about the power of personal accountability.[14] The main idea is simple: "At the heart of the message lies this one simple truth: You can't let your circumstances define who you are and what you do. That kind of thinking only brings a sense of victimization that paralyzes your ability to think clearly, creatively and quickly. Instead, you have to take accountability in order to take charge of shaping your circumstances. Do this and good things, positive things, game-changing things will begin to happen. Easy to say, maybe harder to do."[15]

Because these books were written for a worldwide business audience, I was limited to addressing only what our own individual efforts can produce, as powerful as that can be. Now in a more spiritual context, I can add this important truth: when you combine all of your efforts *with* God's grace and power, there isn't any circumstance that you can't face and eventually "come off conqueror."[16]

Choosing to act can bring real power. Elder David A. Bednar taught, "As you and I come to understand and employ the enabling power of the Atonement in our personal lives, we will pray and seek for strength to change our circumstances rather than praying for our circumstances to be changed. We will become agents who 'act' rather than objects that are 'acted upon' (2 Nephi 2:14)."[17]

When we choose *not* to "act for ourselves," then, by default, we are "acted upon." To be acted upon, in President James E. Faust's words, "means somebody else is pulling the strings."[18] In this condition, we essentially choose to not exercise our agency or become accountable. Instead, we feel we are left without choice—victimized by forces and circumstances we feel are outside of our control that essentially stop us in our tracks. The adversary is anxious for us to feel both hopeless and helpless.[19] Then, he seeks to undermine our faith and tries to convince us that there is nothing we can do but accept our fate.

Interestingly, when we are discouraged and feeling trapped, the principle of doing "all things that lie in our power" may not feel like it amounts to all that much. Meaning, we may not have the energy, strength, or even mental capacity to do what we would normally do if we were feeling whole. In these cases, I believe that the Lord probably doesn't require all that *could* be done; He requires only all that you *can* do in that moment. What's important is that you do what you are able, and then trust, leaving the rest to God.[20]

Now, I've brought this up in past chapters but feel it's worth repeating here: We must acknowledge that there are many who have felt that they have done all they can, yet still do not experience the divine intervention they were hoping for. What then?

Even the Prophet Joseph, one who conversed with God and angels and beheld the most marvelous of heavenly visions, exclaimed, "O God, where art thou? And where is the pavilion that covereth thy hiding place? How long shall thy hand be stayed . . . ?"[21]

Of Joseph's afflictions and adversities in Liberty Jail and his pleas for deliverance, Elder Tad Callister shared: "Sometimes He [God] removes the affliction, sometimes He strengthens us to endure, and sometimes He gives us an eternal perspective to better understand their temporary nature. After Joseph Smith had languished in Liberty Jail for about two months, he finally cried out, 'O God, where art thou?' Instead of providing instant relief, God responded, 'My son, peace be unto thy soul; thine adversity and thine afflictions shall be but a small moment; and then, if thou endure it well, God shall exalt thee on high.'

"Joseph now understood that this bitter experience *was but a dot on the eternal spectrum. . . .* Because of the Savior's Atonement, we can have an eternal perspective that gives meaning to our trials and hope for our relief."[22]

We all probably know someone who feels that God has abandoned them, let them down in some way. They may even be mad at God. Perhaps you feel that way? That He isn't listening to your prayers. Not answering. Blessing your friends and acquaintances while withholding from you. These are real feelings that can emerge from challenging and difficult circumstances, feelings that can easily make things worse. Always, those who feel this way are trying to find the answer to the question, "Why is this happening to me?"

What, Not Why

The "why" question is often difficult to answer. In fact, it's quite often the case that it's not something meant to be understood in this life. I have found that asking "why" often puts us on the wrong path—inviting comparisons to others— another deadly sin! Asking "why" can cause us to tempt God, trying to force an answer out of Him that He is not yet willing to provide. Of course, it should be said that there *are* times He wants us to search out the whys, but this seems more the exception than the rule.

The better question is often "What?" "What is the next step I should take?" "What can I learn from this?" "What more can I do?"[23]

I find that "what?" is a question the Lord seems to readily answer. When we leave the "whys" behind and focus on the "whats," we exercise faith and trust in the Lord and put ourselves in a position to feel blessed and aided in the next steps.

"What?" is a question the Lord
seems to readily answer.

Whys often lead us toward self-pity and anger—the opposites of what this divine pattern encourages: to "cheerfully do all." When we are not cheerful, we are apathetic, depressed, gloomy, sad, heavy-hearted, down, hopeless, lifeless, lethargic, pessimistic, unenthusiastic, upset, unhappy, grave, heavy . . . you get the idea. Actions burdened with these feelings, attitudes, and outlooks are destined to fail.

Whats lead us to positive thinking and acting. They encourage a solve-it mentality—the disposition to look for what more we can do.[24] The 1828 edition of Webster's dictionary, the one used in Joseph Smith's day, defines the word "cheer" as "Life; animation; good spirits; a state of moderate joy or gayety; alacrity." This last word was a new word for me, *alacrity*. Again, the 1828 edition clarifies: "sprightliness; more usually . . . a cheerful readiness . . . or promptitude to do some act; cheerful willingness."

It seems the Lord is clarifying this divine pattern by saying: do all that you can that is within your control, which really cannot be done without the right frame of mind—we should be positive and see opportunity wherever it may exist to impact our circumstances. Then, with total confidence, look for the Lord's hand to be revealed.

Of course, we always hope His hand shows up right away, but that's not what the scripture says or even implies. It doesn't address timing at all. But it does promise that you will see the salvation of God. It may take time. It probably will; often, more than we would like. However, when His arm is revealed, we should know that there will be purpose in His timing.

I will never forget the counsel I heard then BYU President Jeffrey R.

Holland give to students right after I transferred from a junior college near my home in California to BYU–Provo:

"My concern this morning is that you will face some delays and disappointments at this formative time in your life and feel that no one else in the history of mankind has ever had your problems or faced those difficulties. And when some of those challenges come, you will have the temptation common to us all to say, 'This task is too hard. The burden is too heavy. The path is too long.' And so you decide to quit, simply to give up. . . . But in life's most crucial and telling tasks, my plea is to stick with it, to persevere, to hang in and hang on, and to reap your reward."

Elder Holland continued: "I am asking you this morning not to give up 'for ye are laying the foundation of a great work.' That 'great work' is you—your life, your future, the very fulfillment of your dreams. That 'great work' is what, with effort and patience and God's help, you can become. When days are difficult or problems seem unending, I plead with you to stay in the harness and keep pulling. You are entitled to 'eat the good of the land of Zion in these last days,' but it will require your heart and a willing mind. It will require that you stay at your post and keep trying."[25]

Counsel and promises applicable to all of us, not just these lucky college students!

We are reminded several times in the scriptures to "be of good cheer."[26] Staying positive as we wait on the Lord is important. There is no better way to wait. It is helpful to remember and develop the trust to believe that every commandment or admonition from God is designed to be for *our* good and benefit.[27] President Russell M. Nelson taught: "The joy we feel has little to do with the circumstances of our lives and everything to do with the focus of our lives. When the focus of our lives is on God's plan of salvation . . . and Jesus Christ and His gospel, we can feel joy regardless of what is happening—or not happening—in our lives. Joy comes from and because of Him."[28]

Our "cheerful readiness to do some act," will serve us well as we seek to have the blessing of the Lord's hand manifest in our life. Ultimately, His greatest kindness, His most profound act of mercy for us is not to grant some specific blessing we seek, but to save us in the highest degree of the celestial kingdom, "to go no more out, but to dwell with God eternally in the heavens."[29] This is why we can be of good cheer, as the Lord has promised, "The kingdom is yours and the blessings thereof are yours, and the riches of eternity are yours."[30]

Keeping our eyes fastened on the ultimate prize is not only important; it is required. Through the merciful atoning act of a Savior that loves us and would do anything for us, we can overcome and be redeemed. In the end, that is what matters the most and why this divine pattern should be seared into our memory with the fires of conviction.

Notes

1. Doctrine and Covenants 123:17.
2. See 3 Nephi 5:25.
3. Doctrine and Covenants 3:7–8.
4. Jeffrey R. Holland, "For Times of Trouble," BYU devotional, March 18, 1980, https://speeches.byu.edu/talks/jeffrey-r-holland/times-trouble/.
5. Deuteronomy 11:2.
6. Psalm 98:1.
7. Psalm 136:12.
8. Omni 1:13.
9. Mosiah 1:14.
10. Alma 19:36.
11. Mosiah 29:20.
12. 2 Nephi 2:26.
13. Henry B. Eyring, "Do Not Delay," *Ensign*, Nov. 1999.
14. See Roger Connors, Tom Smith, and Craig Hickman, *The Oz Principle: Getting Results Through Individual and Organizational Accountability,* (New York: Portfolio/Penguin, 1998).
15. Roger Connors and Tom Smith, *The Wisdom of Oz: Using Personal Accountability to Succeed in Everything You Do* (New York: Portfolio/Penguin, 2016), x.
16. See Doctrine and Covenants 10:5.
17. David A. Bednar, "In the Strength of the Lord," BYU devotional, October 23, 2001, https://speeches.byu.edu/talks/david-a-bednar/strength-lord/.
18. James E. Faust, "Acting for Ourselves and Not Being Acted Upon," *Ensign*, Nov. 1995.
19. Richard G. Scott said that Satan "would lead you to feel that the walls are pressing in around you and there is no escape or relief. He wants you to believe you lack the capacity to help yourself and that no one else is really interested." ("To Be Healed," *Ensign*, May 1994.)
20. See 2 Nephi 25:23.
21. Doctrine and Covenants 121:1–2.
22. Tad R. Callister, "The Atonement of Jesus Christ," *Ensign*, May 2019.
23. See Jacob 5:47–49.
24. See Jacob 5:47–49.
25. Jeffrey R. Holland, "However Long and Hard the Road," BYU devotional, January 18, 1983, https://speeches.byu.edu/talks/jeffrey-r-and

-patricia-t-holland/however-long
-hard-road/.

26. See Acts 27:22, 25; Matthew 9:2;
Doctrine and Covenants 78:18; 112:4.

27. Elder Robert D. Hales taught: "The
commandments are not a burden or
a restriction. Every commandment of
the Lord is given for our development,

progress, and growth." ("If Thou
Wilt Enter into Life, Keep the
Commandments," *Ensign*, May 1996.)

28. Russell M. Nelson, "Joy and Spiritual
Survival," *Ensign*, Nov. 2016.

29. 3 Nephi 28:40.

30. Doctrine and Covenants 78:18.

DIVINE PATTERNS

PART 4

Enjoying the Divine Privilege to Hear Him

CHAPTER 18

Constant Companion: Entering in by the Way and Showing You All Things

— 2 NEPHI 32:5 —

Several months after I was baptized a member of the Church, I received the Melchizedek Priesthood and was ordained an elder. As a new priesthood holder, I was invited by Bart, a good friend, to attend his priesthood ordination. Right after the Sunday session of stake conference we gathered in the Relief Society room to witness the ordinations occurring in the stake at that time.

As I sat there waiting for Bart's name to be called, I received several very strong spiritual impressions. The first was something specific he should be blessed with that day. I recall thinking that it was odd that I would be receiving this prompting, as I was not the one who would be doing the ordaining. In fact, I didn't even know if I would be joining the circle to assist. Then, another thought popped into my head about something else Bart should be blessed with. This happened several times. Each time I thought to myself, *You've got the wrong guy, I'm not the one acting as voice to ordain my friend.*

Finally, Bart's name was called to come forward. He went to the front of the room, where a member of the stake presidency was there to greet him. They asked who would be ordaining him. He told them who it was, and they then asked that person to come forward. No response. They called for that brother again. Still no response. Clearly, the person Bart had asked to ordain him had not made it, for whatever reason.

So, they turned to Bart and said, "You will need to select someone else to act as voice in your ordination. Who would you like that to be?" My friend quickly glanced around the room, looked at me, then announced my name. I was surprised when he said it, but not shocked.

I think many of the brethren in attendance were caught off guard by the suggestion, as I was such a new member of the Church. But they quickly processed the idea and thought it would be a great experience for me.

I joined the group in the front of the room, conferred the priesthood and ordained my friend an elder, then pronounced the blessings I already knew the Lord wanted him to have.

In the Book of Mormon, we read the promise of this divine pattern: "For behold, again I say unto you that if ye will enter in by the way, and receive the Holy Ghost, *it will show unto you all things what ye should do.*"[1] I know the Holy Ghost showed me what to do by whispering to my mind and heart what I should say to bless my friend Bart. That's one thing about God we should always remember: He knows exactly what is going to happen next. And with the Holy Ghost as our guide, we can be prepared for whatever that may be.

How the Holy Ghost Can Help Us

The Holy Ghost is the third member of the Godhead. He is a personage of spirit and does not have a body of flesh and bones. Once you have entered in "by the way" by being baptized and confirmed, receiving the gift of the Holy Ghost, then you have the *right* to the constant companionship of this member of the Godhead.[2] We stay in "the way" as we walk the covenant path, strive to obey every word of God, and regularly partake of the ordinance of the sacrament.[3]

Consider the promise of having a *constant companion*. The word *constant* means "occurring continuously over a period of time."[4] We can have the constant influence of the third member of the Godhead in our lives. He is a life coach, a counselor, a friend, a teacher, a protector—so much more. And, He does it perfectly. Look at this list of gifts associated with the constant companionship of the Holy Ghost. In no particular order, He will:

- Show us all things that we should do (see 2 Nephi 32:5; Moroni 6:9).
- Tell us what to say (see Doctrine and Covenants 20:26; Luke 12:12).
- Show us where to go (see Doctrine and Covenants 31:11).
- Give us power (see Acts 1:8; 1 Nephi 13:37; Micah 3:8).
- Fill us with joy (see Acts 13:52).
- Fill us with hope and peace (see Romans 15:13).
- Sanctify us (see Alma 13:12).
- Enable us to be born again (see Moses 6:65).
- Fill us with perfect love (see Moroni 8:26).
- Testify to us of the Father and the Son (see 2 Nephi 31:18; Doctrine and Covenants 42:17).
- Teach us (see Doctrine and Covenants 52:9).
- Unfold the mysteries of the kingdom to us (see Doctrine and Covenants 90:14).
- Bring things to our remembrance (see John 14:26).
- Comfort us (see John 14:16–18).
- Help us preach the gospel (see 1 Peter 1:12; Moses 5:58).
- Give us wisdom, understanding, and knowledge (see Exodus 31:3).
- Bring us an innumerable number of gifts of the spirit to enjoy (see 1 Corinthians 12; Hebrews 2:4; Doctrine and Covenants 46).
- Allow us to speak with the tongues of angels (see 2 Nephi 31:13).
- Lead us to do good (see Doctrine and Covenants 11:12).
- Help us write with divine assistance (see Doctrine and Covenants 124:4).
- Help us learn and speak new languages (see Acts 2:4; Articles of Faith 1:7).
- Reprove us when we sin (see Doctrine and Covenants 121:43; John 16:8; Jude 1:19; Helaman 4:24; Doctrine and Covenants 42:23).
- Show us things to come (see John 16:13).
- Help us love others (see Romans 5:5; Galatians 5:22).
- Allow us to testify of Jesus Christ (see 1 Corinthians 12:3).

- Help us be patient and gentle (see Galatians 5:22).
- Help us make decisions (see Doctrine and Covenants 9:8).
- Help us avoid temptation (see 1 Corinthians 10:13).
- Fill us with faith (see 1 Corinthians 12:9).
- Help us discern the truth (see 1 John 4:6).
- Help us know when someone is lying (see Moroni 10:5; Doctrine and Covenants 46:8, 23).
- Bring a remission of sins (see Mosiah 4:3).
- Heal us (see Moroni 10:11; Matthew 14:36).
- Testify to us of truth (see Moroni 10:5, 7; Jacob 7:12).
- Help us judge justly and righteously (see Doctrine and Covenants 11:12).
- Ratify our ordinances so they are accepted by God (see Doctrine and Covenants 76:53).
- Allow us to hear the voice of the Lord (see Doctrine and Covenants 97:1).
- Warn of physical and spiritual danger (see Mosiah 18:34).
- Make it possible for us to see God (see Acts 7:55).

It is quite empowering when we recognize how extensively the Holy Ghost can help us in our lives. Joseph B. Wirthlin, of the Quorum of the Twelve Apostles, quotes Brigham Young and cautions, "I fear that some members of the Lord's Church 'live far beneath our privileges' with regard to the gift of the Holy Ghost."[5] This happens when we do not enjoy these remarkable gifts that come with the companionship of the Holy Ghost.

As a Marvel movie fan, understanding how the Holy Ghost can help us leads me to one certain conclusion: the Holy Ghost has the potential to be every member of the Church's superpower! Sister Ruth L. Renlund, wife of Dale G. Renlund of the Quorum of the Twelve, shared, "You can have a superpower greater than that of any fictional power ever conceived. You can have God's power in your life—the ultimate and very real superpower."[6] So, if anyone ever asks you, "What's your superpower?" tell them, "It's the Holy Ghost!"

The Holy Ghost Can Help Us in Every Aspect of Life

As CEO and cofounder of my own business, I had the opportunity to represent our company in securing a contract to help two large Fortune 500 companies merge their company cultures together as one bought the other. Combined, they would form the sixty-fifth largest company in the world. I was to have a final meeting with the CEO of the purchasing company to finalize their commitment to use our firm. I was a bit nervous about the upcoming meeting. On top of that, I had gotten a cold and wasn't feeling my best.

The Sunday before the big meeting, we had a regional conference broadcast where many stakes were gathering, some 300,000 people, and several Church leaders would be speaking. Because I wasn't feeling well, I was debating whether or not I should attend the meeting but felt the urging to go at the last minute.

I sat through the first hour and thought I might leave at the rest hymn, halfway through. Again, I felt the prompting to stay. As the meeting drew to its conclusion, I thought again that I might leave early, right before the last talk, and avoid the crowd and go home and rest. But, again, I felt the urging to stay.

As it turned out, the final talk was given by then Elder Russell M. Nelson, a member of the Quorum of the Twelve at the time. As he neared the end of his talk, I am almost ashamed to say, I once again considered dodging out before the closing prayer. Now, I did not typically leave a meeting before it was over, but I was just not feeling that great. The urging to stay came again, but it was quite forceful this time: *Stay in your seat; don't miss this!*

As I listened to Elder Nelson's final comments, the very last thing he did in the last two minutes of the meeting was to offer a blessing on all those attending. In the blessing he said something that I don't recall ever hearing before in a situation like this. He said, "I bless you in your professional capacity to have the inspiration to successfully serve those you work with and for." He was speaking to me! He was talking about my "professional capacity." I felt he was reading my mind; this was the blessing I needed. I could now go to my work meeting feeling charged by an Apostle of the Lord with a divine mandate to receive the inspiration I needed to serve my client.

I was grateful for the repeated urgings from the Holy Ghost to go to the meeting and stay in my seat until the last two minutes—to hear the blessing firsthand; to be empowered by a prophet, seer, and revelator.

My business meeting went well, and we were given the contract. The key was finding the right way to be of service to this client. I know Elder Nelson was talking to 300,000 people, but when the Spirit got involved, it felt like he was talking directly to me. The blessing he pronounced could not have been any more precise for what I needed to hear at that time.

Our lives are better, improved, enhanced, and blessed by the power and influence of the Holy Ghost. That influence comes to help us in every aspect of life. I testify that a study of the Holy Ghost, His roles, and His mission will increase your understanding and faith in how the Spirit of God can help and bless you throughout your daily life. President Lorenzo Snow said, "This is the grand privilege of every Latter-day Saint . . . that it is our right to have *the manifestations of the Spirit every day of our lives*."[7]

"The grand privilege of every Latter-day Saint . . . is our right to have *the manifestations of the Spirit every day of our lives*."

—President Lorenzo Snow

What If We Rarely (or Never) Feel the Companionship of the Holy Ghost?

I recall speaking with a good friend and faithful Church member about all the blessings we can receive from the Holy Ghost, and he had quite a strong reaction. He said, "I rarely, if ever, experience these blessings. Because of that, it appears the only option is to beat myself up over not being good enough, not being 'perfect' enough to have the privilege of these blessings."

In answer, I would emphasize that there are a lot of other reasons as to why we may not feel we are experiencing the blessings of the Holy Ghost. I'm sure there are many who have felt, or may feel now, this sense of "spiritual numbness" and do not feel they enjoy the blessings of this companionship.

Spiritual numbness can be the result of many different factors:

- Not obeying the commandments.
- Lack of understanding around how the Spirit speaks to you.
- Experiencing anxiety or depression, and the side effects of the "mood-moderating medications" used to treat them.[8]
- Challenging burdens that are almost too much to handle, like OCD, ADHD, personality disorders, or learning disabilities.
- Extreme fatigue.
- Mental or physical illness.
- Not forgiving yourself or others.
- Overwhelming stress.
- Comparing to others or feeling we've been dealt an unfair hand.
- Anger with others or even God.
- A sense of being preoccupied or just plain old "busyness."
- Feeling a sense of frustration that God isn't listening.
- Or perhaps worst of all—feeling that God doesn't care for you personally, so has sent His Spirit to help those "He likes more." (Of course, the scriptures teach us that God is no respecter of persons,[9] so this one can't be right, even if one happens to feel this way.)

The list could easily keep going. We all have periods of time when the distractions and challenges of life can make it difficult to enjoy the companionship of the Holy Ghost; some feel this more intensely than others.[10]

One psychologist, Debra Theobald McClendon, PhD, writes, "President Boyd K. Packer (1924–2015), President of the Quorum of the

Twelve Apostles, taught that 'our physical body is the instrument of our spirit' and that it houses 'delicate physical senses which have to do with spiritual communication.' *High levels of anxiety can disrupt these 'delicate physical senses'* because it causes our brains to release chemicals that create physiological responses that compete with the Spirit. It can be difficult to differentiate between what our body feels because of spiritual sensations and what it feels because of its release of various stress hormones."[11]

When we go on overload with anxiety and/or depression, or any of the items listed above, it can become difficult or even impossible for us to feel and identify the companionship of the Holy Ghost. The Church website, under "Mental Health," states, "Anxiety is loud and obnoxious, so to speak, making it difficult to feel the Spirit and depend on your faith. Faith is trust in God. The opposite of faith is uncertainty and mistrust. Is it any wonder that anxiety disorders often undermine faith?"[12]

In these moments, it might be well for us to remember these words by President Spencer W. Kimball: "God does notice us, and he watches over us. *But it is usually through another person that he meets our needs.*"[13] When there may seem a barrier between us and God, another person can be inspired to show up and help bridge the gap. For this reason, reaching out to professionals and those around you and confiding in them could be key to helping you effectively cope with these types of challenges.

A Final Thought

Some wonder if it's the Holy Ghost or just coincidence when tender mercies or miracles occur in our lives. I've always felt that two or three coincidences in a row are usually a sign that the divine hand is at work. But we shouldn't miss those times when it's a lone coincidence that has occurred to make the difference in something. That's often how the Spirit works—appearing like a lucky break or stroke of good fortune, a singular fortunate thing that happens that is clearly a blessing to help us on our path.

Elder Ronald A. Rasband shared, "Elder Neal A. Maxwell once explained: . . . '*coincidence* is not an appropriate word to describe the workings of an omniscient God. He does not do things by "coincidence" but . . . by "divine design."'

"Our lives are like a chessboard, and the Lord moves us from one place to another—if we are responsive to spiritual promptings. Looking back, we can see His hand in our lives. . . .

"The Lord is in the small details of our lives, and those incidents and opportunities are to prepare us to lift our families and others as we build the kingdom of God on earth. . . . The Lord's hand is guiding you. By 'divine design,' He is in the small details of your life as well as the major milestones."[14]

And that is the promise of this divine pattern to you: the Holy Ghost will help you with the details of your life. God will never ignore you—it is contrary to His nature and His purpose, "to bring to pass the immortality and eternal life of [you]."[15] He is interested in the facets and details of your life. In fact, He's probably much more involved in your life than you can possibly imagine.

We don't have to be perfect to have the companionship of the Holy Ghost. Elder Kim B. Clark of the Seventy explains, "We do not have to be perfect, but we need to be good and getting better. We need to *strive* to live the plain and simple truths of the gospel. If we take upon us the name of Christ, act with faith in Him to repent of our sins, keep His commandments, and always remember Him [including regularly partaking of the sacrament], we *will* receive the companionship of the Holy Ghost through the mercy and grace of Jesus Christ."[16] It is this companionship of the Spirit, one of the greatest gifts we can receive from God, that will show us all things that we should do.

Notes

1. 2 Nephi 32:5.
2. See Doctrine and Covenants 121:46. See also "Holy Ghost," Gospel Topics, ChurchofJesusChrist.org.
3. See Elder Joseph W. Sitati, Area Presidency Message, "On the Covenant Pathway," *Liahona*, Sept. 2018.
4. "Constant," Lexico.com.
5. Joseph B. Wirthlin, "The Unspeakable Gift," *Ensign*, May 2003.
6. Ruth L. Renlund, "The Power to Change," BYU devotional, December 3, 2019, https://speeches.byu.edu /talks/ruth-l-renlund/power-change/.

7. *Teachings of Presidents of the Church: Lorenzo Snow* (2012), 76.
8. See Daniel K. Judd, *Let's Talk about Religion and Mental Health* (Salt Lake City: Deseret Book, 2021), 96.
9. See 2 Nephi 26:33.
10. For an excellent resource on emotional resilience, see *Finding Strength in the Lord: Emotional Resilience* (2021).
11. Debra Theobald McClendon, "Discerning Your Feelings: Anxiety or the Spirit?" *Ensign*, Apr. 2019.
12. "How can I better understand the difference between warnings from the Spirit and excessive worry?" Mental Health: Help for Me, ChurchofJesusChrist.org.
13. *Teachings of Presidents of the Church: Spencer W. Kimball* (2006), 82.
14. Ronald A. Rasband, "By Divine Design," *Ensign*, Nov. 2017.
15. See Moses 1:39; Matthew 10:29–31.
16. Kim B. Clark, "Eyes to See and Ears to Hear," *Ensign*, Nov. 2015.

CHAPTER 19

*Being Guided: Asking and Seeking
and Receiving and Finding*

— MATTHEW 7:7 —

"Nazanin" left Tehran after her husband ended their marriage and claimed his entitlement to sole custody over their young daughter. With little remaining for her in Iran, she immigrated to Spain and settled in the Mediterranean coastal town of Fuengirola.

Nazanin soon met the missionaries from The Church of Jesus Christ of Latter-day Saints, who taught her the gospel. Because Nazanin did not speak Spanish and only broken English, the elders ordered a Book of Mormon for her in her native language of Farsi. Within only a couple of months Nazanin demonstrated amazing faith and was baptized.

Though she attended church faithfully, her progress was slow. Due to the language barrier, the missionaries were concerned that she still lacked a clear understanding of basic Christian doctrine and of the baptismal covenants she had made.

A few weeks later, on an unrelated matter, President Monte Deere of the Spain Málaga Mission, the mission president of the area, was in contact with one of his missionaries, who had finished his mission in Spain sometime earlier and was now living back in Provo, Utah. President Deere and Elder "Santiago" had been exchanging emails about a recent convert family in Sevilla, Spain, but when the email exchanges became cumbersome, President Deere asked Elder Santiago to email his phone number so they could continue the conversation in real time.

When President Deere called Elder Santiago's number, a woman answered in English but with a strong accent. He was a bit surprised that a woman answered, so he explained, "I am calling for Diego Santiago."

The woman responded, "This is Sister 'Jones.'" President Deere was confused by what connection this "Sister Jones" had to Elder Santiago, but thinking Elder Santiago may be working at the Provo MTC and had given him that phone number, asked, "Is this the MTC? Is there an Elder Santiago there?" The confused Sister Jones finally handed President Deere off to her companion, who spoke better English.

President Deere apologized again and repeated the telephone number he'd been given by Diego Santiago. The woman said, "Well, this is Sister Jones's phone, and the number you called is hers. She is a missionary working in the mission office of the California Los Angeles Mission."

At this point, President Deere was completely confused so started re-assessing the facts: *One, I'm at the mission home in Fuengirola, Spain. Two, I had called a telephone number with an 801 Utah prefix given me by Elder Santiago. Three, that number just happened to reach two sister missionaries serving in California.*

Coincidence would be an understatement.

President Deere suggested to this sister on the phone, "Well, I suppose I've reached a wrong number, but it may interest you to know that I am a mission president presiding over the Spain Málaga Mission. I'm a little surprised that I've somehow called a missionary in California with an 801 telephone number given me by one of my old missionaries in Provo."

After some brief conversation, the sister missionary paused, spoke to Sister Jones for a moment, and then said, "Sister Jones wants to know if you have anyone in your mission who needs to learn the gospel in Farsi?"

Was this really happening? President Deere was flabbergasted.

It turned out, Sister Jones's assignment was to teach investigators by Skype—anywhere in the world—the missionary discussions in Farsi.

Holding back emotion, President Deere managed to say, "Actually yes, we have a recent convert sister here in Spain who needs to hear the gospel in her native Farsi."

They soon traded contact information.

Immediately after the call with Sister Jones and her fellow missionary,

President Deere sent an email to Elder Santiago and learned that the number he had been given was off by one digit.

President Deere in Málaga, Spain.

Sister missionaries in Southern California.

Returned missionary Diego Santiago in Provo, Utah.

All being guided by the Holy Ghost without knowing it at the time.[1]

It was only as events unfolded that each came to recognize the inspiration behind what was taking place. And the beneficiary of all these miracles? Over the next few weeks, Sister Jones taught all of the discussions to Nazanin in Farsi by Skype, allowing her to hear the gospel in her native tongue.

Again, no coincidences. Only God's attention to detail in answering the prayers of a faithful new Iranian convert.

With this divine pattern, when we ask and seek, we shall receive and find. Though this sounds simple and matter of fact, it may not in reality be quite so linear—we often iterate between asking a lot and receiving just enough, then seeking again and finding a bit more. God has His ways of bringing answers and circumstances about in our lives in ways that we can best receive and apply them.

Still, all this may not be as difficult as some may think.

Stop Worrying about It; You Will Be Guided!

In a 2020 Church Education System devotional broadcast called "An Evening with a General Authority," Elder David A. Bednar shared a profound insight on how the Holy Ghost works with us—instruction that is fundamental to our understanding. He began, "We often make it hard on ourselves to receive personal revelation. By that I mean . . . as we honor our covenants, we may *always* have the Holy Ghost to be our constant companion. *But we talk about it and we treat it is as if hearing the voice of the Lord is the rare event,* and that just strikes me as a little curious . . . *we shouldn't be trying to recognize it when it comes, we should be recognizing what happens that causes it to leave. It ought to be with us all of the time.* Not every nanosecond, but if a person is doing his or her best, you don't have to be perfect, *but if you and I are doing our best and we're not committing serious transgression, then we can count on the Holy Ghost guiding us.*"

Elder Bednar continued, "Secondly, I think in the culture of the Church, especially in the western world, we seem to believe . . . *that you have to recognize that you are receiving revelation in the moment that you are receiving revelation* . . . [which is] actually the opposite of what really happens as we receive revelation."

Elder Bednar went on to reinforce the idea that revelation often comes to us without us recognizing it in the moment. Using the example of Nephi in obtaining the brass plates, he pointed out that Nephi really didn't know how things were going to work out while he was attempting to retrieve the plates. Nephi didn't know in "every instant" that he was being guided. It was in looking back on the event that he recognized how the Spirit had been directing him to be successful in obtaining the plates. Nephi himself states that he went forth, "not knowing beforehand the things [that he] should do."[2]

Elder Bednar continued, "Now the reason . . . that's at the very beginning of the Book of Mormon is so . . . every one of us will read it 48 million times in our lives. It's before the Isaiah chapters and I think that's intentional." Elder Bednar explained that repetition is to help us "make the connection that *what happened to him is probably how it ought to be working for us.*" He stated, "I find members of the Church who are terrified: 'I'm going to make a mistake.' Did Nephi make a mistake the first time when they drew lots and [it] didn't work out?"

Here, Elder Bednar made the point—just because Nephi was unsuccessful, it doesn't mean he made a mistake or that he had not been inspired to take the approach he did to retrieve the plates the first time. Elder Bednar continued, "But boy, did he learn a lesson . . . So, [the guidance of the Holy Ghost] doesn't have to be big, dramatic, quick, all at once, and it's just probably the opposite of that; but somehow, we've come to [those] conclusions, and I think those assumptions get in our way."[3]

This is a fresh perspective that ought to help each of us take a sigh of relief when it comes to making decisions and seeking the guidance of the Spirit in our life. Essentially, we are being taught that you can trust the Savior's teachings as you apply this divine pattern: "Ask, and it shall be given you; seek, and ye shall find; knock, and it shall be opened unto you: For every one that asketh receiveth; and he that seeketh findeth; and to him that knocketh it shall be opened."[4] If you are doing your part and striving to live the gospel, you will be guided—whether you know it or not.[5]

> If you are doing your part and striving to live the gospel, you will be guided—whether you know it or not.

Increase Your Spiritual Capacity to Receive Revelation

While serving in the MTC in Provo, Utah, it was Gwen's and my pleasure to hear a General Authority speak almost every Tuesday night for four and a half years. One of those occasions included hearing Elder Bednar promise the missionaries that if they were "a good boy or a good girl, they would be guided by the Holy Ghost." He told them to "stop worrying about it" and have confidence that they would be guided.

In contrast to this, Elder Richard G. Scott of the Quorum of the Twelve Apostles, speaking in the same venue a year or so earlier, taught the missionaries how to listen to the voice of the Spirit using twenty-one principles. In fact, he had a handout for the audience that listed all twenty-one principles in 10-point font that filled the page both front and back. In line with this thinking, Sister Julie B. Beck, former Relief Society General President, echoed the idea that learning the principle of revelation is a skill. She said, "The ability to qualify for, receive, and act on personal revelation is the single most important skill that can be acquired in this life."[6]

How do you reconcile these seemingly opposite messages? "Don't worry about it, just be a good boy or girl" versus "Learn all 21 principles; single most important skill"? Clearly, both are correct; one builds upon the other. Elder Bednar's counsel is the baseline from which we start when it comes to receiving personal revelation and being guided by the Spirit. Elder Scott and Sister Beck were teaching how to refine our ability to hear the Spirit and have that form of revelation more abundantly in our lives.

President Nelson has encouraged members of the Church to listen for the voice of the Lord in their lives and *hear Him*: "The privilege of receiving revelation is one of the greatest gifts of God to His children. Through the manifestations of the Holy Ghost, *the Lord will assist us in all our righteous pursuits.*" He went on to emphasize, "But in coming days, it will not be possible to survive spiritually without the guiding, directing, comforting, and constant influence of the Holy Ghost."[7]

Again, President Nelson teaches: "*We also hear Him more clearly as we refine our ability to recognize the whisperings of the Holy Ghost. . . .* In the Godhead, the Holy Ghost is the messenger. *He will bring thoughts to your mind which the Father and Son want you to receive.* I renew my plea for you to do *whatever* it takes to increase your spiritual capacity to receive personal revelation."[8]

As a stake president, I was working with a member of our stake who was struggling with a very difficult worthiness challenge. It was a sensitive matter and required a membership council that would likely result in having this brother's membership privileges withdrawn. I was concerned for this person and his family and hopeful that they would feel our love and concern for them through it all.

One evening, I received a phone call asking for a last-minute assist with a Scouting campout that one of my sons was attending. As I stood in my closet and began gathering my gear, the thought popped into my mind, "Take a second coat." My initial reaction was *that's silly, why would I need two coats?* I initially ignored the thought and began gathering other things I needed. With a final look before leaving, I again had the thought, *take two coats.* So, I grabbed a second coat and ran to the car.

As I arrived at camp just before dark, things were pretty well in hand—tents were up, Scouts were playing. It was a beautiful evening. However, after about fifteen minutes, an unexpected storm quickly moved in. When everyone began scrambling for their coats, I noticed a young man still walking around in a T-shirt.

"Where's your coat?"

"My mom didn't pack it."

"So, you don't have a—?"

"Nope."

It was at that moment I remembered the second coat I had thrown in the car. I left and grabbed the coat for the now shivering young man.

The significant thing about this experience is not that I was prompted to bring an extra coat that ultimately proved useful, but that I later came to learn that this young man was the son of the individual I was working with on the difficult worthiness issue.

While I'm not even sure if the young man realized I was his stake president, I recognized that if I could receive a prompting to help him with his coat, then I could have confidence in receiving promptings to help his father work through his challenge.

The second coat was for me.

President Nelson promises that we will be guided in our lives: "Take your questions directly to your Heavenly Father in prayer. Ask Him, in the name of Jesus Christ, to guide you. You can learn for yourself . . . how to receive personal revelation. And nothing will make a bigger difference in your life than that! *I promise you that if you will sincerely and persistently do the spiritual work needed to develop the crucial, spiritual skill of learning how to hear the whisperings of the Holy Ghost, you will have all the direction you will ever need in your life.* You will be given answers to your questions in the Lord's own way and in His own time."[9]

> "If you will sincerely and persistently do the spiritual
> work needed to develop the crucial, spiritual skill of
> learning how to hear the whisperings of the Holy Ghost,
> you will have all the direction you will ever need."
>
> —President Russell M. Nelson

We have the absolute assurance that if we are striving to do what's right while walking the covenant path, we will be guided—often we will not even recognize it's happening at the time. Answers *will* come, direction *will* be given, comfort *will* be provided. Consider this powerful truth from President Thomas S. Monson: "Your Heavenly Father loves you—each of you. That love never changes. It is not influenced by your appearance, by your possessions, or by the amount of money you have in your bank account. It is not changed by your talents and abilities. It is simply there. It is there for you when you are sad or happy, discouraged or hopeful. God's love is there for you whether or not you feel you deserve love. It is simply always there."

He concludes, "I promise you that you will *one day stand aside and look at your difficult times, and you will realize that He was always there beside you.*"[10]

It's possible that you may not feel that right now, but it is nonetheless true. Everything the Savior did pointed to lifting, helping, and blessing each of us: "And he will take upon him death, that he may loose the bands of death which bind his people; and he will take upon him their infirmities, that his bowels may be filled with mercy, according to the flesh, that he may know according to the flesh how to succor his people according to their infirmities."[11]

The word *succor* means literally "to run to."[12] That is how a loving God seeks to help us. He will *run* to us, meaning, He will not waste any time in His efforts to lift and assist us, and, gratefully, it will be done in a way that is most eternally advantageous to each of us. That is the promised blessing. As we need help, the Savior promises: "Ask, and *it shall be given you*; seek, and *ye shall find*; knock, and *it shall be opened unto you*."[13] Emphatic statements that leave no doubt as to the intentions of a loving God.

Notes

1. This story was shared in a personal conversation with President Monte Deere, a family friend, who experienced firsthand the events as relayed.

2. 1 Nephi 4:6.

3. "An Evening with a General Authority—Elder David A. Bednar: CES Worldwide Event," February 7, 2020, https://www.Churchof JesusChrist.org/media/video/2020 -02-1000-an-evening-with-a-general -authority-elder-bednar?lang=eng.

4. Matthew 7:7–11.

5. See 3 Nephi 9:20.

6. Julie B. Beck, "And upon the Handmaids in Those Days Will I Pour Out My Spirit," *Ensign*, May 2010.

7. Russell M. Nelson, "Revelation for the Church, Revelation for Our Lives," *Ensign*, May 2018.

8. Russell M. Nelson, "Hear Him," *Ensign*, May 2020.

9. Russell M. Nelson, "Hope of Israel," Worldwide Youth Devotional, June 3, 2018.

   Also, Elder Robert D. Hales taught: "Each of us may feel the influence of the Holy Ghost differently. His promptings will be felt in different degrees of intensity according to our individual needs and circumstances." ("The Holy Ghost," *Ensign*, May 2016.)

10. Thomas S. Monson, "We Never Walk Alone," *Ensign*, Nov. 2013.

11. Alma 7:12.

12. Jeffrey R. Holland, "Come unto Me," BYU devotional, March 2, 1997, https://speeches.byu.edu/talks/jeffrey -r-holland/come-unto/.

13. Matthew 7:7.

CHAPTER 20

*Getting Answers: Trusting in the Lord
and God Directing Thy Paths*

— PROVERBS 3:5–6 —

Life comes at us fast, requiring important decisions and choices, both planned and unplanned. Getting answers from God about how to make good decisions and choices is key to finding happiness and fulfilling the full measure of our creation.[1]

My grandchildren's favorite game is "Monster." Of course, I get to be the monster, count to ten, then chase them around the house trying to catch them. When I do, I put them in the "monster machine"—the nearest couch—where they become the "monster's helper." The object: don't let Grandpa catch you!

One day, while engrossed in an intensive round, and just as I was reaching out to grab one of my little six-year-old grandsons, he looked up at me with fear in his eyes and frantically yelled out, "Pause game!" *What? Pause game?* Apparently, he expected me to freeze, which would then potentially allow him to escape. A clever try to be sure, but this was no video game, this was Monster!

How would it be if we really could "pause game" in life and buy ourselves more time at just the right moment? Maybe we simply aren't ready, are trying to avoid something we don't want to happen, or would just like more time to figure out what to do? Of course, the pause game option doesn't really exist, so we must take life as it comes and deal with the choices as they arise.

As with all divine patterns, this one comes with an important promise: "Trust in the Lord with all thine heart; and lean not unto thine own understanding. In all thy ways acknowledge him, and *he shall direct thy paths*."[2] What a great promise, that He shall direct us. But this blessing is predicated upon our not relying on our own understanding and instead trusting the counsel of the Lord.

Trust in the Lord

What does it mean to trust the Lord? In answer, we know that to "trust" means to have a "firm belief in the reliability, truth, ability or strength of someone or something."[3] Trusting in the Lord means to rely on His promises, live His commandments, to search and believe His words and those of His chosen leaders—to put all of that above our own understanding, particularly when we may not feel we fully understand.

Trusting God doesn't mean to never question; it just means we shouldn't question God. Instead, we question our own understanding of Him and His ways and seek for greater knowledge. Elder Cecil O. Samuelson, former president of BYU and member of the Presidency of the Seventy, taught, "Some seem to believe that faith and questions are antithetical. Such could not be further from the truth. The Restoration itself was unfolded by the proper and necessary melding of both. The Prophet Joseph Smith had both faith and questions . . . the Prophet Joseph Smith used proper questions not only to enhance his knowledge but also to enlarge his faith. . . . Ours is a gospel of questions, and our lives in all of their spheres require thoughtful and appropriate inquiry if we are going to progress. The question is not whether we should ask questions but rather, What are the questions we should be asking?"[4]

In my professional career, we often used an exercise in our team-building sessions called the Trust Fall. More than likely, you've seen it or have done it yourself. The exercise is for someone to stand in the middle of the room on a chair wearing a blindfold.[5] They are instructed to fall backward and told that their teammates will catch them—but they have not actually seen their teammates behind them (they gather in position once the blindfold is on). Thankfully, we have only had one person fall forward in the hundreds of times we have done it—oops!

Trusting God is a lot like the Trust Fall exercise. We just count on the fact that He will be there to catch us—every time. We may not understand all the details, but we get the big picture: we can count on Him; He will never let us down. To that end, Elder Richard G. Scott taught, "To exercise faith is to trust that the Lord knows what He is doing with you and that He can accomplish it for your eternal good even though you cannot understand how He can possibly do it."[6]

With this trust in mind, there are a few common principles that help us receive God's direction when making important decisions in life. In sequence, they include:

1. Study it out and understand the counsel of Church leaders.
2. Seek confirmation.
3. Move forward, until further notice.

This simple framework is an effective way to organize your approach to inviting the Holy Ghost to assist you so that God *can* direct your paths. To illustrate this pattern, I will use the decision of whom to marry—one of the most vital decisions we can ever make. However, these principles can be extrapolated to any decision we are making in life.

First, study it out and understand the counsel of Church leaders. Most of us are familiar with the instruction Oliver Cowdery received from the Lord when he was allowed to translate the Book of Mormon but was unable to. The Lord instructed: "Behold, you have not understood; you have supposed that I would give it unto you, when you took no thought save it was to ask me. But, behold, I say unto you, that you must study it out in your mind."[7]

While this counsel was specifically about translating, Church leaders have cited it often when teaching about decision-making.[8] In short, the Lord expects us to "study with an inquiring mind."[9] He wants us to consider the alternatives, weigh the options, research solutions, gather pertinent data—He wants us to get informed. President Russell M. Nelson taught, "Good inspiration is based upon good information"—another inspired pattern.[10]

"Good inspiration is based upon good information."

—President Russell M. Nelson

It will bless your life immeasurably if you learn to ask, "What has the Lord counseled on this topic through His prophets, other leaders, and the scriptures?" When you answer that question *first*, you prepare yourself to make the best decisions. In fact, the counsel and teachings of our living prophet are paramount. We have been assured that the living prophet will not lead us astray.[11] The Lord promises, "For his word ye shall receive, as if from mine own mouth, in all patience and faith. For by doing these things the gates of hell shall not prevail against you; yea, and the Lord God will disperse the powers of darkness from before you, and cause the heavens to shake for your good, and his name's glory."[12]

Searching out the counsel of Church leaders before making important decisions is always beneficial. For example, when it comes to the important decision of marriage, understanding what Church leaders have counseled on this topic is beyond important—it's mission critical. Speaking to what's at stake with the marriage decision, one BYU religion professor makes this observation: "Far too often I hear such comments as this: 'What if I marry Dr. Jekyll and he turns out to be Mr. Hyde? My sister married a man who seemed wonderful—a returned missionary, a temple-recommend holder. He treated her so well. But within only three years, they were divorced.'"[13] Things were not as they appeared. Unfortunately, we have all seen this play out too many times. How do we avoid such challenging circumstances? While it may not be entirely preventable, the counsel of Church leaders is helpful here.

President Gordon B. Hinckley has said that other than the decision to come unto Christ, marriage "will be the most important decision of your life. . . . Marry the right person in the right place at the right time."[14] And, these wise words from President Dallin H. Oaks: "If you wish to marry well, inquire well."[15]

So, what does it mean to inquire well? One sister asked, "Isn't it enough to know that your future husband has a temple recommend? Doesn't it mean that someone is living a worthy life when a bishop and stake president have signed off? Why can't a woman rely on that in terms of understanding that the man she is marrying is living a righteous life?" (Of course, a man could and should ask the same of a woman.)

President Oaks continues: "The best way to *avoid divorce* from an unfaithful, abusive, or unsupportive spouse is to *avoid marriage to such a person*."[16] Using the first principle in our sequence to *study it out and understand the counsel of Church leaders*, you could begin by compiling a pre-marriage checklist to make sure the person is not "unfaithful" (pornography or law of chastity issues), "abusive" (verbally, emotionally, or physically), or "unsupportive" (selfish, or not encouraging of your faith).

You have every right to ask the necessary questions and make the needed observations of a potential spouse to alleviate any concern you may have in these areas. Elder Neil L. Andersen said, "I once told a university audience that I believed that if one had a history of immorality or pornography, *the person he or she is planning to marry deserves, should she or he desire, to know that history.* Secrets are devastating to an eternal companionship, and things of the past that emerge years later, even if one has been forgiven, can stir doubt and mistrust. *My counsel is to be completely honest with the person with whom you are contemplating living through the eternities,* realizing that these discussions come well after your relationship has developed."[17]

You *both* should be willing to have the necessary conversations and be forthcoming about any problems in these or any other areas. It's not a matter of trust when there is so much on the line.[18]

Elder David A. Bednar taught that inspired questions come before inspired answers,[19] an important pattern when it comes to studying it out in our minds. The scriptures and teachings of Church leaders help to inform the "study it out" phase, allowing thoughts to be shaped by inspiration from the Holy Ghost.

Second, seek confirmation. To "confirm" means to "establish the truth or correctness of something," or to "reinforce someone in an opinion, belief or feeling."[20] Spiritually, it is to gain a witness from God that the course *we have chosen* is correct. That witness can range from a simple feeling of peace (more common),[21] all the way to a burning of the bosom (less common).[22] It might involve a stupor of thought,[23] where you become confused or less clear or uncomfortable with the idea, or it could be the opposite—you have total clarity in your mind and heart.[24]

Important note: Elder Richard G. Scott cautions, "Two individuals who have allowed themselves to violate the laws of chastity during court-ship cannot expect to clearly perceive the answer to their prayer regarding marriage."[25]

When Elder Merrill C. Oaks of the Seventy served as bishop in a BYU ward, he was approached by a young woman asking for counsel about a marriage proposal. She was praying to know if she should marry a certain young man but had received no answer. Over subsequent weeks, each time Bishop Oaks checked in with her, she still hadn't received an answer. He assured her to keep trying—that the Lord would be there. Meanwhile, the young man was growing impatient.

Finally, Elder Oaks relates, "The key came to me in a moment of clear enlightenment. I told her she was expecting the Lord to completely make the decision for her, but He would not do that. Even a decision as impor-tant as marriage requires us to exercise our own agency. . . . I asked her to make two lists. On one list she was to place the things she liked about him and all the positives about marrying him. On the second list she was to outline all her doubts and anything she did not like about him or that was a negative. After a few days she was to evaluate the lists, make a tenta-tive decision on her own, and then go to the Lord for confirmation of her decision.

"The following Sunday she asked for a recommend for her temple marriage. I asked her if she was now sure. She felt certain it was right to marry him. I questioned how she had received her answer. She explained that each day as she looked at the two lists, she was crossing things off the list of negatives and adding to the list of positives. Her words were something like, 'I just began to feel good about getting married, and I knew that my prayers were being answered.'"[26]

As this example shows, often the Lord simply wants us to make the choice and be accountable for it—that's how we learn and grow. It is always His intent to teach us to exercise our free will as we learn to become more like him.[27]

Third, move forward, until further notice. Sister Sharon Eubank related some wise counsel shared by President Boyd K. Packer of the Quorum of the Twelve Apostles that she heard in a leadership-training meeting. A bishop in the congregation commented: "I've been a bishop for five months. I've called a lot of people, [but] I don't know if I'm doing it right. I don't feel a lot of positive revelation when I'm doing this; it just feels logical, and it feels like the right thing to do." Sister Eubank relates that President Packer stood up and said:

"Bishop, the light is always green, except if it's yellow or red."

Sister Eubank then shared President Packer's clarification: "When you are trying to make decisions . . . don't get frozen up with all of these feelings of 'what if'; go with your feelings the best you can. [Move forward with] whatever looks good, and the Lord takes the assignment [that] if you need to be cautioned, if you need to be stopped, He'll let you know, as long as you are asking for His help. But otherwise, go forward in faith. . . . You may even go down a little wrong road [and] he'll help you back up. . . . You'll learn some things down those little roads, but the light is always green, except if it's yellow or red."[28] The idea: we move forward until the Lord gives us further notice that we need to make some type of course adjustment.

The Lord generally reveals His will over time, allowing us to develop and grow along the way. Elder Richard G. Scott stated, "*Seldom will you receive all at once a complete answer from the Lord. It will come a piece at a time.* . . . Moreover, *it will seldom come as the prayer is offered*, rather in quiet moments when the Spirit can most effectively touch your mind and heart."[29]

The Lord generally reveals His will over time,
allowing us to develop and grow along the way.

Now I should point out that there are those who feel God did not give them the "red light" when it was needed. For example (staying with our marriage discussion), we all probably know too many people in the Church who did "all the right things" but were later disappointed when their marriage ended in pain or divorce. Unfair and devastating. They are left to ask, "Why didn't the Lord warn me before we were married?"

Here are a few interrelated principles to consider as we try to understand why warnings may not seem to come when we would expect them (for anything in life):

1. Purpose. The Lord told the prophet Isaiah: "For my thoughts are not your thoughts, neither are your ways my ways, saith the Lord. For as the heavens are higher than the earth, so are my ways higher than your ways, and my thoughts than your thoughts."[30] There may be purpose in our misfortune that we can't see or understand right now. Maybe the warning didn't come because God has purpose in it. We read in the *Liahona*, "Yes, some might rashly blame Heavenly Father for not preventing the bad things that happen to us and our loved ones. Some even become embittered. But after we have passed the portals of death and see with an eternal perspective, we will undoubtedly praise Him for His mercy, His love, and His wisdom in allowing precisely those experiences that are designed to help us reach our full eternal potential and become even as He is."[31]

2. Choice. God is not always going to prevent us from making mistakes or having difficulties by removing all the adversities and challenges of life. Remember, test, trial, challenges—opposition in all things[32]—are the very nature of the mortal proving experience God has designed, and He has designed it perfectly for each one of us. Allowing us to make choices is a part of that process, leads to learning and growth, and is "one of life's great privileges."[33] But for every choice, there are accompanying positive or negative consequences. Being shielded from these consequences is not always in our best interest—especially in the eternal scheme of things.[34]

3. Agency. While we may do all we can to exercise righteous principles, other parties may not do the same. The free exercise of their agency (they may lie, deceive, hurt others, steal, etc.) is a guiding principle in mortality even though it has negative consequences on others. Yes, we can expect to be protected and warned, but such is not always in accord with the mind and will of God. People striving to live righteously and doing the right things do become victims in this mortal world. The only solace in those circumstances is to remember that "whether in this life or the next, all will be made right."[35]

As a side note, there may also be the occasion when the warnings were missed. Perhaps the "study it out" phase was not rigorous enough or our emotions were so compelling that we were distracted from noticing the intimate feelings of the Spirit. Even in these cases, it is important to remember, "There is not anything about your life that gets bent or broken that He cannot fix and will fix."[36]

In the end, we may feel we have walked through fire and been tested to the very core, but holding on to our trust in God, knowing He will not abandon us, is everything.[37]

One Path to Eternal Life

The covenant path leads to only one destination: eternal life. Our Heavenly Father will do everything He can to direct us in that journey. It's what He cares most about.[38] Consider this instruction from the *Gospel Principles* manual: "Those who receive exaltation in the celestial kingdom through faith in Jesus Christ will receive special blessings. The Lord has promised, 'All things are theirs' (D&C 76:59). These are some of the blessings given to exalted people:

1. They will live eternally in the presence of Heavenly Father and Jesus Christ (see D&C 76:62).
2. They will become gods (see D&C 132:20–23).

3. They will be united eternally with their righteous family members and will be able to have eternal increase.

4. They will receive a fullness of joy.

5. They will enjoy everything that our Heavenly Father and Jesus Christ have—all power, glory, dominion, and knowledge (see D&C 132:19–20)."[39]

In addition, those who are exalted "shall inherit thrones, kingdoms, principalities, and powers, dominions, all heights and depths" and they shall go on "to their exaltation and glory in all things, as hath been sealed upon their heads, which glory shall be a fulness and a continuation of the seeds forever and ever."[40]

God will provide direction, guidance, counsel, and power to help you in your life as you apply the divine pattern of trusting and acknowledging Him in all the ways we've talked about. That direction will most often come in subtle ways—sometimes without our even knowing that it has. But come it will if we are humble and willing to receive what He has to give.

Notes

1. Elder Joseph B. Wirthlin once said: "Our goal should be to fill the measure of our creation as sons and daughters of our Heavenly Father—that is, to reach exaltation and eternal life." ("Never Give Up," *Ensign*, November 1987.)

2. Proverbs 3:5–6.

3. "Trust," Lexico.com.

4. Cecil O. Samuelson, "The Importance of Asking Questions," BYU devotional, November 13, 2001, https://speeches.byu.edu/talks/cecil-o-samuelson/importance-asking-questions/.

5. You can get hurt doing this exercise; it should be performed only by someone competently trained in the safety of the activity.

6. Richard G. Scott, "Trust in the Lord," *Ensign*, Nov. 1995.

7. Doctrine and Covenants 9:7–8.

8. For example, see Elaine S. Dalton, "Zion Is the Pure in Heart," BYU devotional, September 13, 2009, https://speeches.byu.edu/talks/elaine-s-dalton/zion-pure-in-heart/; Richard G. Scott, "Using the Supernal Gift of Prayer," *Ensign*, May 2007; Russell M. Nelson, "Choices," *Ensign*, Nov. 1990.

9. See Russell M. Nelson, "Begin with the End in Mind," BYU devotional, September 30, 1984, https://speeches.byu.edu/talks/russell-m-nelson/begin-end-mind/.

10. "Pray, Then Listen: President Nelson Counsels Members to Seek Revelation," *Church News*, April 1,

2018, https://www.Church
ofJesusChrist.org/church/news
/pray-then-listen-president-nelson
-counsels-members-to-seek
-revelation?lang=eng.

11. Ezra Taft Benson, "Fourteen
Fundamentals in Following the
Prophet," BYU devotional, February
26, 1980. See also "The Living
Prophet: The President of the Church,"
*Teachings of the Living Prophets Student
Manual*, ChurchofJesusChrist.org;
Doctrine and Covenants 1:38.

12. Doctrine and Covenants 21:5–6.

13. Michael A. Goodman, "Inquire Well to
Marry Well," *Ensign*, Aug. 2017.

14. Gordon B. Hinckley, "Life's
Obligations," *Ensign*, Feb. 1999.

15. Dallin H. Oaks, "Divorce," *Ensign*,
May 2007.

16. Dallin H. Oaks, "Divorce," *Ensign*,
May 2007.

17. Neil L. Andersen, *The Divine Gift of
Forgiveness* (Salt Lake City: Deseret
Book, 2019), 209–10.

18. Elder L. Whitney Clayton counsels:
"Where there is respect, there is also
transparency, which is a key element of
happy marriages. There are no secrets
about relevant matters in marriages
based on mutual respect and transparency." ("Marriage: Watch and Learn,"
Ensign, May 2013.)

19. "New 'Face to Face' Event," *Church
News*, https://www.thechurchnews
.com/archives/2015-04-02/new-face
-to-face-event-34671.

20. "Confirm," Lexico.com.

21. See Doctrine and Covenants 6:23.

22. See Doctrine and Covenants 9:8.
Dallin H. Oaks explained, "What does
a 'burning in the bosom' mean? Does
it need to be a feeling of caloric heat,
like the burning produced by combus-
tion? If that is the meaning, I have

never had a burning in the bosom.
Surely, the word 'burning' in this
scripture signifies a feeling of comfort
and serenity. That is the witness many
receive. That is the way revelation
works." ("Teaching and Learning by
the Spirit," *Ensign*, March 1997.)

23. See Doctrine and Covenants 9:9.

24. See Doctrine and Covenants 8:2–3.

25. Richard G. Scott, "Making the Right
Choices," BYU devotional, January 13,
2002, https://speeches.byu.edu
/talks/richard-g-scott/making-right
-choices/.

26. Merrill C. Oaks, "How to Get an
Answer," *New Era*, Aug. 2001.

27. Spencer W. Kimball taught, "In
selecting a companion for life and
for eternity, certainly the most *careful
planning* and thinking and *praying and
fasting* should be done to be sure that,
of all the decisions, this one must not
be wrong. . . . *Emotions must not wholly
determine decisions*, but the mind and
the heart, strengthened by fasting and
prayer and serious consideration, will
give one a maximum chance of marital
happiness." ("Oneness in Marriage,"
Ensign, Mar. 1977.)

28. Sharon Eubank, Young Adult English
Area Devotional with President
Ballard, March 7, 2021.
    Also, this counsel from Elder
David A. Bednar: "We should always
pray for guidance and direction. We
should always seek for the constant
companionship of the Holy Ghost.
But we should not be dismayed or
discouraged if answers to our petitions
for direction or help do not necessarily come quickly. Such answers rarely
come all at once. Our progress would
be hindered and our judgment would
be weak if every answer was given to us
immediately and without requiring the

price of faith, work, study, and persistence." ("A Reservoir of Living Water, BYU devotional, February 4, 2007, https://speeches.byu.edu/talks/david-a-bednar/reservoir-living-water/.)

29. Richard G. Scott, "Making the Right Choices," BYU devotional, January 13, 2002, https://speeches.byu.edu/talks/richard-g-scott/making-right-choices/.

30. Isaiah 55:8–9. See also Chapters 2 and 20.

31. "Questions and Answers: Why does our all-loving Heavenly Father allow bad things to happen to innocent people?" *Liahona,* Feb. 2001.

32. See 2 Nephi 2:11.

33. Russell M. Nelson, "Choices," *Ensign,* Nov. 1990.

34. "Being human, we would expel from our lives physical pain and mental anguish and assure ourselves of continual ease and comfort, but if we were to close the doors upon sorrow and distress, we might be excluding our greatest friends and benefactors.

Suffering can make saints of people as they learn patience, long-suffering, and self-mastery. The sufferings of our Savior were part of his education." (Spencer W. Kimball, *Faith Precedes the Miracle,* 98.)

35. Neil L. Andersen, "What Thinks Christ of Me?" *Ensign,* May 2012. See also Chapters 3, 4, and 21.

36. Boyd K. Packer, "The Instrument of Your Mind and the Foundation of Your Character," BYU devotional, February 2, 2003, https://speeches.byu.edu/talks/boyd-k-packer/instrument-mind-foundation-character/. See also Chapters 7, 14, and 19.

37. See Russell M. Nelson, "Choices," *Ensign,* Nov. 1990.

38. The Father "wants your eternal happiness even more than you do" (Richard G. Scott, "Trust in the Lord," *Ensign,* Nov. 1995).

39. "Chapter 47: Exaltation," *Gospel Principles,* ChurchofJesusChrist.org.

40. Doctrine and Covenants 132:19.

CHAPTER 21

Overcoming Adversity: Receiving the Comforter and Being Filled with Hope

— ROMANS 15:13 —

I will never forget the story President Henry B. Eyring shared in general conference about conversations he had with a district president he once served with in the eastern United States. "More than once, as we were driving to our little branches, he said to me, 'Hal, when you meet someone, treat them as if they were in serious trouble, and you will be right more than half the time.' Not only was he right, but I have learned over the years that he was too low in his estimate."[1]

And so it is with each of us. We all have "serious troubles" now and then. In fact, if the test of mortality is working, it's probably more now than then. God has perfectly matched our trials and troubles with the experiences He knows we need to prepare us for the wonders to come.[2]

On this topic, Elder Jeffrey R. Holland, quoting Neal A. Maxwell, shared: "'One's life . . . cannot be both faith-filled and stress-free.' It simply will not work 'to glide naively through life,' saying as we sip another glass of lemonade, 'Lord, give me all thy choicest virtues, but be certain not to give me grief, nor sorrow, nor pain, nor opposition. Please do not let anyone dislike me or betray me, and above all, do not ever let me feel forsaken by Thee or those I love. In fact, Lord, be careful to keep me from all the experiences that made Thee divine. And then, when the rough sledding by everyone else is over, please let me come and dwell with Thee, where I can boast about how similar our strengths and our characters are as I float along on my cloud of comfortable Christianity.'"[3]

We are meant to experience adversity, trial, and tribulation—it *is* the mortal experience.[4] Still, sometimes we underestimate just how blessed we are to be members of The Church of Jesus Christ of Latter-day Saints. We don't always appreciate that peace is the *absence of conflict*;[5] that living the gospel helps us avoid so much of the turmoil and strife that is part of everyday life for so many in the world.

As a mission president, I often told our missionaries a well-known phrase: "Everything will work out in the end, so, if it hasn't worked out yet—it's not the end!" That is the promise found within this divine pattern. We can receive the Holy Ghost, also known as the Comforter,[6] who will bring us guidance, peace, and *hope* in this life (and ultimately, eternal life in the world to come) to aid us in dealing with our troubles and challenges. In the book of Romans, we read: "Now the God of hope fill you with all joy and peace in believing, that ye may abound in hope, through the power of the Holy Ghost."[7]

> Everything will work out in the end. If it hasn't worked out yet—it's not the end!

As we walk the covenant path, God is so in the details of our lives—whether we believe it or not—that the things we experience, the challenges and blessings, will all ultimately work to our benefit and help us obtain our eternal goal. Elder Chi Hong (Sam) Wong of the Seventy taught, "He knows not only the details of our lives. God knows the details of the details of our lives."[8] That's not a typo; the truth Elder Wong is speaking is that God *is* in the details. Way in. As I have said before, if you are not seeing or feeling this in your life yet, please hang on. God *will* be there for you.

Tailored to You

I mentioned earlier that I've had both shoulders and both hips replaced as a result of my cancer treatments. I recall sitting in the doctor's office after receiving the news that I would need my fourth and final replacement. The doctor then arrived and explained that he had just been with another patient, a young thirteen-year-old boy who had recently received his twelfth joint replacement, the result of a rare disease. I was astonished that someone so young would have to face a trial so great—it made my four replacements pale in comparison.

This is one of the things I have learned about adversity: just look around and you will find someone worse off. Counting your blessings is a very real thing. It's like spare pennies in a jar—you have more than you think. The adversities we face are uniquely tailored to each of us. The Divine Hand is busy at work, making sure we have the experiences we need to prepare us for the marvels and blessings of the life to come. And Elder Richard G. Scott assures us that the Father "would not require you to experience a moment more of difficulty than is absolutely needed for your personal benefit or for that of those you love."[9]

My middle daughter, Kim, encountered a fairly unique challenge in her life that I share with her permission. As a new mother and from almost out of the blue, she began having anxiety. In fact, it struck in a most unusual way. She got scared leaving the house and would have panic attacks every time she went to church and received the sacrament. Clearly, her anxiety and sense of panic could drive her away from partaking of the sacrament, but she made a promise to the Lord that she would not allow herself to be deprived of this ordinance. This went on for an entire year.

As she struggled, she shared: "Heavenly Father reassured me by letting me know that someday, it would all be okay. I just needed to keep trying and do my best." That's often the answer that comes—it's not that the burden will be lifted or removed, but that God will help us bear the burdens we face.[10]

In Kim's case, the anxiety she was feeling was so overwhelming that she was not sure how it could ever go away. On top of this, she was greeted with the news of a pregnancy with a second child, which she worried would compound the intense anxiety she was feeling. But it was then that she felt the Holy Ghost comfort her with peace as she settled in with the news. She had the strong spiritual impression that the birth of her next child would actually help her heal. After Carter was born, her anxiety began to gradually subside until it completely disappeared. In this instance, she was ultimately blessed to have the burden lifted, just like what eventually happened for the people of Alma who endured their burdens until the day came when the Lord said, "On the morrow I will deliver you out of bondage."[11]

Elder David A. Bednar taught, "The unique burdens in each of our lives help us to rely upon the merits, mercy, and grace of the Holy Messiah (see 2 Nephi 2:8). As we are yoked with Him through sacred covenants and receive the enabling power of His Atonement in our lives, we . . . pray for the strength to learn from, change, or accept our circumstances rather than praying relentlessly for God to change our circumstances according to our will. We will become agents who act rather than objects that are acted upon (see 2 Nephi 2:14). *We will be blessed with spiritual traction.*"[12]

Spiritual Traction

In my professional consulting and training work I often refer to the principle of traction. I like to first show a picture of a fairly worn tire, where the tread is almost gone—essentially bald. Imagine what happens when you are stuck in the mud then hit the gas with tires like that. They just spin, throwing mud everywhere, but the car won't move. Or can't. You're stuck. But what if you have tractor tires? You know the kind—big, thick-treaded monsters designed specifically for getting out of a soggy pasture. Hit the gas with tires like that and you take off. That's traction.

I imagine spiritual traction being like those tractor tires—perfectly designed to get you unstuck from the trials and adversity of life. This kind of spiritual traction comes from applying important faith-promoting principles. Consider three:

1. Understand there is purpose in your trial.
2. Realize that God will not leave you alone.
3. Choose to let God prevail in your life.

While there is no single approach for discovering the strength to face your challenges, there is a common element—faith in the Lord Jesus Christ and His unwavering commitment and life's mission to *save you*.[13]

First, you begin to gain spiritual traction when you understand there is purpose in your trial. Elder Richard G. Scott of the Quorum of the Twelve Apostles taught, "Trials, disappointments, sadness, and heartache come to us from two basically different sources. Those who transgress the laws of God will always have those challenges. The other reason for adversity is to accomplish the Lord's own purposes in our life that we may *receive the refinement that comes from testing.* It is vitally important for each of us to identify from which of these two sources come our trials and challenges, for the corrective action is very different."[14] Here, Elder Scott suggests there are two types of adversity: that which comes from personal transgression and everything else. This latter category includes trials arising from our mistakes, the sins and mistakes of others, and the natural difficulties of our mortal life.

Second, spiritual traction comes from realizing that God will NOT leave you alone in your moment of despair. President George Q. Cannon once taught: "No matter how serious the trial, how deep the distress, how great the affliction, [God] will never desert us. He never has, and He never will. He cannot do it. It is not His character [to do so] . . . He will [always] stand by us. We may pass through the fiery furnace; we may pass through deep waters; but we shall not be consumed nor overwhelmed. We shall emerge from all these trials and difficulties the better and purer for them."[15]

However, for someone in the throes of deep, long-lasting adversity where they may be feeling abandoned by God—despite priesthood blessings, fasting, and prayers—feeling deserted can be overwhelming. Those buried by such despair often don't feel any "balm of Gilead."[16] While the Holy Ghost can bring hope, what if you feel He doesn't? Where do you find strength then?

For the Holy Ghost to do His work—to bestow the spiritual gift of long-suffering—we need to let the trials and adversities of life, however long they may be, *soften* and not harden us.[17] The antidote: humility, not pride or anger; prayers of gratitude rather than bouts of murmuring; trust rather than fear; faith rather than doubt. Otherwise, those dark and negative emotions can short-circuit the connection the Lord may be trying to establish through the Holy Ghost. Hope comes from that connection. Hopelessness comes with the disconnect. Moroni teaches us: "And the remission of sins bringeth meekness, and lowliness of heart; and because of meekness and lowliness of heart cometh the visitation of the Holy Ghost, *which Comforter filleth with hope.*"[18]

Third, to obtain real spiritual traction in life as you work to meet challenges and overcome adversity, choose to let God prevail in your life. President Russell M. Nelson taught the Church this principle when he said, "We can choose to let God prevail in our lives, or not. We can choose to let God be the most powerful influence in our lives, or not. . . . Are *you* willing to let God prevail in your life? Are *you* willing to let God be the most important influence in your life? Will you allow His words, His commandments, and His covenants to influence what you do each day? Will you allow His voice to take priority over any other? Are you *willing* to let whatever He needs you to do take precedence over every other ambition? Are you *willing* to have your will swallowed up in His?"[19]

"Are *you* willing to let God prevail in your life? Are *you* willing to let God be the most important influence in your life?"

—President Russell M. Nelson

To prevail means to "prove more powerful than opposing force; to be victorious; be widespread in a particular area at a particular time; persuade (someone) to do something"[20] Synonyms include triumph, gain the victory, carry the day, conquer, overcome, gain/achieve mastery, rule, reign, be present, be current, be the order of the day, be established, be in effect; endure, survive, persist. All words and ideas that capture the essence of how God could be in our lives, should we choose it.

President Nelson then promised, "When your greatest desire is to let God prevail, to be part of Israel, so many decisions become easier. So many issues become nonissues! . . . And what is the Lord willing to *do* for Israel? The Lord has pledged that He will 'fight [our] battles, and [our] children's battles, and our children's [battles] . . . to the third and fourth generation'! . . . As you choose to let God prevail in your lives, you will experience for yourselves that our God is 'a God of miracles.'"[21]

I'm reminded of a missionary who served in our mission and was very shy. I will call him Elder Jenkins. Knocking on a door of a stranger was the last thing in the world he wanted to do. It was even hard for him to talk to Church members or other missionaries. Because of this it was not uncommon for me to get a call from the district leaders who would say, "We are here at Elder Jenkins's and he has locked himself in the bathroom again. He doesn't want to go on team-ups and talk to people. What should we do?"

Yet, Elder Jenkins faced his fears and stayed with it. He chose to let God prevail in his life. He did his part by facing difficult personal challenges and not retreating. He kept working and serving, even though talking to people was the last thing on the planet he wanted to do.

One day I looked at a report I had received from the missionaries working in the office. They had listed who the top baptizing missionaries were in the mission, so we might learn from what they were doing to see how we could better share the gospel. To my great surprise, Elder Jenkins was at the top of the list! Truly, he let God prevail in his life, and his weakness as a missionary literally became a strength as he humbly kept at it.[22] I love this guidance from President Thomas S. Monson: "May we ever choose the harder right instead of the easier wrong."[23]

Sometimes, either due to the trials we face or the absence of blessings, we can feel that life is treating us unfairly, that others have it better, that we are getting the short end of the stick. Elder Dale G. Renlund provides timely counsel: "Some unfairness cannot be explained; inexplicable unfairness is infuriating . . . but I declare with all my aching heart that Jesus Christ both understands unfairness and has the power to provide a remedy. . . . In unfair situations, one of our tasks is to trust that 'all that is unfair about life can be made right through the Atonement of Jesus Christ.' Jesus

Christ overcame the world and 'absorbed' all unfairness. Because of Him, we can have peace in this world and be of good cheer. If we let Him, Jesus Christ will consecrate the unfairness for our gain. He will not just console us and restore what was lost; He will use the unfairness for our benefit. . . . Your faith in Heavenly Father and Jesus Christ will be rewarded more than you can imagine. All unfairness—especially infuriating unfairness—will be consecrated for your gain."[24]

Sometimes, we may not be physically, emotionally, or spiritually able to feel the divine empathy Elder Renlund describes. Feelings of peace can feel stomped on pretty hard when one is desperate, destitute, or even suicidal—challenges with mental and physical health can lead to spiritual numbness. It's just so easy to miss God's empathy and love when one is really struggling. Important to know is that God will not stop reaching out, finding ways to signal He *is* there and ready to help. Most likely, one feeling so trodden under foot will need help from someone who has eyes to see and ears to hear to help in their time of need.

As we seek to have the companionship of the Holy Ghost, the promise is that the Comforter will fill us with hope.[25] That hope is an expectation that God will provide us the needed spiritual traction to bear our burdens well and, ultimately, bring us back to Him.[26] God be thanked for that hope attained through the gift of the Holy Ghost—made possible by the Atonement of Jesus Christ and His personal desire, commitment, and ability to save us.

Notes

1. Henry B. Eyring, "Try, Try, Try," *Ensign*, Nov. 2018.
2. See Doctrine and Covenants 98:14. Also, Elder Bruce R. McConkie said, "As to the individual trials [or] problems that befall any of us, all we need say is that in the wisdom of Him who knows all things, and who does all things well, *all of us are given the particular and specific tests that we need in our personal situations*."("The Dead Who Die in the Lord," *Ensign*, Nov. 1976.)
3. Jeffrey R. Holland, "Waiting on the Lord," *Ensign*, Nov. 2020. See also Neal A. Maxwell, "Lest Ye Be Wearied and Faint in Your Minds," *Ensign*, May 1991.
4. See 2 Nephi 2:11. See also https://www.ChurchofJesusChrist.org/study/liahona/2006/08/the-fulness

-of-the-gospel-the-purpose-of
-life?lang=eng.

5. "Peace," Lexico.com.

6. See John 14:26.

7. Romans 15:13.

8. Chi Hong (Sam) Wong, "They Cannot Prevail; We Cannot Fall," *Ensign*, May 2021.

9. Richard G. Scott, "Trust in the Lord," *Ensign*, Nov. 1995.

10. See Mosiah 24:14–15.

11. Mosiah 24:16.

12. David A. Bednar, "Bear Up Their Burdens with Ease," *Ensign*, May 2014.

13. See Moses 1:39.

14. Richard G. Scott, "Trust in the Lord," *Ensign*, Nov. 1995.

15. George Q. Cannon, "Remarks," *Deseret Evening News*, March 7, 1891, 4.

16. A substance that came from Gilead, beyond the Jordan used in biblical times to heal and soothe (see "The Balm of Gilead," *Ensign*, Nov. 1977).

17. See Galatians 5:22. Long-suffering is an attribute of God. It is also a Christlike attribute that we are asked to develop. It is also a gift of the Spirit.

18. Moroni 8:26.

19. Russell M. Nelson, "Let God Prevail," *Ensign*, Nov. 2020.

20. "Prevail," Lexico.com.

21. "Prevail," Lexico.com.

22. See Ether 12:27.

23. Thomas S. Monson, "Choices," *Ensign*, May 2016.

24. Dale G. Renlund, "Infuriating Unfairness," *Liahona*, May 2021.

25. See Moroni 8:26.

26. See "Hope," Gospel Topics, ChurchofJesusChrist.org.

DIVINE PATTERNS

PART 5

Striving to Stand Firm, Faithful, and True

CHAPTER 22

*Accessing the Power of the Atonement
of Jesus Christ: Always Remembering
Him and Having His Spirit to Be with You*

— DOCTRINE AND COVENANTS 20:77, 79 —

I recall an experience I had as a brand-new mission president. I was invited to attend a stake conference where Elder Marlin K. Jensen of the Seventy was presiding. I'm not sure I have ever met a kinder man. The agenda for the meetings that Sunday morning did not have me scheduled to attend the new convert meeting. Looking back, it's silly that I didn't clarify, but for some reason my brain just didn't process it, so I didn't attend.

I did show up on time to the next meeting however, where I was greeted by Elder Jensen, who of course, asked why I hadn't been in the new convert meeting. I explained that I didn't attend because I wasn't included on the agenda. Elder Jensen looked me in the eyes and must have been thinking, *Really? Did you as a mission president need a formal invite to attend a new convert meeting?* Instead, he simply said, "President, I'm so sorry, we will do better."

I will never forget how this good man, this inspired Church leader, handled that moment. Later, he taught in a leadership meeting—no doubt I was among those who served as the inspiration for his training—that he had learned that whenever he meets someone, *he assumes that person is doing the best they can.* This powerful and loving approach only made me want to do and be better.

What compelled Elder Jensen to be so meek, lowly, and grateful? In my view, it's because he is a recipient of the power of the Atonement of Jesus Christ. It permeates his thoughts and actions and guides how he reacts to the circumstances he faces. While the Savior's Atonement is clearly about overcoming sin and gaining redemption, it is also so much more than that.

What Is the Atonement of Jesus Christ?

During a recent Face-to-Face video discussion, President Henry B. Eyring and Elder Jeffery R. Holland took these two questions:[1]

1. What exactly is the Atonement of Jesus Christ, and how can I receive its blessings?
2. How do I access the Atonement?

President Eyring began answering the question by saying: "The first thing to do is to get a few facts straight. *The Atonement was something Jesus Christ did. It's not a thing itself.* He atoned for our sins, and He paid the price to allow us to be forgiven and to be resurrected. So, it's what He did that qualified Him to give us forgiveness, to change our hearts. It's the Holy Ghost doing that, not the Atonement as if it's a thing itself. And so, *when you feel forgiveness, that's not the Atonement; that's the Savior giving you a feeling of forgiveness because of the Atonement.*"[2]

"When you feel forgiveness, that's not the Atonement; that's the Savior giving you a feeling of forgiveness because of the Atonement."

—President Henry B. Eyring

Given the significance of what President Eyring said, let me add my own summary of some of his key points:

- The "act" of the Atonement is separate from the "power" of the Atonement.
- Jesus qualified to receive that power by performing the Atonement.
- The Father gave power to Jesus to forgive and strengthen us.
- When we feel forgiven, we are not feeling "the Atonement," we

are feeling the Holy Ghost—who is able to act because of the Atonement.

In the same Face-to-Face discussion, Elder Jeffrey R. Holland commented, "*If we understand the Atonement, we're going to be meek and lowly and very grateful.* 'And because of meekness and lowliness of heart cometh the visitation of the Holy Ghost.'"

Elder Holland continued, "We've just been swept right into the celestial kingdom here on the strength of the Atonement of Christ because it made us meek. It made us lowly. It made us grateful. It made us know somebody helped us. And that brings the Holy Ghost. *I don't know that I had ever quite tied the gift of the Holy Ghost as an extension of the Savior's Atonement.*"[3]

Again, let me summarize Elder Holland's comments:

- The gift of the Holy Ghost is a direct extension of the Savior's Atonement.
- The act of the Atonement was necessary to enable the gift of the Holy Ghost.
- We access the power (and all the blessings) of the Atonement by being meek, lowly, and grateful, which brings the Holy Ghost into our lives.

Addressing this point, President Russell M. Nelson taught, "Under the Father's great eternal plan, it is the Savior who suffered. It is the Savior who broke the bands of death. It is the Savior who paid the price for our sins and transgressions and blots them out on condition of our repentance. It is the Savior who delivers us from physical and spiritual death.

"There is no amorphous entity called 'the Atonement' upon which we may call for succor, healing, forgiveness, or power. Jesus Christ is the source. . . . [His] atoning sacrifice—the central act of all human history—is best understood and appreciated when we expressly and clearly connect it to Him."[4]

Accessing the Power of the Atonement of Jesus Christ

The Atonement of Jesus Christ brings *real power* to help us obtain a celestial glory. That was, and is, the aim of the Savior's Atonement—to facilitate our becoming joint heirs with Christ and receive eternal life and become exalted. The power that comes from the Atonement of Jesus Christ has been characterized by contemporary Church leaders as having two dimensions:

1. The "cleansing" or "redeeming power"
2. The "strengthening, or enabling, power"

These two powers are not "separate and discrete," but are "connected and complementary."[5] Elder Kim B. Clark of the Seventy (and former president of BYU–Idaho) taught: "If you turn to Christ and repent of your sins, He will forgive you and cleanse you and change your heart. *This is the redeeming power of the Atonement.* If you turn to Christ when you face challenges and need capacity beyond your own, He can strengthen you and magnify your capacity. *This is the strengthening power of the Atonement.*"[6]

Most of us are very familiar with the concept of the redeeming power of the Atonement of Jesus Christ, through which He gives us the ability to repent and be forgiven of our sins. But we may not be as familiar with the strengthening or enabling power of the Atonement. Elder David A. Bednar clarifies, "I frankly do not think many of us 'get it' concerning [the] enabling and strengthening aspect of the Atonement, and I wonder if we mistakenly believe we must make the journey from good to better and become a saint all by ourselves through sheer grit, willpower, and discipline, and with our obviously limited capacities."[7]

It is essential for us to understand that Jesus Christ, because of the act of His Atonement—and through His loving grace—gives us access to *real power* to redeem, strengthen, and enable us. The prophets, seers, and revelators of our day have all testified of this principle. President Dallin H. Oaks taught, "Our Savior's Atonement does more than assure us of immortality . . . and give us the opportunity to be cleansed from sin by repentance and baptism. His Atonement also provides the opportunity to call upon Him who has experienced all of our mortal infirmities to give us the strength to bear the burdens of mortality."[8]

President Nelson teaches us that the Savior's Atonement provides "access to godly power—*power sufficient to deal with the burdens, obstacles, and temptations of our day*."[9] The message: the Savior can help us as we strive to overcome challenges, weakness, bad habits, and imperfections in our lives. In fact, the enabling power of the Atonement is a real power from God that gives us the ability not just to endure our challenges, *but to thrive despite them.*

Elder Kim B. Clark makes this powerful statement: "There is no sin, no guilt, no shame, no fear, no loneliness, no heartache, no loss, no depression, no sadness, no terror, no pain, no challenge, no weakness that Jesus has not experienced and overcome. He has all power over all things."[10] Indeed, we should have reason to believe that God will help us with our challenges in ways that we could not do ourselves. Often, we just need to be willing to see it.

"Olivia" had a challenging young life. She struggled as a teen, feeling depressed, and, for a period of time, suicidal. She ended up marrying a man with a very different background and upbringing from her. Her first pregnancy turned out to be quite high-risk, because she was also a diabetic. Her first child, a son, was eventually diagnosed with autism. After suffering two miscarriages, she was blessed with twins—which also meant double the challenge, double the trouble and, of course, double the blessings (and double the fun!). Added to this, her husband was diagnosed with cancer early in their marriage. Looking down the road, she realized she may eventually become the sole provider for her family, so she began preparations to get a master's degree. Needless to say, she was constantly overwhelmed and felt like her life was destined for challenge and problems.

However, her mother pointed out that from where she sat, Olivia was indeed being blessed, though Olivia could not see it.

Her mother stated that Olivia had been able to bear the burdens that she was facing because the Lord was reaching out with extra help, which might be easy to miss if you were not looking for it. For example, Olivia's son was having trouble with friends at school. One day, in the middle of the family's anxiety over her son's problem, a little girl began sitting with him at lunch. A little act to be sure, but given the circumstances, a miraculous answer that showed the Lord was in it.

Add to this, Olivia had to miss work to help her husband with cancer treatments. One day when returning to work, she found an envelope on her desk containing $700, collected by colleagues concerned for her welfare. That amount happened to be the exact amount of the wages she had lost by taking time off to go to the doctors with her husband.

The problem for Olivia was that her trials were so hard and so loud, she struggled to perceive the blessings and godly power manifested in her life—real power given to help her make it through the struggle. God was indeed helping, something she was eventually able to truly see.

This divine pattern of accessing the power of the Atonement of Jesus Christ and relying on Him to help in "every time of trouble" means that as we "always remember Him," we "may always have his Spirit to be with" us. Then, as we humble ourselves, the redeeming and strengthening powers of the Atonement will operate in our lives through the power of the Holy Ghost.[11]

As we humble ourselves, the redeeming and strengthening powers of the Atonement will operate in our lives through the power of the Holy Ghost.

Why Do We Need the Atonement of Jesus Christ?

Most likely, anyone reading this book has at least a basic understanding that without the Atonement of Jesus Christ, mankind would remain in a "lost and . . . fallen state, and ever would be save they should rely on this Redeemer."[12] Abinadi teaches in the Book of Mormon, "And now if Christ had not come into the world . . . there could have been no redemption. And if Christ had not risen from the dead, or have broken the bands of death that the grave should have no victory, and that death should have no sting, there could have been no resurrection."[13]

The purposes of the Atonement of Jesus Christ are many.

1. We all sin and therefore suffer spiritual death and are cut off from the presence of God. (Christ makes us clean and mercifully pays the demands of justice, bringing us back into God's presence).[14]

2. We all have weakness. (The Savior strengthens and enables us with capacity beyond our natural abilities and can compensate for our inadequacies).[15]

3. We suffer illness, pain, grief, depression, and mental distress. (Jesus brings relief to our mental and physical suffering.)[16]

4. We all make mistakes and are sometimes disobedient. (He can erase our mistakes and make restitution to others we injure in the many ways we cannot.)[17]

5. We die and are separated from loved ones who suffer physical death. (Christ will raise us from the grave, allowing us to see our departed loved ones again.)[18]

6. We experience fear, stress, and anxiety. (He can hush our fears and soothe our souls.)[19]

7. We live in a wicked world. (Jesus brings peace and calms the daily storms of life.)[20]

8. Life can be "infuriatingly unfair."[21] (He provides a remedy in every situation to make all things right.)[22]

The plan of salvation is the great plan of happiness, restoring those who access the power of the Atonement of Jesus Christ to the presence of God and to a state of "never-ending happiness."[23] It is imperative for us to remember how this "precious gift of eternal life" comes to us.[24] The prophet Nephi declares, "It is only in and through the grace of God that ye are saved."[25] That is, as we make our best effort to meet the "conditions of repentance,"[26] God's grace strengthens us every step of the way as we walk the covenant path, making up for what our efforts cannot cover, and allowing us to be "reconciled" to Him.[27] This "grace is a gift from Heavenly Father given through His Son, Jesus Christ. The word *grace*, as used in the scriptures, refers primarily to [the] enabling power and spiritual healing offered through the mercy and love of Jesus. . . . It strengthens us to do good works we could not do on our own. The Lord promised that if we humble ourselves before Him and have faith in Him, His grace will help us overcome all our personal weaknesses."[28]

Brother Bradley R. Wilcox, then on the Sunday School General Board, related, "Grace is not a booster engine that kicks in once our fuel supply is exhausted. Rather, it is our constant energy source. It is not the light at the end of the tunnel but the light that moves us through the tunnel. Grace is not achieved somewhere down the road. It is received right here and right now. It is not a finishing touch; it is the Finisher's touch (see Hebrews 12:2)."[29]

Key to experiencing the grace of God (the Savior's power) in our lives is receiving the constant companionship of the Holy Ghost. *Through the Holy Ghost we gain access to the power of the Atonement of Jesus Christ.* It is this important divine pattern—to always remember Him and have His Spirit—that enables us to survive the storms of our mortal journey and, ultimately, inherit eternal life. You can rely on the Savior and the power of His Atonement: a power that comes from a merciful, loving, and generous God.

Notes

1. Worldwide Face-to-Face with President Eyring and Elder Holland, March 4, 2017, https://www.Churchof JesusChrist.org/media/video/2017 -03-1000-face-to-face-with-president -eyring-and-elder-holland?lang=eng.
2. Worldwide Face-to-Face with President Eyring and Elder Holland, March 4, 2017, https://www.Churchof JesusChrist.org/media/video/2017 -03-1000-face-to-face-with-president -eyring-and-elder-holland?lang=eng.
3. Worldwide Face-to-Face with President Eyring and Elder Holland, March 4, 2017, https://www .ChurchofJesusChrist.org /media/video/2017-03-1000-face

-to-face-with-president-eyring-and
-elder-holland?lang=eng.

4. Russell M. Nelson, "Drawing the
Power of Jesus Christ into Our Lives,"
Ensign, May 2017.

5. David A. Bednar, "The Atonement and
the Journey of Mortality," *Ensign*, Apr.
2012.

6. Kim B. Clark, "The Redeeming and
Strengthening Power of the Savior's
Atonement," *Ensign*, Apr. 2016.

7. David A. Bednar, "In the Strength of
the Lord," BYU devotional, October
23, 2001, https://speeches.byu.edu
/talks/david-a-bednar/strength-lord/.

8. Dallin H. Oaks, "Strengthened by the
Atonement of Jesus Christ," *Ensign*,
Nov. 2015.

9. Russell M. Nelson, "Drawing the
Power of Jesus Christ into Our Lives,"
Ensign, May 2017.

10. Kim B. Clark, "The Redeeming and
Strengthening Power of the Savior's
Atonement," *Ensign*, May 2016.

11. See Doctrine and Covenants 3:8;
20:77.

12. 1 Nephi 10:6.

13. Mosiah 16:6–7.

14. See 3 Nephi 27:19 (problem); Alma
42:14–15 (solution).

15. See Ether 12:27 (problem); Philippians
4:13 (solution).

16. See Genesis 3:16–19 (problem); Alma
7:12 (solution).

17. See Alma 42:12 (problem); Mosiah
15:9, 12 (solution).

18. See 1 Corinthians 15:22 (problem);
Mormon 9:13 (solution).

19. See Matthew 24:21 (problem);
Deuteronomy 31:6, 8 (solution).

20. See 2 Timothy 3:13 (problem);
Matthew 11:28–30 (solution).

21. See Dale G. Renlund, "Infuriating
Unfairness," *Liahona*, May 2021.

22. See Isaiah 48:10 (problem); Isaiah
41:10 (solution).

23. Mosiah 2:41.

24. Helaman 5:8; Doctrine and Covenants
14:7.

25. 2 Nephi 10:24.

26. Alma 42:13; Doctrine and Covenants
138:19.

27. See 2 Nephi 10:24–25.

28. "Grace," Gospel Topics,
ChurchofJesusChrist.org; see also
Ether 12:27.

29. Bradley R. Wilcox, "His Grace Is
Sufficient," BYU devotional, July 12,
2011, https://speeches.byu.edu/talks
/brad-wilcox/his-grace-is-sufficient/.

CHAPTER 23

Search, Ponder, and Pray: Hungering and Thirsting after Righteousness and Being Filled

— 3 NEPHI 12:6 —

Have you ever felt that you were just going through the motions spiritually, checking the boxes but not really gaining much from the effort? As with anything in life, that would be considered normal—our spiritual lives are no exception. Most growth comes in nonlinear patterns, not straight lines. There are ups and downs, setbacks and disappointments—many plateaus.

It's human nature to be on the lookout for some new insight, approach, or idea that will spark accelerated growth and renewed energy. However—and this is not meant to disappoint—when it comes to spirituality, there really isn't anything new. It seems that what is taught in Primary *really is* the answer. We see this time and again in general conference—the same basic ideas, doctrines, and principles on how we can become better disciples, repeated with each passing year. Why is that? Are we missing something? There must be more . . . right?

Aubrey Milligan Zalewski, a college-aged Church member, posted on her blog, "I value these Primary answers and the standards they represent, and I've tried to live by them. *But they haven't always seemed like enough.* Despite my best efforts to live righteously, my life has gone through waves of spiritual highs and lows. And in those lows, I've felt worse than imperfect; I've felt the pain of seeing my potential and then looking down at the ever-widening gap between who I want to be and who I am.

"During these times of self-doubt, I begin focusing on who I am not. Yes, I go to church, but I don't always feel the Spirit. Yes, I read my scriptures every day, but my study is lacking. Yes, I pray, but it feels one way. And yes, I am temple-worthy, but visits are few and far between. Feeling completely inadequate, I work to change. But inevitably, I fall short.

"The Church has this list of Primary answers, or standards, we are to live by, and when we do so, we are promised happiness. But I live those standards, and I'm still unhappy. Either there is something wrong with me or there is something wrong with God—and I can't bring myself to believe the latter. But the problem isn't my imperfection, and it certainly isn't God; the problem is that I am focusing too much on the standards and too little on the reason we have them."[1]

Everyone wants evidence that their faith is not in vain; that God *really* does live and that He *really* does love them. It seems we need a continuous flow of signs throughout our lives to keep the fires of faith brightly burning. After all, shouldn't "signs follow them that believe"?[2] Our testimonies are living testimonies, not something we do once and then put on the shelf. When the evidence that God is real seems lacking in the moment, when nothing "miraculous" seems to be happening in our lives, "spiritual drifting" can occur.[3]

Spiritual Drifting

Our family enjoys boating now and then. I will always remember the nerve-racking experience of learning how to park a boat in a slip at the dock for the first time. Our assigned slip happened to be between two beautiful (and expensive) boats. That heightened the stakes of missing my slip by drifting too far to the left or right—potentially damaging someone else's prized possession.

If you've ever done any boating, you know that boats don't stay stationary in the water for very long—they float and move in the direction of the most recent current caused by the wind, other boats, or your own motor. The trick to parking a boat is calculating the drift into your moves. It takes power from the motor to make sure you counteract the drift so the boat goes where you want it to go.

The same is true of our spirituality. The currents of the world caused by culture, friends, media, or our own actions will shift our direction. It's only by applying spiritual power that we can counteract the drift and maintain the desired course. But what if there is no gas in our spiritual tanks? What if, when we need it most, we call for that spiritual power and it's not there?

Sister Elaine S. Dalton, then Second Counselor in the Young Women General Presidency, spoke of the occasion when Gordon B. Hinckley sealed her and her husband in the temple. There, he counseled them to study the scriptures daily, remember their prayers both morning and night, pay their tithing, and remain worthy. Then he said, "There will come times in your life when you will need immediate blessings. You will need to live in such a way that they will be granted—not out of mercy but because you are worthy." She recounts, "I didn't comprehend then what that meant, but in the 38 years that have followed, we have called upon our Father in Heaven for many 'immediate blessings.' Daily, these holy habits and righteous routines have helped steady us on the path that leads back into our Father's presence."[4]

You may have several examples from your own life when such "immediate blessings" have been granted. You may also have other examples when blessings didn't come. In that case, I am certain that if Heavenly Father were to talk with you privately about your life and how He has helped you, He would provide a compelling explanation tailored just for you as to why things didn't happen the way you had hoped. From that perfect explanation (literally), you would see that He was always with you, on your side, pulling for you, and you would probably recognize that He did bless you more abundantly than you had ever supposed.

For now, it takes faith, trusting in Him, trusting that the "perfect" explanation you hope to receive someday will indeed come.[5]

Regarding this divine pattern, the New Testament says that the Savior taught, "Blessed are they which do hunger and thirst after righteousness: for they shall be filled."[6] *Filled with what?* Third Nephi in the Book of Mormon answers this question: "filled with the Holy Ghost."[7] As you and

I hunger and thirst after righteousness, we are filled . . . with the Holy Ghost!

The visual of hungering and thirsting after righteousness is so simple, yet so perfect. Who can't relate to what it feels like to be hungry? Consider the description by Elsa Bruer, an Auschwitz concentration camp survivor from the Holocaust of World War II who was on starvation rations ("not enough to live, and not enough to die"): "Hunger is when you don't eat for . . . days and weeks. When you can't . . . fall asleep because you were hungry . . . the only thing we were talking about or thinking about was food . . . hunger took over everything."[8]

Personally, I've never been that hungry, but how compelling would the urge to eat be under those conditions? I think that's what the Savior was teaching—we should feel that compelled about righteousness. We must personally be hungering and thirsting, seeking and searching after righteousness, so we can then be filled with the Holy Ghost. No one can do this for you; you must do it for yourself.

But how do we do this? The leaders of the Church have long taught two simple "righteous routines" or "holy habits" that God has ordained for us to seek after Him. They are what you would expect to hear:

1. Pray daily.
2. Search and ponder the scriptures daily.[9]

Pray Daily

When I was a young college student, I would have the occasion to travel from Provo, Utah, back home to Southern California. It had been some time since making the drive, and my '72 Opel was on life support. I was worried about the long drive, but even more concerned about the freeway traffic going through Los Angeles.

Before leaving Utah that morning, I started with a prayer for safe travels. After many hours, when I dropped down Interstate 15 into the LA basin, I renewed my prayers. It was pretty exhilarating to get back to driving high speeds, "California close" (bumper to bumper)—something a prayer or two can definitely help with. About this same time, I had the thought come to me, *What would you do if the car in front of you suddenly swerved into the next lane to avoid something like a chair that had fallen off someone's truck and landed on the road in your lane?* (Yes, my thought was that specific!) Under these driving conditions, there would be little time to react. As I played out this detailed scenario in my mind, I determined that if the car in front of me suddenly swerved, I would instinctively follow.

It wasn't but a half hour later that the car immediately in front of me suddenly swerved into the next lane. Because of my previous mental exercise, I also swerved and followed the car. As I looked over my shoulder, I saw a large, upholstered chair lying on its side in the traffic lane we had just been in. Had I not swerved, I would have undoubtedly hit the chair, which, at the time, appeared to be larger than my '72 Opel! I know the prompting to ponder this specific situation was an answer to my prayers that morning.

I believe those in dire need who want the Lord's blessings, give up on prayer too soon because they no longer feel anyone is listening. Prayer is the first thing we should do when trying to reignite our faith and the last thing we should give up when we are struggling.[10] If you are struggling in any way, I encourage you to keep praying—keeping it simple. Perhaps *pick one thing you are thankful for and one thing you truly need in life right now.* Then, begin looking for evidence that God is listening and helping you. When that prayer is sincere and coupled with genuine effort to take a step toward God, I know you will see His hand in your life.[11]

> Prayer is the first thing we should do when trying to reignite our faith and the last thing we should give up when we are struggling.

President James E. Faust, then Second Counselor to President Gordon B. Hinckley in the First Presidency, stated, "*There is no limit on the number of times or how long we can pray each day. There is no quota of* how many needs we wish to pray for in each prayer. . . . He is reachable at any time and any place."[12] God hears every prayer.[13]

That said, we should guard against getting casual in our prayers. The substance of our prayers may not change a lot from day to day over a given period of time, but that's okay. There are many things I pray for every day and have done so for many months or even years. The key is to be sincere and grateful. We follow the simple model the Savior taught when addressing His Father, specifically thanking Him for blessings, asking for what we need, then closing in the name of Jesus Christ.[14]

God wants to hear from you.[15] He needs to hear from you so that you can authorize Him through the expression of your agency to act on your behalf. No matter what, be sure to pray.[16]

Search and Ponder the Scriptures Daily

Elder Robert D. Hales of the Quorum of the Twelve Apostles once taught that "when we want to speak to God, we pray. And when we want Him to speak to us, we search the scriptures."[17]

"When we want to speak to God, we pray.
. . . When we want Him to speak to us,
we search the scriptures."

—Elder Robert D. Hales

We can find great strength in the stories, counsel, and experiences shared in the scriptures. Recall the relatively short story of the Israelites in the Old Testament who were following Moses in the wilderness. They had become "much discouraged because of the way. And the people spake against God, and against Moses."[18] So the Lord sent fiery serpents among the people to humble them, and many died. The people began to repent and came to Moses and asked him to ask the Lord to take away the serpents. "And the Lord said unto Moses, make thee a fiery serpent, and set it upon a pole: and it shall come to pass, that every one that is bitten, when he looketh upon it, shall live."[19] And that is where the story ends in the Old Testament.

However, in the Book of Mormon, we learn more: "But there were many who were so hardened that they would not look, therefore they perished. Now the reason they would not look is because they did not believe that it would heal them."[20] All people had to do was look in order to live, but they wouldn't. Alma asks, "O my brethren, if ye could be healed by merely casting about your eyes that ye might be healed, would ye not behold quickly, or would ye rather harden your hearts in unbelief, and be slothful, that ye would not cast about your eyes, that ye might perish?"[21]

An important way we "look to God and live" in our day is to study the scriptures. As hard as that may be for some, it is a relatively easy thing that God asks us to do. We should make it a priority, every day. Elder Gerrit W. Gong, of the Quorum of the Twelve Apostles, teaches "searching" and "pondering" the scriptures, not just reading them.[22] It is only when we move from reading, to searching, to pondering, that we can have the spiritually strengthening exercise the Lord intends for us to have.[23] Anything less is like leaving the main course on the table, which moves us closer to a starvation diet—not enough to kill you, but not enough to keep you alive.

To ponder what we read means to "think about something carefully."[24] As you thoughtfully and prayerfully *think about what you have read*, you will feel the Holy Ghost teach and guide you.[25] Elder Spencer J. Condie of the Seventy noted that the scriptures facilitate the companionship of the Holy Ghost when we are faced with important decisions: "You may be facing decisions about a mission, your future career, and, eventually, marriage. As you read the scriptures and pray for direction, you may not actually see the answer in the form of printed words on a page, *but as you read you will receive distinct impressions and promptings*, and, as promised, the Holy Ghost 'will show unto you all things what ye should do' [2 Nephi 32:5]."[26]

While there are many wonderful things we can study in the Church, it's important to remember this promise from President Russell M. Nelson: "My dear brothers and sisters, I promise that as you prayerfully study the Book of Mormon *every day,* you will make better decisions— *every day.* I promise that as you ponder what you study, the windows of heaven will open, and you will receive answers to your own questions and direction for your own life. I promise that as you daily immerse yourself in the Book of Mormon, you can be immunized against the evils of the day, even the gripping plague of pornography and other mind-numbing addictions."[27]

Getting into the habit and spending time in the scriptures will keep you spiritually fed, while not doing so in a day when the word of God is so available is like starving yourself to death at a grocery store—you have to do it on purpose. Remember these words from Alma: "Now behold, my brethren, I would ask if ye have read the scriptures? If ye have, how can ye disbelieve on the Son of God?"[28] We nourish our bodies every day with food and water. It should be no surprise that our spirit needs to be nourished in just the same way.

Elder David A. Bednar describes scripture study as the primary means for our "drink[ing] deeply from the reservoir of living water [the words of Christ]."[29] He outlines three basic ways to read the scriptures: "(1) *reading* the scriptures from beginning to end, (2) *studying* the scriptures by topic, and (3) *searching* the scriptures for connections, patterns, and themes." He then offers, "In my judgment, diligently searching to discover connections, patterns, and themes is in part what it means to 'feast' upon the words of Christ. This approach can open the floodgates of the spiritual reservoir, enlighten our understanding through His Spirit, and produce a depth of gratitude for the holy scriptures and a degree of spiritual commitment that can be received in no other way."[30]

This divine pattern is about putting the most important things first in our lives. These two holy habits of daily prayer and searching and ponder- ing the scriptures daily are key to maintaining your spirituality, testimony, and eternal perspective. They are foundational to growing your testimony and facilitating personal revelation. They are a main ingredient in the daily bread and water that feed your spiritual survival. Their relevance to your feeling connected to heaven cannot be underestimated. They are an important way you hunger and thirst after righteousness and are filled with the wonderful and irreplaceable gift of the Holy Ghost.

Notes

1. "When Primary Answers Don't Seem Like Enough," BYU blog post, February 2, 2017, https://speeches .byu.edu/posts/primary-answers -dont-seem-like-enough/.

2. Ether 4:18.

3. See Paul B. Farnsworth, "Avoiding Spiritual Drift," BYU devotional, July 13, 2010, https://speeches.byu .edu/talks/paul-b-farnsworth/avoid ing-spiritual-drift/.

4. Elaine S. Dalton, "Look toward Eternity!" *Ensign*, Nov. 2006.

5. Doctrine and Covenants 101:32–33.

6. Matthew 5:6.

7. 3 Nephi 12:6.

8. Dan Whipple, "Starvation Rations—A Holocaust Survivor's Story: Part II," *The Colorado Independent*, https:// www.colora doindependent.com/2007/07/17 /starvation-rations-a-holocaust-survi vors-story-part-ii/.

9. For example, see Richard G. Scott, "For Peace at Home," *Ensign*, May 2013.

10. See 2 Nephi 32:7–9.

11. See Doctrine and Covenants 88:63.

12. James E. Faust, "The Lifeline of Prayer," *Ensign*, May 2002.

13. See Richard G. Scott, "Recognizing Answers to Prayer," *Ensign*, August 2003.

14. See "The Way to Pray," *Liahona*, February 1992.

15. "*Lie #1:* God doesn't want to hear from you anymore. Not after you've ignored Him for so long. *The truth:*

God always wants to hear from you, even if it's been a while. Elder Juan A. Uceda of the Seventy has taught: 'At the very moment we say, "Father in Heaven," He hears our prayers and is sensitive to us and our needs.'" (David Dickson, "Seven Lies Satan Wants You to Believe," *New Era*, January 2017.)

16. See Doctrine and Covenants 19:38.

17. Robert D. Hales, "Holy Scriptures: The Power of God unto Our Salvation," *Ensign,* Nov. 2006.

18. Numbers 21:4–5.

19. Numbers 21:8.

20. Alma 33:20.

21. Alma 33:21.

22. See Gerrit W. Gong, "Our Campfire of Faith," *Ensign*, Nov. 2018.

23. "When I say 'study,' I mean something more than reading. . . . You should care more about the amount of time you spend in the scriptures than about the amount you read in that time. I see you sometimes reading a few verses, stopping to ponder them, carefully reading the verses again, and as you think about what they mean, praying for understanding, asking questions in your mind, waiting for spiritual impressions, and writing down the impressions and insights that come so you can remember and learn more." (D. Todd Christofferson, "When Thou Art Converted," *Ensign*, May 2004.)

24. "Ponder," Lexico.com.

25. See "Revelation," Gospel Topics, ChurchofJesusChrist.org.
26. Spencer J. Condie, "Becoming a Great Benefit to Our Fellow Beings," *Ensign*, May 2002.
27. Russell M. Nelson, "The Book of Mormon: What Would Your Life Be Like without It?" *Ensign*, Nov. 2017.
28. Alma 33:14.
29. David A. Bednar, "A Reservoir of Living Water," BYU devotional, February 4, 2007, https://speeches.byu.edu/talks/david-a-bednar/reservoir-living-water/.
30. David A. Bednar, "A Reservoir of Living Water," BYU devotional, February 4, 2007, https://speeches.byu.edu/talks/david-a-bednar/reservoir-living-water/.

CHAPTER 24

*Overcoming Weakness: Becoming Humble
and Weakness Being Made Strong*

— ETHER 12:27 —

One of our former missionaries, who I will call "Doug," posted an update on social media. He said, "Liking people can be hard. Loving people can be insanely difficult. This has been ever true in my life. Normally, my natural inclination is to dismiss things that are 'problems' to me—to cast them out of my personal world so I can enjoy my peace. This has been effective but has not allowed me to have compassion or empathy for others."

Doug continued, "Having a desire to fix this natural weakness, I decided about a year and a half ago to put incredible effort into 'thinking' about other people. The idea of thinking about another person to many people is like breathing air—their natural inclination is to be around people and like them.

"Wanting to improve in this area, I started removing almost all influences of violence from my life, including movies, TV shows, or games. When I prayed, I began to pray for other people by name with as much intent as I prayed for myself."

Doug later shared the outcome of his efforts to overcome his weakness: "The results have been small, but wonderful. I had a customer enroll in my program [at work]. We spent a lot of time and money . . . with him. He then decided after starting the program that he didn't want to do it anymore. Agreements had been signed and he was past the refund window. He became angry and bitter and threatening. I'm used to dealing with this. Normally, I would let justice have its way with him. But I thought, 'Clearly this man is in such a bad position in his life that this money means more to him than his dignity. He is losing it and I have a chance to remove some bitterness from the world right now.' At great loss to me, I gave him his money back and sent him on his way. Whether this was right or wrong or ethical or justified, it doesn't matter. I'm just glad that I was able to think of him as a person. I had said to myself, 'I have the power to be kind or the power to be just.' In the past, I would have never thought of such a sentiment."

Doug concluded: "I've now had many little events like this. It's nothing amazing . . . but for me it has removed all conflict and discord that I might feel for other people. . . . Of course, Jesus Christ is the ultimate example of peace, empathy, and service. He is at the core of why I am trying to change."

To one degree or another, Doug has described what we all deal with—the often lifelong pursuit of overcoming our weakness.

Weakness Is a Mortal Condition

In the Book of Mormon, we learn something significant about the "weakness" we experience in mortal life. The Lord said: "And if men come unto me I will show unto them their weakness. I give unto men weakness that they may be humble; and my grace is sufficient for all men that humble themselves before me; for if they humble themselves before me, and have faith in me, then will I make weak things become strong unto them."[1]

It was the Lord's response to Moroni's concern about his weakness in writing compared to his strength in speaking (note the Lord did not immediately solve this by suddenly making him mighty in writing) that triggered this well-known scriptural response.

The Lord Himself teaches us that:

- If we come unto God, He will show us our weakness.[2] (This is hard for us to see without His help. Drawing closer to God always leads to greater self-awareness).[3]
- He gives *all of us* weakness so we will be humble. (Weakness is a

planned part of our mortal condition designed to keep us humble; to be mortal is to have weakness).[4]

- His grace will allow weak things to become strong for us, provided we are humble and have faith. (Grace is the power of the Atonement of Jesus Christ. It is an enabling power that compensates, makes up for, counterbalances, restores, and rectifies the effects of our condition of weakness).[5]
- If we are meek, the grace of God can protect us from our mortal weakness. (If God deems it so, we can be protected from the negative impact our state of mortal weakness can have on ourselves and others).[6]

Perhaps one of the more apparent ways God turned Moroni's weakness to a strength was to endow his words with the power of the Holy Ghost, the great compensator. When we read Moroni's words, the Spirit witnesses to us in ways that cause the truths to speak deeply to our hearts. Moroni's promise may not mean that our particular weakness will become a strength, (though that can happen), but that weak things will become strong as the Lord compensates for our weakness in a myriad of different ways.

This mortal weakness opens the door to the individual struggles that each of us can feel troubled by throughout our lives. Nephi himself reflects upon his new role as family and priesthood leader with the death of his father, Lehi, in 2 Nephi chapter 4. He is overcome with a sense of great humility, having witnessed many mighty miracles, angels and visions: "Nevertheless, notwithstanding the great goodness of the Lord, in showing me his great and marvelous works, my heart exclaimeth: O wretched man that I am! Yea, my heart sorroweth because of my flesh; my soul grieveth because of mine iniquities. I am encompassed about, because of the temptations and the sins which do so easily beset me."[7] Wretched man? Nephi? Clearly, in a moment of great humility, Nephi recognizes his own mortal imperfections, challenges, and struggles. My takeaway from all of this: no one is immune. We are all left with the task, as disciples of Christ, to strive to overcome this state of weakness and the associated individual weaknesses that grow from it, looking to God that He will make that weakness, in the end, strong: "if they humble themselves before me, and have faith in me, then will I make weak things become strong unto them."[8] It is the process of overcoming weakness that I wish to focus on in this chapter.

Weaknesses Are Inadequacies, Not Sins

With my decades of work in human performance, personally coaching hundreds of leaders around the world in a wide variety of settings, it has become clear to me that our inherent personality styles can account for many of our greatest strengths, as well as our most prominent weaknesses. In fact, because personality style nearly always highly correlated with both the positive and negative feedback leaders received, I made it my practice to first "personality type" whoever I was working with. This would help me quickly understand where the person was coming from, how they processed information and, generally, how they looked at the world: were they more interested in people or tasks, did they tend to like to be in charge or prefer to stay out of the limelight, were they more analytical about things or did they prefer speed and spontaneity, did they tend to be an extrovert or an introvert? While it is not always cut and dried, each of us has general tendencies that highly correlate with known personality styles.[9]

Undoubtedly, our unique personalities, while molded by experiences in this life, had their beginnings in the life before. Elder Neal L. Maxwell taught, "Genes and environment by themselves will never provide an adequate explanation for human differences because there is a third factor in the equation of this life: all that occurred before we came here . . . trailing traits from our lengthy and extensive experience in the pre-mortal existence."[10] In my view, a discussion of overcoming weakness would be incomplete without acknowledging the role our personality traits plays in the process—traits that likely developed long before we arrived in mortality.

A review of the research on personality styles reveals that there are inherent weaknesses, as well as strengths, for each personality type—common traits among those who tend to identify with that specific style. One big takeaway: we all have strengths and weaknesses that are often similar to those of people who share our style type. In other words, you are not alone, but actually have plenty of company in your efforts to improve and overcome your specific weaknesses, especially those related to your personality style.

With regard to those weaknesses, the good news is that your weaknesses don't make you unworthy, nor do they require repentance: *They are inadequacies, not sins.* Wendy Ulrich, a psychologist and Relief Society general advisory council member, stated, "It is crucial to understand that while *sin* inevitably leads us away from God, *weakness,* ironically, can lead us toward Him. . . . We commonly think of sin and weakness as merely different sized black marks on the fabric of our souls, different severities of transgression. *But the scriptures imply that sin and weakness are inherently different, require different remedies, and have the potential to produce different results. . . .* The implications of this familiar scripture (Ether 12:27) are profound and invite us to distinguish sin (encouraged by Satan) from weakness (described here as a condition that is with us because of our imperfections in mortality)."

Sister Ulrich continues, "*We cannot simply repent of being weak—nor does weakness itself make us unclean.* We cannot grow spiritually unless we *reject* sin, but we also do not grow spiritually unless we *accept* our state of human weakness, respond to it with humility and faith, and learn through our weakness to trust in God. . . . Even when we sincerely repent of our sins, obtain forgiveness, and become clean again, we remain weak. We are still subject to illness, emotion, ignorance, predispositions, fatigue, and temptation. *But limitations and inadequacies are not sins and do not keep us from being clean and worthy of the Spirit.*"[11]

Bottom-line: *making a mistake is not sinning and weakness is not sin.*[12] Thankfully, the impact and effects of these weaknesses, in addition to our sins, pains, and sicknesses, can also be overcome through the power of the Atonement of Jesus Christ. One caution worth mentioning: Sister Ulrich points out that sometimes, "Satan . . . play(s) to our weakness to entice us to sin."[13] Is it possible that what some might perceive to be a weakness is actually a sin? Fortunately, our loving Savior, who is our advocate with the Father, "knoweth the weakness of man and how to succor them who are tempted."[14] With God's help, we can learn the difference and access His grace to overcome.

Making a mistake is not sinning
and weakness is not sin.

We Should Understand Our Weaknesses

When I was a young boy, the game of the day was Little League baseball. I wasn't a natural, but I really enjoyed it. I still have a cap on my front tooth from when I was eight years old and caught the ball with my mouth instead of the glove! Ouch!

Moving from Little League to Pony League was a bit of a transition. The balls flew faster and the runners were quicker. I played second base. My inspiration on the team were two players, the Evans twins, who were standouts physically. When they threw the ball from the outfield, it looked like a missile shooting across the grass. Both eventually became professional baseball players.

Compared to those regularly sitting on the bench, I was probably a better player. However, compared to those on the starting lineup, not so much. Compared to the Evans twins, not at all. I was even replaced at second base at one point by a guy with a cast on his throwing arm—now that one really hurt!

My point? What we are good at is a relative thing. I may not be the best baseball player, but I play a mean guitar . . . uh, until I sit with a friend who is a natural and has played a fraction of the time that I have and they just blow me away! There is always someone better or worse than we are. The dictionary defines weakness as "a state or condition of lacking strength; a quality or feature regarded as a disadvantage or fault"—an apt description of what it means to be mortal. Wendy Ulrich points out, "Out of this general state of human weakness we experience specific weaknesses such as variations in mental or physical well-being, vulnerability to desires and appetites, predispositions to various physical and emotional states, or differing levels of talents or abilities. All these varying attributes come with the territory of having a mortal body."[15] With this broad understanding, it is easy to see that both strengths *and* weaknesses are a relative thing (another reason we should never compare).

Weaknesses are also normal, as mentioned previously. Elder Bruce C. Hafen wrote: "Our Father's plan subjects us to temptation and misery in this fallen world . . . if you have problems in your life, don't assume there is something wrong with you. Struggling with those problems is at the very core of life's purpose. . . . *If you're seeing more of your weaknesses, that just might mean you're moving nearer to God, not farther away.*"[16] As that happens, consider these four different types of weakness you might see in yourself—noting that all weaknesses are not equal in importance:

Type 1—Urgent: *Weakness that affects your worthiness.* Think of the temple recommend questions—this kind of weakness could affect your standing before God and your standing in the kingdom of God. This weakness is significant and requires your best effort and should be prioritized for immediate attention. Often, habitual/addictive behaviors fall into this category. Nothing in your life should be more important than conquering these challenges.

Important to understand in this quest to overcome these *urgent* weaknesses is this great truth taught by Elder Randy D. Funk: "No amount of personal improvement on our part can make us clean from the sins we have committed or whole from the wounds we have suffered without the Atonement of Jesus Christ. He is our Redeemer."[17] Our redemption, deliverance, recovery, healing, liberation, rescue, and salvation are all centered in, and dependent upon, our Savior, Jesus Christ.

Type 2—Pressing: *Weakness that relates to your ability to fulfill your mission on earth and your effectiveness in building the kingdom of God.* God has given each of us a multifaceted mission to fulfill upon this earth.

Eliminating personal obstacles that keep you from successfully fulfilling this mission should demand your full attention. This is particularly true if weakness impedes your relationship with your spouse (an important part of a life's mission for many).

Type 3—Situational: *Weakness that impedes your personal progress.* This type of weakness doesn't necessarily affect your worthiness or even hinder your life's mission, but it can present some level of obstacle and challenge for you and others. It may simply be something you are not that good at yet (e.g., Little League baseball). Weakness in this area can take on more importance as you focus on your pursuit of personal progress, purifying your life and drawing closer to God.

Type 4—Lifelong: *Weakness related to personality.* This weakness deserves your sincere effort, though for many, may present the most constant frustration in the personal progress category. Lifelong weakness may not be easy to change and can take a lifetime and beyond to overcome.

As these categories show, there are different types of weakness that plague us in this mortal world, and it's important to differentiate them so you can prioritize as you work to strengthen them. For example, if you need to work on obtaining your temple recommend because you are not attending church but have put all your efforts into improving your Ultimate Frisbee game, then you are probably need to reassess your priorities. Pick the most important first.

The Holy Ghost Will Help You Work on Your Weakness

For us to actively be working on our weakness, we have to understand what it is. This takes a strong dose of self-honesty. President Dieter F. Uchtdorf counsels, "being able to see ourselves clearly is essential to our spiritual growth and well-being. If our weaknesses and shortcomings remain obscured in the shadows, then the redeeming power of the Savior cannot heal them and make them strengths. Ironically, our blindness toward our human weaknesses will also make us blind to the divine potential that our Father yearns to nurture within each of us."[18]

245

The most compelling way to discover the weakness we most need to overcome is by the influence and power of the Holy Ghost. Personally, I have felt the Spirit teach me about my own weakness many times. It's not always pleasant, but it is powerful, and ultimately, positive.

As we make every effort to deal with our weakness, beginning with the most urgent, we should do so with the expectation that God will help weak things become strong. That could range from eliminating the weakness by making it strong to simply making us stronger by compensating for weakness.[19]

Elder Gérald Caussé, Presiding Bishop of the Church, taught that accessing the power of the Atonement of Jesus Christ will help us overcome our weakness: "The Spirit of the Lord, or the Holy Ghost, is *the agent of the Atonement.* Thanks to His gentle influence we can feel the love of the Savior and receive His grace in our lives. *When the Spirit accompanies us, we become aware of a powerful transformation taking place within us as our weaknesses are transformed into strengths and our natural abilities are magnified and enhanced beyond even what we believe is possible.* The Spirit sanctifies us and progressively raises us beyond our mortal condition."[20]

I like to think of these three steps to working on overcoming weakness:[21]

- Humbly realize: Become fully aware of (something) as a fact; understand clearly; like Nephi, "because that my heart is broken and my spirit is contrite!"[22]
- Faithfully address: Think about and begin to deal with (an issue or problem), exercising faith in Christ that He *will* help.[23]
- Strive to overcome: To defeat (someone or something); to successfully deal with or gain control of (something difficult).[24]

Please note that "overcome" *doesn't* necessarily mean "eliminate," which is to "completely remove or get rid of something."[25] Successfully dealing with weakness through life may simply mean you learn to manage weakness and "successfully deal with it" to your dying breath.

We have all heard the inspiring Emerson quote repeated often by

President Heber J. Grant: "That which we persist in doing becomes easier for us to do; not that the nature of the thing is changed, but that our power to do is increased."[26] Over time, we may feel frustrated and disappointed that dealing with our own weakness has *not* become easier, but in reality that may not be the point. Our weakness serves an important purpose in that honestly *trying to overcome* may count as much as truly overcoming.

> Our weakness serves an important
> purpose in that honestly *trying to overcome*
> may count as much as truly overcoming.

The Real Blessing Comes in Being Humble

It would appear that the grand design in being given weakness is to help us become humble: "I give unto men weakness that they may be humble."[27] In *Preach My Gospel*, we read: "Humility is willingness to submit to the will of the Lord and to give the Lord the honor for what is accomplished. It includes gratitude for His blessings and acknowledgment of your constant need for His divine help."[28] Often, the phrase to "be meek and lowly of heart," is used in conjunction with being humble—they are almost inseparable. The Savior is meek and humble: "*for I am meek and lowly in heart.*"[29]

Our ability to be humble, meek, and lowly of heart is an essential ingredient to our "drawing into our lives" the grace and subsequent power of Jesus Christ.[30] In *Gospel Topics*, we read: "In addition to needing grace for your ultimate salvation, *you need this enabling power every day of your life.* As you draw near to your Heavenly Father in diligence, humility, and meekness, He will uplift and strengthen you through His grace (see Proverbs 3:34; 1 Peter 5:5; D&C 88:78; 106:7–8). Reliance upon His grace enables you to progress and grow in righteousness. . . . If you ever become discouraged or feel too weak to continue living the gospel, remember the strength you can receive through the enabling power of grace."[31] President Uchtdorf testified, "His grace refines us. His grace helps us become our best selves."[32]

This divine pattern begins by recognizing our weakness and adopting a sense of deep, genuine humility regarding ourselves, which then allows for God to help us—often leading to an even greater sense of humility towards God's loving kindness. It's often a bit circular, but it leads to a form of heavenly help that includes real power that strengthens us and, in many cases, shields us from what could be the devastating effects of weakness.

In the end, the question isn't, are you weak? The real question is, are you humble?

Notes

1. Ether 12:27.
2. "Looking more closely at what the Lord is teaching us here, we see that He first says that He gives men and women *weakness*, singular, *which is part of our mortal experience as fallen or carnal beings. We have become natural men and women because of the Fall of Adam. But through the Atonement of Jesus Christ, we can overcome our weakness, or our fallen natures.*

   "He then says that His grace is sufficient and that *if* we will humble ourselves and have faith in Him, *then* He will "make weak *things* [plural] become strong unto [us]." In other words, as we first change our fallen natures, our weakness, then we will be able to change our behaviors, our weaknesses." (Kevin S. Hamilton, "Then Will I Make Weak Things Become Strong," *Liahona*, May 2022.)
3. See Ether 12:27.
4. See Ether 12:27. Also, to be "mortal" is to *be subject to death*. ("Mortal," lexico.com.)
5. See Dieter F. Uchtdorf, "The Gift of Grace," *Ensign*, May 2015.
6. See Ether 12:26.
7. 2 Nephi 4:17, 18.
8. Ether 12:27.
9. See "Big Five personality traits," Wikipedia, https://en.wikipedia.org /wiki/Big_Five_personality_traits.
10. *Neal A. Maxwell, in The Neal A. Maxwell Quote Book* (Salt Lake City: Bookcraft, 1997). See also Neil O. Annandale, "Personality Theory and Pre-mortal Life," *Issues in Religion and Psychotherapy*, Vol. 29, No. 1 (2004), Article 5, https://scholarsar chive.byu.edu/irp/vol29/iss1/5.
11. Wendy Ulrich, "It Isn't a Sin to Be Weak," *Ensign*, Apr. 2015.
12. Brigham Young said, "Let all Latter-day Saints learn that the weaknesses of their brethren are not sins. When men or women undesignedly commit a wrong, do not attribute that to them as a sin." (*Teachings of Presidents of the Church: Brigham Young* [1997], 220.)

13. Wendy Ulrich, *Weakness Is Not Sin* (Salt Lake City: Deseret Book, 2009), 5.
14. Doctrine and Covenants 62:1. Also, Wendy Ulrich explained: "It is not always easy to tell the difference between sin and weakness. We can think we are dealing with weakness when we are really in a state of sin; this is an extremely dangerous position because then we don't repent and qualify for forgiveness but remain in our sinful state. We can also think we are dealing with a sin we just can't seem to repent of when we are really dealing with a weakness; this is also a dangerous position because we can easily become discouraged, give up on ourselves and God, stop trying, give in to sin, or deny ourselves the joy and peace that are rightfully ours as those we are actually clean before the Lord." (*Weakness Is Not Sin* [Salt Lake City: Deseret Book, 2009], 35.)
15. Wendy Ulrich, *Weakness Is Not Sin* (Salt Lake City: Deseret Book, 2009), 35.
16. Bruce C. Hafen, "The Atonement: All for All," *Ensign*, May 2004.
17. Randy D. Funk, "Come into the Fold of God," *Liahona*, May 2022.
18. Dieter F. Uchtdorf, "Lord, Is It I?" *Ensign*, Nov. 2014.
19. President Brigham Young: "There is not a single condition of life [or] one hour's experience but what is beneficial to all those who make it their study, and aim to improve upon the experience they gain." (*Teachings of Presidents of the Church: Brigham Young* [1997], 179.)
20. Gérald Caussé, "For When I Am Weak, Then Am I Strong," BYU devotional, December 3, 2013, https://speeches.byu.edu/talks/gerald-causse/weak-strong/.
21. See "How Do I Develop Christlike Attributes?" *Preach My Gospel* (2018), 121.
22. "Realize," Lexico.com. See also 2 Nephi 4:32.
23. "Address," Lexico.com.
24. "Overcome," Lexico.com.
25. "Eliminate," Lexico.com.
26. *Teachings of Presidents of the Church: Heber J. Grant* (2002), 35.
27. Ether 12:27.
28. "How Do I Develop Christlike Attributes?" *Preach My Gospel* (2018), 121.
29. Matthew 11:28–30.
30. Moroni 8:26. See also Russell M. Nelson, "Drawing the Power of Jesus Christ into Our Lives," *Ensign*, May 2017.
31. "Grace," Gospel Topics, ChurchofJesusChrist.org.
32. Dieter F. Uchtdorf, "The Gift of Grace," *Ensign*, May 2015.

CHAPTER 25

*Staying on the Path: Continually Holding Fast
to the Rod of Iron and Partaking of the Fruit*

— 1 NEPHI 8:30 —

Previously, I told the story about my son Seth, who was struggling to connect with friends in elementary school.[1] As you may recall, I joined him at his school for lunch and ended up having a miraculous experience playing soccer with his classmates. While that experience was helpful, it didn't solve the problem. The following year, things became more desperate, to the point that we decided to homeschool him for a while.

The challenge was very real, so I offered to give Seth a father's blessing. In that blessing, he was promised that the day would come when he would have "friends without number." I recall finishing the blessing and feeling that it was a bold declaration, considering the circumstances he was facing.

Fast-forward a few years to the state of Washington and the night before we had completed our assignment and were leaving the mission field. The mission home was packed with people. Most were not there to see Gwen or me—they were there to see now sixteen-year-old Seth! All night long, throngs of friends cycled in and out of the mission home.

A few days later, sitting on the edge of his bed back home in Utah, we reflected on all that had happened. As we talked, I looked up at the wall beside Seth's bed, a wall completely covered in photographs of his friends. There had to be a couple hundred pictures. We thought back to the blessing he had received many years earlier and the promise that he would have "friends without number."

Then, just two years after that discussion, he became captain of both the cross-country and track teams, then received the "Spirit Award" in his high school, recognizing one male and one female student out of two thousand. The receipt of this award marked for him a clear turnaround from those desperate days before, when feeling accepted seemed so unlikely.

Seth's journey is very much an illustration of how (and when) the Lord brings blessings into our lives. Working through our troubles, not giving up, turning to the right people for support, maintaining our faith, having hope, waiting for the Lord's timing, and having trust in Him—in short, holding to the iron rod and enduring to the end. For Seth, this process took years before he realized the blessings he wanted.

It's all very much the journey that Father Lehi taught from his vision of the Tree of Life. Of those who partake of eternal life, he said, "And *they did press their way forward, continually holding fast to the rod of iron*, until they came forth and *fell down* and partook of the fruit of the tree."[2] This divine pattern promises that if we continually hold fast, we *will* partake of the fruit. And that fruit, the gift of eternal life, "is most precious and most desirable above all other fruits; yea, and it is the greatest of all the gifts of God,"[3] a gift promised to fill your soul "with exceedingly great joy."[4]

Must We Be Perfect to Make It?

Do we have to be perfect to become exalted and receive eternal life? The answer is no—but we do have to be *perfected*. Of course, there was only one perfect person who lived or who will ever live on the earth, the Savior, Jesus Christ. Our eternal perfection will not come in this life, but in the life to come.[5]

Elder Gerald N. Lund, then director of curriculum and instruction for the Church Educational System, clarified the distinction between being *perfect* and being *perfected*. He said, "*Perfect* can also mean 'having all flaws and errors removed.' A better way to state the original question might be: 'Do we have to be *perfected* to be exalted?' Here the scriptural answer is a resounding yes. In numerous references, the Lord says that no unclean thing can enter his presence. (See 1 Ne. 10:21; Alma 7:21; 3 Ne. 27:19; Moses 6:57.) Obviously, then, we must repent of those flaws identified as sins and become clean before we can be exalted. But what of other flaws—those that don't qualify as sins but are nevertheless imperfections?"[6] In answer, even our weaknesses will need to be perfected. As to the timing, the Prophet Joseph said it best: "It will be a great work to learn our salvation and exaltation even beyond the grave."[7]

Elder Lund goes on to explain that we can be far less than perfect in this life and still have the hope of exaltation. He said, "Elder Bruce R. McConkie described what it takes to be saved: 'What we do in this life is chart a course leading to eternal life. . . . If we make that firm determination and are in the course of our duty *when this life is over, we will continue in that course in eternity. . . . If we go out of this life loving the Lord, desiring righteousness, and seeking to acquire the attributes of godliness, we will have that same spirit in the eternal world,* and we will then continue to advance and progress until an ultimate, destined day when we will possess, receive, and inherit all things.'"[8]

The bottom line: if we are doing our best and walking the covenant path, then, through the loving grace and mercy of Jesus Christ, we can be assured that we *will* be perfected and exalted (meaning, we will attain the highest degree of the celestial kingdom).

If we are doing our best and walking the covenant path, then through the loving grace and mercy of Jesus Christ, we *will* be perfected and exalted.

President Russell M. Nelson speaks of "mortal perfection" versus "eternal perfection." Of those who the scriptures say attained mortal perfection, President Nelson says: "This does not mean that these people never made mistakes or never had need of correction. . . . Mortal perfection can be achieved as we try to perform every duty, keep every law, and strive to be as perfect in our sphere as our Heavenly Father is in his. If we do the best we can, the Lord will bless us according to our deeds and the desires of our hearts . . . We need not be dismayed if our earnest efforts toward perfection now seem so arduous and endless. Perfection is pending. *It can come in full only after the Resurrection and only through the Lord.* It awaits all who love him and keep his commandments. It includes thrones, kingdoms, principalities, powers, and dominions. It is the end for which we are to endure. It is the eternal perfection that God has in store for each of us."[9]

God is not expecting perfection from us in this life (though mortal perfection is the direction we should be pursuing). But He is working *to* perfect us—if we are willing. The question is, are we "anxiously engaged" in walking the covenant path?[10] Sister Elaine Jack, then General President of the Relief Society, quoted Proverbs and counseled to "ponder the path of thy feet," to reflect on the path we are following and to make sure it is the covenant path.[11]

The Covenant Path Leads to the Temple

President Russell M. Nelson taught: "*The temple is the object of every activity, every lesson, every progressive step in the Church.* All of our efforts in proclaiming the gospel, perfecting the Saints, and redeeming the dead lead to the holy temple."[12] The rod of iron from Lehi's dream has been described by the Brethren as consisting of the scriptures, personal revelation from the Holy Ghost, and the words of living prophets.[13] Given President Nelson's instruction, we should understand that holding fast to the rod of iron will always lead to the temple and regular participation in the saving ordinances of the house of the Lord.

In this regard, it is reassuring to know that as we participate in the gathering of Israel on the other side of the veil by performing proxy work in the temple for others, we can have confidence that they will most likely accept those ordinances. President Henry B. Eyring related that most, if not all, of our departed ancestors for which temple work is being done will accept the gospel.[14] In fact, it may well be that the majority of our Heavenly Father's children enter the highest degree of glory in the celestial kingdom—at least, it will be "many" and not "few."[15]

President Gordon B. Hinckley taught that the work performed in the temple *is a continuation of the Atonement of Jesus Christ* when he said, "These temples, which now dot the earth, are necessary to the total fulfillment of the Savior's Atonement."[16] It is interesting to consider that the work we do in the temple is, in some sense, a continuation of the Atonement of Jesus Christ, which is what makes us saviors on Mount Zion.[17] President Hinckley teaches, "We literally become saviors on Mount Zion. What does this mean? Just as our Redeemer gave His life as a vicarious sacrifice for all men, and in so doing became our Savior, even so we, in a small measure, when we engage in proxy work in the temple, become as saviors to those on the other side who have no means of advancing unless something is done in their behalf by those on earth."[18] Truly, it is a unique blessing to participate with the Savior in the most sacred of works.

We should do everything in our power to hold a current temple recommend. We are taught that it is a symbol of our faithfulness.[19] As a symbol, like flying a flag, it's a representation of where our loyalties lie. It represents that we acknowledge that we are walking the covenant path and are covenant keepers. Recall that President Russell M. Nelson taught, "A covenant made with God is not restrictive, but protective. . . . Covenants do not hold us down; they elevate us beyond the limits of our own power and perspective."[20] With that understanding, we should "make an appointment regularly with the Lord" to be in the temple.[21]

The promised blessings available to us from consistent temple worship are numerous:

- The ordinances of the temple can "fill [your] life with power and strength that is available *in no other way*."[22]
- "Increased personal revelation and peace will fortify your commitment to stay on the covenant path."[23]
- "There is no place in the world where [you] can feel closer to the Lord."[24]
- The temple can bring great peace to your soul.[25]
- "Temple attendance creates spirituality."[26]
- You will experience "increased faith, so that conversion to the Savior becomes deep and abiding."[27]

- Regular temple attendance will help you recognize and feel God's power.[28]
- You can find "new ways to deal with the challenges you face . . . [and] receive spiritual guidance."[29]
- You will feel "increased protection from temptations and the intensifying influence of the adversary."[30]
- "The blessings [God] gives you [are not] limited to your time in the temple, [but] He will bless you in all aspects of your life" for your service there.[31]
- Both men and women will learn how to draw upon the priesthood power they have been endowed with in the temple.[32]
- "The Lord will bring the miracles He knows you need as you make sacrifices to serve and worship in His temples."[33]
- Your mind will be moved upon by the Holy Ghost, and inspiration will follow your attendance at the temple.[34]
- The temple can help you "get [your] true physical and spiritual bearings."[35]
- You will see more clearly your "place amidst the things of the universe" and "among the purposes of God."[36]
- You will be better able to place yourself where you belong and better able to value and to weigh, to separate and to organize the common, ordinary duties of your life so that the little things do not oppress you or take away your vision of the greater things that God has given you.[37]
- Participation in the temple can bring "increased ability and motivation to learn and repent."[38]
- Healing blessings await you there, including "increased assistance to mend troubled, broken or anxious hearts and make the wounded whole."[39]
- "Increased family blessings, no matter your current, past, or future family situation or how imperfect your family tree may be."[40] Relationships between husband and wife as well as other family relationships will be blessed and strengthened.[41]

- You will draw closer to your departed ancestors as you serve and help them receive the ordinances of salvation. They, in turn, are then better able to help you.[42]
- Through temple service "you will find not only protection from the temptation and ills of the world, but you will also find personal power—power to change, power to repent, power to learn, power to be sanctified, and power to turn the hearts of your family members to each other and heal that which needs healing."[43]
- As you place your burdens before the Lord in the temple, you will be filled with a new spirit and confidence in the future. "He will hold you and cradle you and lead you step by step along that pathway that leads to the celestial kingdom."[44]
- You are promised more "increased joy through an increased ability to feel the love of the Lord."[45]

Compelling promises, to be sure, to those who attend the temple.

Endure to the End and Expect the Blessings of Heaven

The straight and narrow path we walk is the covenant path. It *begins* with the first principles and ordinances of the gospel (the doctrine of Christ), faith, repentance, and baptism, where we make our first covenants along that path. President George Q. Cannon taught: "When we went forth into the waters of baptism . . . *He bound Himself also by covenant to us that He would never desert us, never leave us to ourselves, never forget us, that in the midst of trials and hardships, when everything was arrayed against us, He would be near unto us and would sustain us.* That was His covenant."[46]

Thereafter, every covenant we make better strengthens and enables us to keep the commandments of God and walk the covenant path. That's how God has designed it. The ordinances and covenants of the gospel are intended to fortify us and give us real power to help us make the journey and partake of the fruit.[47]

The ultimate reward is described by the prophet Nephi: "Wherefore, if ye shall press forward, feasting upon the word of Christ, and *endure to the end*, behold, thus saith the Father: Ye shall have eternal life.[48]

What does it mean to endure to the end? In *Preach My Gospel*, we read that it means "to remain true to the commandments of God despite temptation, opposition, and adversity throughout life."[49] President Russell M. Nelson calls enduring to the end "a dominant theme of the scriptures" and a responsibility that is "uniquely yours."[50] Meaning, at least in part, no one can do it for you. Enduring to the end is something you must do for yourself, and it may be different than what it looks like for others.

Stephen E. Robinson, then department chair in Ancient Scripture at BYU, taught, "Enduring to the end means, in general, entering into the gospel covenant (through faith in Christ, repentance, baptism, and receiving the Holy Ghost) and then remaining faithful to that covenant. . . . Enduring to the end is keeping those promises throughout our lives—no matter what. It means we don't quit because of life's difficulties or temptations."[51]

Worthwhile repeating here: it is never too late to get back on the path once we have left it, and from that point on, endure to the end.[52] For those who do endure, they have this promise: "Everyone who will live the gospel of Jesus Christ daily and endure to the end will gain eternal life— this is the promise of the Lord."[53]

It is never too late to get back on the path, and from that point on, endure to the end.

As you walk the covenant path and continually hold to the rod of iron, making an earnest effort to endure and really striving to overcome all the temptations, challenges, hardships, and tests of mortal life that have been customized to your unique situation, *you will* partake of the fruit and enjoy that which is most precious above all the gifts of God.

Notes

1. See Introduction.
2. 1 Nephi 8:30.
3. 1 Nephi 15:36.
4. 1 Nephi 8:12. Note that the fruit of the tree is commonly referred to as the "love of God" (see 1 Nephi 11:22), which is to be understood in its broadest context. Here, Elder David A. Bednar added an important insight: "The fruit on the tree is a symbol for the blessings of [Jesus Christ's] Atonement. Partaking of the fruit of the tree represents the receiving of ordinances and covenants whereby the Atonement can become fully efficacious in our lives." ("Lehi's Dream: Holding Fast to the Rod," *Ensign*, Oct. 2011.)

    The most significant manifestation of the love of God is found in what Elder Vaughn J. Featherstone describes as the "most exquisite, supernal act of charity ever performed in all eternity," the Atonement of Jesus Christ. ("A Man After God's Own Heart," BYU devotional, September 12, 1995, https://speeches.byu.edu /talks/vaughn-j-featherstone/man -gods-heart/.)

    Additionally, Elder Jeffrey R. Holland taught that the tree of life is a symbol of Jesus Christ. He said: "The images of Christ and the tree [are] inextricably linked. . . . At the very outset of the Book of Mormon, . . . Christ is portrayed as the source of eternal life and joy, the living evidence of divine love, and the means whereby God will fulfill his covenant with the house of Israel and indeed the entire family of man, returning them all to their eternal promises" (*Christ and the New Covenant* [Salt Lake City: Deseret Book, 1997], 160, 162).

    Finally, it should be understood that the fruit represents the fullness of joy found in eternal life (exaltation) (see 1 Nephi 15:36 and Doctrine and Covenants 14:7). This is best summed up in a statement found in the Book of Mormon Gospel Doctrine Teacher's Manual: "Emphasize that eternal life is the 'most sweet' and 'most precious' blessing we can receive. Because of God's love for us, this blessing is available to us through the Atonement of Jesus Christ." ("Lesson 3: The Vision of the Tree of Life," Book of Mormon: Gospel Doctrine Teacher's Manual [1999], 11–15, ChurchofJesusChrist .org.)
5. See Marvin J. Ashton, "On Being Worthy," *Ensign*, May 1989; Bruce R. McConkie, "Jesus Christ and Him Crucified," BYU devotional, September 5, 1976, https://speeches .byu.edu/talks/bruce-r-mcconkie /jesus-christ-crucified/.
6. Gerald N. Lund, "Are We Expected to Achieve Perfection in This Life?" *Ensign*, Aug. 1986.
7. *Teachings of Presidents of the Church: Joseph Smith* (2007), 268.
8. Gerald N. Lund, "Are We Expected to Achieve Perfection in This Life?" *Ensign*, Aug. 1986; Bruce R. McConkie, "The Seven Deadly Heresies," BYU devotional, June 1, 1980, https://speeches.byu.edu /talks/bruce-r-mcconkie/seven -deadly-heresies/.
9. Russell M. Nelson, "Perfection Pending," *Ensign*, Nov. 1995.
10. Doctrine and Covenants 58:27.

11. Elaine L. Jack, "Ponder the Path of Thy Feet," *Ensign*, Nov. 1993.

12. Russell M. Nelson, "Prepare for Blessings of the Temple," *Ensign*, Mar. 2002.

13. See Neil L. Andersen, "Hold Fast to the Words of the Prophets," BYU devotional, March 4, 2007, https://speeches.byu.edu/talks/neil-l-andersen/hold-fast-words-prophets/.

14. Henry B. Eyring, "Hearts Bound Together," *Ensign*, May 2005. See also *Teachings of Presidents of the Church: Wilford Woodruff* (2006), 191.

15. The Savior's declarations that "many are called, but few are chosen" (Matthew 22:14) and "strait is the gate, and narrow is the way, which leadeth unto life, and few there be that find it" (Matthew 7:14) are in reference to those who come to earth, live beyond the age of accountability, and do not accept the gospel when they had the opportunity to do so (either during their time on earth or in the spirit world). Of these, we are to understand that here will be relatively few, compared to the earth's population, that will fully embrace the gospel. However, when you take into consideration all the children who died before the age of accountability throughout the history of the earth (experts put this at around fifty percent of the population), as well as those who will come to earth during the Millennium (could be even more than ever came to earth prior to that period), where children will grow up "without sin unto salvation" (D&C 45:58), then the numbers begin to add up and the words "many will be saved" are justified. (See https://ourworldin-data.org/child-mortality-in-the-past; Bruce R. McConkie, "The Salvation of Little Children," *Ensign*, Apr. 1977.)

16. *Teachings of Presidents of the Church: Gordon B. Hinckley* (2016), 312.

17. See Obadiah 1:21.

18. Gordon B. Hinckley, "Closing Remarks," *Ensign*, Nov. 2004.

19. See Dieter F. Uchtdorf, "Temple Blessings," *Ensign*, Aug. 2010.

20. Russell M. Nelson, "Personal Preparation for Temple Blessings," *Ensign*, May 2001.

21. Russell M. Nelson, "Becoming Exemplary Latter-day Saints," *Ensign*, Nov. 2018.

22. Russell M. Nelson, "COVID-19 and Temples*," Liahona*, May 2021.

23. See Russell M. Nelson, "As We Go Forward Together," *Ensign*, Apr. 2018.

24. Thomas S. Monson, "Blessings of the Temple," *Ensign,* Oct. 2010.

25. Thomas S. Monson, "Blessings of the Temple," *Ensign,* Oct. 2010.

26. *Teachings of the Presidents of the Church: Howard W. Hunter* (2015), 184.

27. Dale G. Renlund, "Family History and Temple Work: Sealing and Healing," *Ensign*, May 2018.

28. See Doctrine and Covenants 109:22, 26.

29. "Temples," *True to the Faith*, ChurchofJesusChrist.org;Robert D. Hales, "Temple Blessings," *Ensign,* Feb. 2014.

30. Dale G. Renlund, "Family History and Temple Work: Sealing and Healing," *Ensign*, May 2018.

31. "Temples," *True to the Faith*, ChurchofJesusChrist.org.

32. See Russell M. Nelson, "Sisters' Participation in the Gathering of Israel," *Ensign*, Nov. 2018.

33. See Russell M. Nelson, "Becoming Exemplary Latter-day Saints," *Ensign*, Nov. 2018.

34. *Teachings of Presidents of the Church: Gordon B. Hinckley* (2017), 317.

35. Dieter F. Uchtdorf, "First Presidency Message: Temple Blessings," *Ensign*, Aug. 2010.

36. *Teachings of Presidents of the Church: Howard W. Hunter* (2015), 184.

37. *Teachings of Presidents of the Church: Howard W. Hunter* (2015), 184.

38. Dale G. Renlund, "Family History and Temple Work: Sealing and Healing," *Ensign*, May 2018.

39. Dale G. Renlund, "Family History and Temple Work: Sealing and Healing," *Ensign*, May 2018.

40. Dale G. Renlund, "Family History and Temple Work: Sealing and Healing," *Ensign*, May 2018.

41. See *Teachings of Presidents of the Church: Howard W. Hunter* (2015), 185.

42. See Doctrine and Covenants 110:14–15; James E. Faust, "The Phenomenon That Is You," *Ensign*, Nov. 2003.

43. Dale G. Renlund, "Family History and Temple Blessings," *Ensign*, Feb. 2017.

44. Ronald A. Rasband, "How to Claim Temple Blessings," *Ensign*, July 2016.

45 Dale G. Renlund, "Family History and Temple Work: Sealing and Healing," *Ensign*, May 2018.

46. George Q. Cannon, *Gospel Truth,* sel. Jerreld L. Newquist, 2 vols. (1974), 1:170.

47. Elder Neil L. Andersen taught: "My dear young friends, God *will* help you, and He stands ready to bless you. As our loving Father, He has given us ordinances that help us feel His power in our lives—the power of godliness. Think of this scripture: 'In the ordinances . . . , the power of godliness is manifest" (Doctrine and Covenants 84:20)."

Elder Andersen goes on to describe the four ordinances and blessings that invite power into our lives: 1. Power in the sacrament, 2. Power in the temple, 3. Power in your patriarchal blessing, 4. Power in priesthood blessings. ("The Power of Godliness through Priesthood Ordinances and Blessings," *For the Strength of Youth*, Aug. 2021.)

48. 2 Nephi 31:20. See also 3 Nephi 27:16; 15:9; 27:13–22.

49. "The Gospel of Jesus Christ," *Preach My Gospel* (2018), 70.

50. Russell M. Nelson, "Endure and Be Lifted Up," *Ensign*, May 1997.

51. Stephen E. Robinson, "Enduring to the End," *Ensign*, Oct. 1993.

52. See W. Christopher Waddell, "Just as He Did," *Ensign*, May 2019.

53. Christopher Golden Jr., "Small and Simple Things," *Ensign*, Nov. 2007.

CONCLUSION

The divine patterns we have talked about in this book are but a small, curated sampling of the many promised blessings God has made to His children. As said before, these pattens are not the only way He might bless or help us. They are simply patterns to be observed and followed, and, as we do, we will come to know Him in deeper, richer ways so we can more readily see the blessings he bestows on us so abundantly throughout our lives. There is not adequate time in one book to cover all the scriptural patterns that can be found—it would take volumes! In fact, it is quite revealing to see how generous, kind, and giving our Father in Heaven is—so many powerful blessings available to those who seek Him. *Seek and ye shall find*—an overarching pattern that sums it all up. *Seek*, and you will find the blessings you want and need. *Seek*. God is ready, even anxious, to bestow them.

As said many times throughout this book, we seek God's blessings by following the divine patterns that He has revealed in the scriptures. As we strive to give our best efforts to live these principles, we must recognize that patience and faith are required—knowing that the blessings will come in His own time, in His own way, and according to His own plan. The plan He has for you.

That said, God is not a vending machine. We don't deposit our token of effort with the expectation that the ordered blessing will come forth immediately. Rather, God is a wise parent who has your best interest at heart: to bring you back into His presence to live with Him eternally in the highest degree of the celestial kingdom. He knows what you really need but will not micromanage your life. He has given you your agency and wants you to be an "agent" unto yourself.[1] He will, however, entertain your requests, as you act and turn to God for His help and work to ensure you have what's best for your long-term interests. He may even entertain some frivolous wants along the way, because He values your agency so highly.

God loves each of His children. That includes you and those you love. President M. Russell Ballard taught: "Our Father in Heaven loves all of His children equally, perfectly, and infinitely."[2] In writing to members of the Church in Rome, the Apostle Paul taught of the abiding connection God has with us: "For I am persuaded, that neither death, nor life, nor angels, nor principalities, nor powers, nor things present, nor things to come, nor height, nor depth, nor any other creature, shall be able to separate us from the love of God, which is in Christ Jesus our Lord."[3] The love God has for you and me will never change; despite anything we might do.

I hope you never have reason to question His love for you, or the lengths He is willing to go to bless and help you in your life. If you do, I hope you quickly come to know that He really is there for you. He will never step away from you. Never. That is my belief, my experience, and my witness.

For those who have come to believe that God is deaf and distant, that blessings have been delayed, withheld, or even altogether denied, perhaps a word or two in this book has given you renewed hope. Maybe even given you the perspective that there is reason in His delay, purpose in His withholding, and wisdom in His denial. God can be trusted. He always acts in our best interest. He has the wisdom, knowledge, and power to arrange our circumstances in unthinkable ways, to solve problems using unimaginable solutions. In the book of Job, we read: "God thundereth marvellously with his voice; great things doeth he, which we cannot comprehend."[4]

In many ways, God is incomprehensible. We don't always understand His ways. However, "the day shall come when you shall comprehend even God, being quickened in him and by him."[5] And, in that day, you shall understand why He has done what He has done in your life.

And making it all possible . . . the grace of the Lord Jesus Christ. A grace so merciful and powerful that it qualifies you to receive the blessings that are part of God's plan for you—a plan that includes never-ending joy. Sounds pretty good. It is a generous, wonderful, merciful, and brilliant plan.

So, don't delay. Seek out the blessings of heaven in your life to a greater degree than you may be doing today. The blessings are there. Waiting. You will be the beneficiary of your efforts and will then bless the lives of those around you. More importantly, you will authorize God to intervene in your life in miraculous ways. He wants to continue to convince you that He is, indeed, a God of miracles and that He is *your* God, *your* Father, and *your* friend.

Notes

1. See Doctrine and Covenants 58:27–28.
2. M. Russell Ballard, "Equality through Diversity,'" *Ensign*, Nov. 1993.
3. Romans 8:38–39.
4. Job 37:5.
5. Doctrine and Covenants 88:49.

ACKNOWLEDGMENTS

Where to begin? A life full of mentors in the form of caring friends who were members of the Church—some were my leaders, others were simply loving ward members—have shaped my understanding of what it means to truly live the gospel and be a disciple of Jesus Christ. To all of them—Doc and Cozette Wallace, Garth and Verna Rogers, Robert and Ruth Durrans, Jack and Loa Young, Bob Bramwell, Brother Eastwood, Nolan Draney, Brother and Sister Adams—really too many to try to name them all here, I express my gratitude and appreciation.

Those mentors extend into my service in the Church—missions and callings—and have provided such a rich experience in furthering my understanding of the gospel of Jesus Christ. I will be forever grateful for those experiences and how they have shaped and reinforced my faith.

More specifically to this book, several focus groups and book reviewers and readers have offered important input and observations that made meaningful contributions. To each of them I express my thanks. Their time and attention given to the manuscript was very helpful. In this regard, I am very appreciative to Chad Webb, Greg Jackson, Katie Connors, Lisa Laycock, Larissa Chase, Stacie Christensen, Emily Barlow, Cathy Ginn, Sonya Stucki, and Gaye Willis for their review, input, and encouragement.

Many individuals have allowed me to use their stories or refer to their experiences, that all may benefit. Thank you to each of them for allowing that to happen. Their personal experience deepens our understanding and encourages our faith.

ACKNOWLEDGMENTS

I am especially beholden to David Pliler and Terri Chase. Their input, suggestions, research, feedback, and encouragement have significantly impacted what is written here. It truly was a journey that I am so grateful they were willing to make with me. To both of them I express the greatest appreciation.

To Lisa Roper, my product director, and the production team at Deseret Book, including Tracy Keck, Richard Erickson, Garth Bruner, Breanna Anderl, and Kristen Evans, I am especially indebted. Lisa's encouragement and support have been instrumental in bringing this book forward. The input from the Deseret Book editorial review board has been especially useful and has produced a better work than if left entirely to my own devices. Thank you for that.

Finally, to my wife, Gwen, who read several versions of the same chapter numerous times, thank you. I appreciated both the blank stares as well as the positive reviews. And to my children, who offered faithful encouragement, I extend my thanks. I especially appreciate that they allowed me to share their own stories of challenge and faith. Reliving those experiences as I shared them in this book reminded me once again of just how indebted we really are to God.

In the end, my hope is that my children and, especially, my grandchildren will see this book as a reminder of my testimony of the gospel and my love for our Savior Jesus Christ. To Him I owe everything good that has happened in my life. I am so grateful to worship such a loving, forgiving and empowering God.